WORKING
THE
NORTH

WORKING
THE
NORTH

**LABOR AND THE
NORTHWEST DEFENSE
PROJECTS 1942–1946**

WILLIAM R. MORRISON
KENNETH A. COATES

UNIVERSITY OF ALASKA PRESS
1994

HD
8/09
NG72
M67
1994

Library of Congress Cataloging-in-Publication Data

Morrison, William R. (William Robert), 1942-
  Working the North : labor and the Northwest defense projects
1942-1946 / William R. Morrison, Kenneth A. Coates.
      p.   cm.
  Includes bibliographical references and index.
  ISBN 0-912006-72-2 : $30.00 -- ISBN 0-912006-73-0 (pbk) : $20.00
  1. Working class--Northwest, Canadian--History--20th century.
  2. World War, 1939-1945.   I. Coates, Kenneth A.   II. Title.
  HD8109.N672M67   1993
  305.5'62'097192--dc20   93-41687
                                                              CIP

International Standard Book Number: cloth 0-912006-72-2
                                      paper 0-912006-73-0

Library of Congress Catalogue Number: 93-41687

Printed in the United States by McNaughton & Gunn, Inc.

This publication was printed on acid-free paper that meets the minimum
requirements for the American National Standard for Information Science—
Permanence of Paper for Printed Library Materials ANSI Z39.48-1984.

Publication coordination by Pamela Odom.
Production by Debbie Van Stone.
Book and cover design by Paula Elmes, Publications Center, Center for Cross-
   Cultural Studies.

For the people of
Northern British Columbia,
whose vision and commitment led to
the establishment of the
University of Northern British Columbia.

CONTENTS

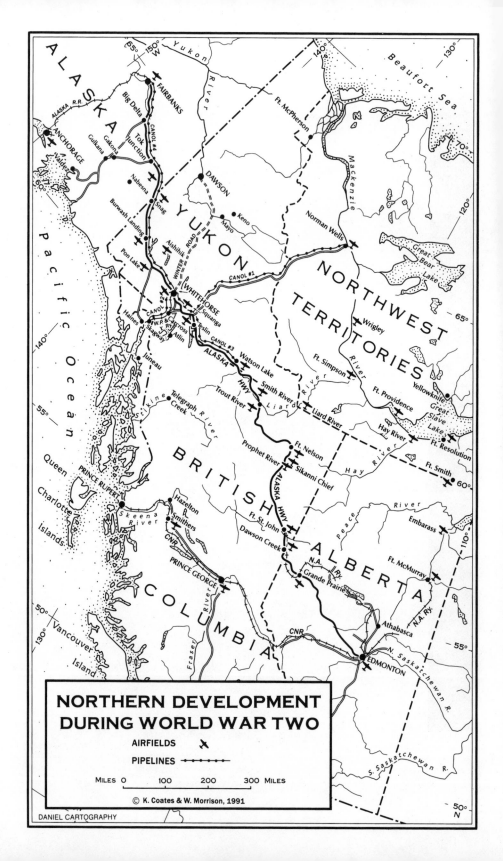

NORTHERN DEVELOPMENT
DURING WORLD WAR TWO

AIRFIELDS ✈

PIPELINES •••••••

MILES 0   100   200   300 MILES

© K. Coates & W. Morrison, 1991

DANIEL CARTOGRAPHY

PREFACE

The documentary material on which this book is based comes chiefly from four major archival sources: the National Archives of Canada (NAC), the National Archives of the United States (NA), the archives of the United States Army Corps of Engineers (ACE), and the Yukon Territorial Archives (YTA). Other important archives such as the Glenbow-Alberta Institute were also consulted. The particular collection from each archives is noted in the footnotes. We owe a tremendous debt to a number of archivists (always the life-support system for historians), particularly Terry Cook and Doug Whyte at the National Archives of Canada, the staff of the National Archives of the United States, the Office of the Chief Historian of the United States Army Corps of Engineers (particularly Dr. John Greenwood and Martin Gordon), the Edmonton Municipal Archives, and the friendly and helpful staff of the Yukon Territorial Archives.

The book also draws on personal interviews conducted with people who had worked in the far northwest during the war and a series of questionnaires filled out by people who could not be interviewed.[1] These people were contacted partly through advertisements in newspapers, and through our appearances on regional radio programs, but mostly through the mailing lists kept by organizations which hold regular reunions of military and civilian veterans of the projects. Many of these people are elderly, for the civilians who worked on these projects were on the average older than those in the military, and many were well into their eighties when we contacted them. Their response to our request for interviews, photographs, and other memorabilia was unfailingly generous and made us aware of our responsibility to the history of their experiences; we hope that we have done justice to them. It is noteworthy that none of the respondents put any restriction on the information they provided. We have nonetheless attempted to deal responsibly with this information, some of which is quite sensitive, and in some cases have concealed the identity of the informant or the subject. A list of the many people who provided information appears in the bibliography; we thank all of them for their kindness and generosity. We wish to acknowledge the assistance of Norman Allison, Donald Amos, C. E. "Red" Anderson, Marvin and Mabel Armitage, Thelma Ashby, A. G. Askew, Kaare Aspol, Coreen Bafford, Duncan Bath, Chuck Baxter, J. E. Bedford, Bill Bennett, Charles Biller, Robert and Dell Black, H. M. Blackwood, Homer Blackwood, Bob and Lil Brant, Agnes Brewster, Barbara Brocklehurst, Vera Brown, A. Brutto, Howard Burrel, D. K. Campbell, Phyllis Church, Ruth Clemo, Aleatha and Marshall Close, Dick and Marge Coates, Muriel Coats, Gileen Colcleugh, Muriel Gwen Collip, J. D. Cooper, C. T. Cotton, Crawford Cowieson, Syliva Cranston, G. B. Criteser, W. H. Croft, Bob and Barb Dempster, Hugh Devitt, Evelyn Dobbin, G. C. Drake, Tom Dunbar, George Ford, Alex Forgie, R. Fowler, Lorne Frizzell, Merle and Audrey Gaddy, Stacia Gallop, Raymond Ganser, J. Garbus, Harry George, Gordon and Lorna Gibbs, M. E. Golata, W. A. Gorham, Willis Grafe, Rex Graham, P. and M. Greenan, Nancy Greenwood, Harold Griffin, Cyril Griffith, L. G. Grimble, Clarence Haakenstad, Selmer Hafso, Fred Hammond, Harvey Hayduck, J. D. Hazen, Chuck Hemphill, Ed Herzog, Richard Hislop, M. Hope, John Hudson, Gunnar Johnson, Mary Johnson, Vernon Kennedy, Charles Knott, Con and Dot Lattin, Phyllis Lee, Brig. Gen. H. W. Love, Laura MacKinnon, Mickey and Effie McCaw, A. C. McEachern, R. C. McFarland, Helen McLean, Donald Miller, Adam Milne, Bruce Milne, Roy Minter, J. Mitchell,

T. E. Moylneux, John Mueller, Claus-M. Naske, Walter Nelson, E. O'Neill, Bob Oliphant, R. A. Panter, Ben and Addie Parker, Ena Parsons, Joan Patterson, Gerry Pelletier, Frank and Ester Peters, Walter Polvi, Hampton Primeaux, A. J. S. Protherow, William T. Pryor, Jim Quong, Peggy Read, Cale Roberts, K. L. Rudhardt, Donald Saunders, Ray Savela, L. H. Schnurstein, Carl Schubert, June Scully, Bernice Sillemo, Bud and Doris Simpson, Earl and Barbara Smith, Earle Smith, Lake Southwick, Frank and Agatha Speer, Mildred Spencer, Frank Steele, Cliff and Colette Stringer, John and Ruth Stringer, Jolyne Sulz, Jim and Iris Sutton, Norman Swabb, Duane Swenson, Ray Talbot, Jim Tedlie, Joan Thomas, Jean Waldon, E. R. Walker, H. Walker, Paul E. Warren, Harvey Weber, Bub and Barb Webster, Olga Whitley, E. J. Wiggans, J. Williams, Wendell Williamson, L. E. Willis, L. Williscroft, Bruce F. Willson, Vern and Alice Wilson, Henry Wright, and Peggy Wudel.

The questionnaires contained forty questions, covering a wide variety of topics. Civilian respondents were asked why they volunteered for northern service, what their initial impressions of the north were, whether they encountered racial, national or sex discrimination, what living conditions—food, housing, and so forth—were like, if they were satisfied with their wages, what contact if any they had with the indigenous people, what relations were like with management, and other questions of this kind. Ample space was provided for general and specific observations beyond what was asked for. Some of the people who answered the questionnaires did so in a simple, perfunctory manner. Others sat down with pen or typewriter and provided long and thoughtful answers to our questions. Some sent us copies of personal correspondence or photographs, and others provided tape-recorded reminiscences. We were surprised to find that the number of women who replied was proportionately greater than their percentage of the northern civilian work force. This may be due to the greater willingness of women to respond to such inquiries, or that women have more interest in maintaining networks of wartime friends and co-workers; or perhaps it is because proportionately more women from the period are alive than men, since female longevity is greater than that of men, and the women workers from the region tended to be younger than the men.

There is therefore no "scientific" basis for selection of these people; rather, they are self-selected, and the one thing they have in common is that they all have fairly happy memories of their experiences in the Northwest. Although they describe hardships, the overall tone of the interviews and questionnaires is positive; for many of them, it was the most exciting episode of their lives. Those who have no fond memories of the period do not, of course, belong to these organizations.

The result of the interviews and the written questionnaires was a substantial collection of oral history relating to the construction of the defense projects in the far northwest. Most of the responses were useful, while a small number reflect the hyperbole which inevitably colors reflections of the fairly distant past. What was particularly helpful was the respondent's attention to the private details of their lives and work experiences—the tents and dormitories, the food, the mail service, how they cashed their pay checks, their relationship with fellow workers, bosses, and the local population.

For the less positive side of the episode, then, we have relied not entirely on the workers' memories recorded fifty years after the event, but on contemporary documentary material. Of particular value are the files kept by those who censored the mail; here one finds what the soldier-workers and civilians, black as well as white, were thinking and saying at the time. With this kind of evidence to work with it would be futile to attempt any kind of statistical analysis of the evidence. This book is a work of interpretation based on the analysis of documentary material, written in comparison with the oral material, interpreted through the filter of historical knowledge, and, as with all historians, our own attitudes towards the subject.

An example of how we have handled our material is the question of racism in the Northwest. Virtually all the people interviewed in the late 1980s stated that there was little racial conflict in the region during the war, that black and white workers lived and toiled in harmony, while the documentary evidence shows that in many cases quite the opposite was true. Only a very few expressed the feelings of racism which in fact were endemic during that era. The fact that none of our correspondents was black would have a good deal to do with this present attitude. We believe the documents in this case, though it is impossible to quantify the amount of racism, and probably a waste of time even to try.

Such approaches to historical investigation have, of course, been adopted in the past, though it is likely that increasingly tight budgets for research may well force scholars to rely increasingly on a kind of interview-by-mail technique similar to that used here. Given the fact that our topic is in the relatively recent past, we have had an opportunity that most historians do not have—to speak to many of the subjects of our study. Perhaps the most interesting discovery of this process was that the men and women who worked in the Northwest that we were able to contact were truly anxious to have their stories told. The history of the northwest defense projects has been told on a number of occasions, but always from the perspective of politicians, senior military officers, and civilian managers; seldom have the workers' voices been heard.[2] We only hope that our reconstruction of their experience is an accurate representation of those dynamic and momentous times.

That this project has reached completion is due in substantial measure to the support and encouragement of others. We are thankful for the financial support received from the Social Sciences and Humanities Research Council of Canada, Brandon University's Research Committee, the President's Research Committee at the University of Victoria, and the Senate Research Committee and the Centre for Northern Studies at Lakehead University. We have benefited tremendously from the counsel and insight of our friends and colleagues, especially Peter Baskerville, Ian MacPherson, Eric Sager, Claus-M. Naske, Shelagh Grant, Richard Diubaldo, and Heath Twichell. They bear no responsibility for any errors contained in this book, but must share in whatever merits it may have.

A note on spelling. Anyone writing on this subject runs afoul of a difference in the Canadian and American practice of spelling words that end (in Canada) in -*our*, words such as colour, honour, neighbour, and especially labour. This book contains the word "labour" (Canadian) and "labor" (American) several hundred times. To lessen confusion (though since we must cite our sources and formal titles accurately it cannot be eliminated), and to make the text look less odd, we have adopted the American spelling in the text, in deference to the fact that the book is the product of an American university press. We have similarly adopted the American spellings of words such as "center," "theater," and "defense."

NOTES

1. Many of these interviews were conducted by our research assistants, Judith Powell, Jacob Marshall, and Brenda Clark, whom we thank for their efforts.

2. Recently other voices have begun to be heard on this theme: John Schmidt, *This was No @#$%% Picnic: 2.4 Years of Wild and Woolly Mayhem in Dawson Creek* (Hanna, Alberta: Gorman and Gorman, 1991): Earl Gingrich, *Eastern Passage to the Alaska Highway* (self-published, 1986); Cyril Griffith, *Trucking the Tote Road to Alaska, 1942-1943: Memories of the Early Days of the Alaska Highway* (self-published, 1989).

INTRODUCTION

In the days when all history was political history, it used to be that working people were left out of history books. For generations, historians focused on the great men— and once in a while on the great women—of the past. History was about kings, politicians and businessmen, military leaders and religious leaders. No one cared much about the life and community of the working class—the men and women who worked in the factories, aboard the ships, in the construction camps and on the farms. Happily, the long-entrenched and deliberate "ignore-ance," to use the pointed word of Michael Frish, of working people has been offset by a new generation of historians who begin their inquiries into the past with the lot and experience of the "common people." Those who wish to study labor history, therefore, no longer need to justify the selection of workers as the primary unit of analysis. Thanks to the work of those who have done so much to set the agenda and to raise the questions, this field of inquiry is widely accepted as legitimate, vital, and of fundamental scholarly importance.

Unfortunately, however, this general observation does not hold for the Northwest, defined here to include Alaska, the Yukon Territory, the Northwest Territories, and the northern sections of British Columbia and Alberta, whose historiography remains locked in the questions and topics that preoccupied North American historians a generation or so ago. While much of this work is useful and often very competent, it does not compensate for the failure of northern historians to add workers to their studies. Most historical studies of Alaska and the Canadian north remain south-centered, concerned more with the creation of northern policy than with the struggles of aboriginal societies or working people on the far distant frontier, or they are anecdotal and narrative treatments of the characters or unique events of the Northwest.

Equally, however, North American labor historians have been notably reluctant to turn their attentions northward. They are particularly interested in industrial processes—the struggle to organize the large industries and the battle for control of the workplace that engulfed the working class in the years of the industrial revolution. With a few exceptions, including Robert Robson's study of mine workers in northern Manitoba[1] and Ian Radforth's examination of lumber workers in northern Ontario,[2] there have been few attempts to analyze the experience of northern workers; the work of Alaskan historians, which usually highlights Alaskan exceptionalism, remains outside the main currents of contemporary historical scholarship.[3] As a consequence, labor historiography, which has only recently broken away from urban and factory-based workers, has yet to incorporate the experience of northern, frontier workers into the history of the North American working class.[4]

Our studies, which have focused on the Canadian north, suggest that this omission is an important one, both for an understanding of the evolution of northern society and of the historical experience of the working class. Although the northern work force was quite small in any given year, transiency and turn-over was such that thousands of North American workers could claim some northern experience during their working lives. Their experience is crucial for what it reveals about continental attitudes towards the North and about worker and management relations in peripheral or frontier settings.

This study—which concerns workers on the World War II defense projects in the Northwest—emerged in a somewhat roundabout fashion. We were drawn to the "Army of Occupation" through a study of the building of the Alaska Highway and related projects.

As we researched this fairly specific theme, we were startled by the complexity and scale of the American invasion of the Northwest between 1942 and 1946. What began as a single volume on the Army of Occupation became two: a general study of the impact of the American projects on the region,[5] and this book on the role of working men and women in the construction of these projects.

The existing historical studies of the northwest defense projects have focused on diplomatic and political questions, issues that have been studied extensively.[6] While these themes may be vital in national and international terms, they reveal very little about the impact of the invading forces on the Northwest and the impact of the Northwest on the incoming soldiers and workers. Nor do they advance our understanding of the North as a specific regional society and economy.

If we had one concern in tackling this assignment, it was that we would be unable to convince others of its importance. The North has, after all, long been historiographically peripheral, the number of people working there usually small, and many of their experiences deemed to be unique to the region. To many North American historians, Alaska and the Canadian north remain the preserve of antiquarian and narrative historians, and of a scholarship that rarely speaks to wider issues. Whatever little truth there may be in this, we do not believe that it holds for the period of World War II. The construction of the northwest defense projects created a most unusual mix of national, class, and regional processes that calls for detailed study, if only because of its scale. In 1943, at their peak, over 60,000 workers were in the Northwest of North America, from Edmonton to Norman Wells, and from Dawson Creek to Fairbanks. Over 40,000 of these workers were in the Canadian northwest, creating a most unusual situation of foreign nationals outnumbering the local population.

But the magnitude of the activity is not the only important aspect of the period. Most of the workers were Americans, employed by U.S. companies and agencies but usually working on Canadian soil. There were several thousand Canadians involved as well, the majority of whom came from outside the North. Most worked for Canadian contractors and remained on Canadian soil, but some found employment with American companies; a number also worked for American government agencies. The complexity of the situation goes further. Much of the initial work was completed by soldiers, many of whom were black, a much ignored element of the work force. In addition, dozens of northern Native people found temporary construction-related jobs, from guiding and laboring to doing laundry and selling handicrafts; several hundred women also came north to work. This was, in sum, a complex and varied labor force, subject to a wide range of government regulations, working under different wage schedules, and bringing very different expectations to the North. The two things they had in common was the North—the cold winter, long summer days, mosquitoes, isolation, separation from community and family, and relentless boredom—and the fact that they were working people.

In this book, we explore the experience of workers—American and Canadian, military and civilian, black, white and Native, male and female, government and private sector—involved with the construction of the northwest defense projects. We also hold to a very broad definition of "experience." We are concerned with the recruitment of workers, wage rates and living conditions, workers' expectations about the region and their reaction to the North, the adaptation of skills and technology to subarctic conditions, efforts by managers to control and regulate the workers through legal process, and the promotion of after-hours activities.

There is a tendency to deal with northern history in isolation, and to argue that the climate and geography of the region make it an exceptional case. This historiographic isolation has been very destructive of understanding, for much of what happens in the North can be properly understood only in the context of broader patterns and processes. Similarly, the northern experience is not irrelevant, as has been implicitly suggested, to the greater understanding of North American life generally.[7] This book is not intended solely as a contribution to regional or even national historiography. Instead, we are determined that the study of the experience of working people in the Northwest during World War II should make as broad a contribution as possible.

A number of scholars[8] in Canada and the United States have examined aspects of the recruitment and management of labor by large industrial and/or state enterprises in the first half of the

ARMY CAMP AT WHITEHORSE IN WINTER.
YTA, Robert Hays collection, 5692.

ARMY CAMP AT WHITEHORSE, SUMMER 1942.
YTA, Carter collection, 1548.

twentieth century. Economic conditions, the operation of the labor market, or wartime circumstances forced corporations and the state to recruit, manage and control labor in new environments, often far removed from urban centers and head offices. The issue of management at a distance has increased steadily through this century, in both urban factories and hinterland resource ventures and construction activities.

In the past, the owner managed his own factory, often lived near the plant, and hence had direct oversight over the company's operations. As the economy evolved towards what Marxist scholars describe as monopoly capitalism, coming increasingly under the control of large, monopolistic and transnational corporations, the structure and nature of management changed dramatically. A single corporation might own and operate several factories, construction sites, mines, or lumber camps, scattered widely across a region or nation and even overseas. Management styles had to be redrawn accordingly. Corporations and state enterprises established industrial bureaucracies, using local managers and supervisors, trusted by the owners and trained in the techniques of scientific management, to control the workers and to ensure the efficient operation of the work-site.

In northern or remote areas, the problems of management and control were particularly acute, if only because of the difficulty of communicating between the field and head office. Further, with only a tiny regional labor force, adjustments to the working staff were slow and costly. Hinterland labor relations, therefore, tested the strength and resilience of the new model of labor recruitment and management. War added a further strain, due to the combination of a radically altered labor force, as hundreds of thousands took up arms, and an acute need for resources and productivity.

This book examines the processes of labor recruitment and management, the conditions of work, and the response of the working people, under a combination of these circumstances. The Northwest—Alaska, the Yukon and Northwest Territories, northern British Columbia and Alberta—were clearly hinterlands, far distant from the regular corporate and governmental lines of control. Also, during the chaotic days of 1942 and 1943, as the United States and Canada braced for a possible Japanese invasion, this region played

MEMBERS OF 18TH ENGINEERS REGIMENT
AT THE PONTOON FERRY ON KLUANE LAKE, SUMMER 1942.
YTA, MacBride Museum collection, 3555.

host to a remarkable series of construction projects—the Northwest
Staging Route, the Alaska Highway, and the CANOL (Canadian Oil)
pipeline—as well as a myriad of small construction projects undertaken at the same time.

We think of this book not as labor history but as an aspect of
northern history—a history of workers in a particular time and place,
and on a specific set of projects. We are not labor historians, but
historians of the North, and we seek in this book not to validate any
particular ideology but to examine and analyze the experiences of a
large number of temporary northerners, in this case, workers. Our
purpose is to examine the role and patterns of labor in the Northwest
during World War II, and to look closely at the lives of the workers
there. In the process, we hope to shed light on the response of
government and company managers to the unusual circumstances
surrounding the projects, and the reaction of working people to the
conditions encountered in the Northwest. We are particularly interested in the ability of workers to change their circumstances or to

exercise some measure of control over their lives. We have also attempted to illustrate the impact that working people had on the pattern of living and working in the region. Our goal as far as the historical professional is concerned is essentially twofold: to bring the role of *northern* workers to the attention of labor historians, and to bring the role of northern *workers* to the attention of northern historians.

The first chapter of this book outlines the nature of northern society, and patterns of northern labor, in the years before World War II. We have included a separate chapter on soldiers as workers, because their experiences were different in many respects from those of civilian employees. The next two chapters consider the question of recruiting workers for the northern projects and their experience as employees in the region. Although the number of Native and female workers on the northern projects was comparatively small, their activities have to be considered separately. The northern experience of these Canadian and American workers extended beyond hours of work, and managers were particularly anxious to control the activities of their employers off the work site. We have thus included chapters on the efforts made by project managers to fill their hours away from work with recreational and leisure activities. Because of the urgency of the work, as well as the fact that it was occurring in a remote region under military control, there was little labor protest or radicalism during the war years; still, workers found numerous ways of responding to, and occasionally protesting, working conditions, wages, and subarctic isolation.

In preparing this work, we have been fortunate to have had the assistance of many of the men and women who worked on the northwest defense projects. They have readily shared their memories and memorabilia, helping us to understand the wartime construction projects in a way that archival documents simply would not permit. If this book succeeds in getting inside the experience of workers in the Northwest during World War II, it is largely due to their generosity.

NOTES

1. Robert Robson, "Flin Flon: A Study of Company-Community Relations in a Single Enterprise Community," *Urban History Review* (February 1984).

2. Ian Radforth, *Bushworkers and Bosses: Logging in Northern Ontario, 1900-1980* (Toronto: University of Toronto Press, 1987).

3. For a review of the work of Alaskan historians, see W. R. Morrison, "Alaska History," in *The Northern Review* 5 (Summer 1990).

4. For a useful exception to this pattern, see G. O. Williams, "Share Croppers at Sea: The Whaler's 'Lay' and Events in the Arctic, 1905-1907," *Labor History* 29, no. 1 (1988).

5. K. S. Coates and W. R. Morrison, *The Alaska Highway in World War II: The U.S. Army of Occupation in Canada's Northwest, 1942-1946* (Norman, Okla.: University of Oklahoma Press and Toronto: University of Toronto Press, 1992).

6. In, for example, Stanley W. Dziuban, *Military Relations Between the United States and Canada 1939-1945* (Washington: Department of the Army, 1959); K. S. Coates, ed., *The Alaska Highway: Papers of the 40th Anniversary Symposium* (Vancouver: University of British Columbia Press, 1985); P. S. Barry, *The Canol Project: An Adventure of the U.S. War Department in Canada's Northwest* (Edmonton: published by the author, 1985); Shelagh Grant, *Sovereignty or Security? Government Policy in the Canadian North, 1939-1950* (Vancouver: University of British Columbia Press, 1988); David Remley, *Crooked Road: The Story of the Alaska Highway* (New York: McGraw Hill, 1976).

7. The absence of the North in broad thematic surveys is indicative of this inattention to the region. For the United States, see Patricia Limerick, *The Legacy of Conquest*. All the standard national survey texts of Canada and the United States reflect a southern bias. As this relates to working people, see Bryan Palmer, *The Canadian Working Class Experience: The Rise and Reconstitution of Canadian Labour* (Toronto: Butterworths, 1983) and D. Morton with Terry Copp, *Working People* (Ottawa: Deneau, 1984).

8. Laurel Sefton Macdowell, *Remember Kirkland Lake: The History and Effects of the Kirkland Lake Gold Miners' Strike, 1941-42* (Toronto: University of Toronto Press, 1983); Craig Heron and R. Storey, eds., *Working in Steel: The Early Years in Canada 1883-1935* (Toronto: McClelland and Stewart, 1988); C. Heron, ed., *On the Job: Confronting the Labour Process in Canada* (Kingston: McGill-Queens' University Press, 1986); Rex Lucas, *Minetown, Milltown, Railtown: Life in Canadian Communities of Single Industry* (Toronto: University of Toronto Press, 1971). For American work in this field, see Daniel Nelson, *Managers and Workers: Origins of the New Factory System in the United States, 1880-1920* (1975) and Sandford Jacoby, *Employing Bureaucracy: Managers, Unions and the Transformation of Work in American Industry, 1900-1945* (1985).

1

LABOR AND THE FAR NORTHWEST BEFORE THE INVASION

In all the volumes written about the Northwest, historians and other writers have been preoccupied with the colorful characters and thrilling tales which are so plentiful in northern latitudes. This approach, however, has emphasized one aspect of the picture at the expense of others, and important parts of the northern experience have been virtually ignored. The role of working people, for instance, has been almost completely omitted from accounts of the North. This is unfortunate, given the importance of labor in such processes as the Klondike gold rush, the northern fur trade, and the construction of the White Pass and Yukon Railway. The single best example of the role of labor in the region is provided by the northwest defense projects undertaken in 1942, when the number of imported workers far outstripped the total population, Native and non-Native, of the entire Yukon and Northwest Territories.

In the forty years before the outbreak of World War II a unique society had developed in the region stretching from the Mackenzie River valley to Alaska, one that was self-contained, yet bearing the marks of isolation, neglect, and economic insecurity. It was into this society that the northwest defense projects and their tens of thousands of workers arrived, almost without warning, in the summer of 1942. For most people, the economic history of the region had been a void, briefly illuminated by the burst of a magnificent skyrocket. Few people knew or cared much about the region's affairs except for one short spectacular episode which occurred from 1897 to 1899—the Klondike gold rush. After that was over, the region became dark again, ignored by outsiders, entering a long period of decline and struggle for economic survival. The energy of the gold rush spent itself in a series of small echo-booms which ran from Atlin, British Columbia, to Fairbanks and Tanana in Alaska, to some small finds in the Northwest Territories. Yet though the region declined, it did not die. After the disappointed gold seekers and their camp followers left, there was still mineral wealth in the Northwest. But now the individualist frenzy of the gold rush era was replaced by the hard capitalist realities of corporate ownership and large-scale mining. The great concessionaires bought up the gold-bearing Klondike ground, and poured capital into power stations, aqueducts, and mammoth dredges, ensuring that the extraction of mineral wealth would continue—but now it would be machines, not men, that moiled for gold.

Not all the mineral wealth of the Northwest lay in gold, for there were promising discoveries of other metals in the first decades of the twentieth century, ranging from copper deposits in the Whitehorse area to radium at Great Bear Lake. Deposits of silver in the Yukon's Elsa and Keno district breathed new life into the territory's economy in the 1920s, and the opening of the Yellowknife gold mines did the same for the Mackenzie River valley in the 1930s. In the interior of Alaska, too, gold mining remained the backbone of the economy. The primary work force of the region was made up of hardrock miners, dredge operators, and the crews of the railway and the sternwheelers that provided the main form of transportation.

But mining was not the only foundation of northern economic life. Although the fur trade no longer enjoyed the high profile and sense of adventure that had surrounded the industry in the eighteenth and nineteenth centuries, it remained a vital sector of the northern economy.[1] In the Mackenzie River basin before World War II, the Hudson's Bay Company was supreme. It had faced stiff competition early in the century, but it outwaited its rivals during economic slumps, forcing them out of business or buying them out. In Alaska and the Yukon, the situation was much more competitive. One firm, the locally owned Taylor and Drury Company, dominated the Yukon fur trade, but it was rivaled by a number of small, independent operators who survived in the trade for a few years at a time. In Alaska, a number of independent traders competed for the valuable fur resources harvested by the Native people of the Alaskan interior.

The northern fur trade, famous for the quality of the subarctic pelts, successfully rode out the depression of the 1930s. Native people dominated the trapping side of the trade, although they had to share it with "bushmen" who came north to escape the depression in the south.[2] The fur traders helped to keep open the north's lines of communication and supply, particularly on the smaller rivers not served by the major transportation companies. The trade no longer attracted much outside interest, but it remained vital to the society and economy of the north.

The relative stability of gold mining and the northern fur trade protected the Northwest from the worst effects of the Great Depression. While the rest of North America suffered through a prolonged economic crisis, the Yukon and the interior of Alaska plodded quietly along. The region experienced little of the excitement and energy that had accompanied the gold rush, and the economic returns were meager in comparison to the halcyon days of 1898, but for a small number of people who stayed in the North, gold mining and the fur trade provided a security that was woefully lacking Outside.

The Northwest was not a region where the permanent residents created the economy; rather, it was one where the economy determined the size and makeup of the population. When the economy boomed, people swarmed in and the population soared. When it slackened, people left, and the population went into a prolonged decline. A direct correlation existed between the resource production of the region and its population; as with all boom communities, people left quickly once the easy wealth had been taken out.

Both the Yukon and the interior of Alaska suffered a steady decline of population in the aftermath of the gold rush, a decline

Table 1.1
RESOURCE PRODUCTION IN THE FAR NORTHWEST, 1920–1950

	Gold (thousands of ounces)[3]		Silver (thousands of ounces)	
	YT	NWT	YT	NWT
1920	72		19*	
1925	48		905*	
1935	35*		201*	
1940	80	55	2,259	59.5
1945	31.7	8.6	25	2
1950	93	200	3,302	62

*includes NWT

Yukon: Other Minerals[4]

	Coal (short tons)	Copper (lbs)	Cadmium (lbs)	Lead (lbs)
1920	763	277,712		
1925	730			1,875,442
1935	835			231,418
1945				119,516
1950	3,703		56,410	12,885,518

Northwest Territories

	Natural Gas (M cu ft)	Crude Oil (bbl)
1935		5,115
1940	1,500	18,633
1945	1,500	345,171
1950	33,335	186,729

Table 1.2
REGIONAL POPULATION, 1900–1951.[5]

	Yukon Territory			Northwest Territories		
	Native	White	Total	Native	White	Total
1901	3,302	23,917	27,219			
1911	1,489	7,023	8,512	15,904	1,292	17,196
1921	1,390	2,767	4,157	7,115	873	7,988
1931	1,628	2,602	4,230	8,716	1,007	9,723
1941	1,508	3,406	4,914	9,456	2,572	12,028
1951	1,563	7,533	9,096	10,660	5,344	16,004

	Alaska[6]			
	Native	White	Military	Total
1900	29,542	30,450		65,592
1910	25,331	36,400		64,356
1920	26,558	28,228	250	55,036
1930	29,983	29,045	250	59,278
1940	32,456	39,566	500	72,524
1950	33,863	74,373	20,047	128,643

which accelerated during the First World War, then experienced a slow reversal throughout the 1920s and 1930s. The Mackenzie district, on the other hand, had seen little commercial development other than that connected with the fur trade before 1930, except for a brief flurry of oil exploration at Norman Wells in 1920. In 1930 the non-Native population of the Northwest Territories was barely 1,000, and the region still moved largely to the rhythm of the lives of its indigenous population.

The Northwest in this era was a classic demographic frontier. The non-Native population was young, mobile, and mostly male. Few women or children ventured north, and those who did seldom remained for long. There were of course exceptions—Martha Black, the doyenne of the Yukon, who came north in 1898 and stayed for sixty years, or Laura Berton, who came to the Yukon as a school-teacher and remained to raise a family. But the non-Native population of the North was predominantly made up of single men, many no longer young, who had come in search of adventure and wealth. Most of them found a good measure of the former, typically in brutally harsh winters, isolation, and privation, but not much of the latter.

Table 1.3

POPULATION OF THE YUKON BY AGE, RACE, AND GENDER, 1941.[7]

	Native		Non-Native	
Age	Male	Female	Male	Female
0–4	135	135	99	100
5–9	119	113	95	91
10–14	116	107	67	59
15–19	84	80	44	44
20–24	80	79	140	89
25–34	108	117	529	231
35–44	77	71	364	106
45–54	52	60	258	79
55–64	45	37	290	79
65–69	20	18	165	24
70+	30	24	256	18

Some, their fantasies of new bonanzas rudely shattered, stayed only as long as their temperament, determination, or finances permitted, then fled south. Others established a kind of quasi-residence in the North, working there in the summer, but returning to the south every winter.[8] Then as now, the primary characteristic of non-Native northern society was a remarkable transiency, showing few signs of stability or long-term commitment.

Natives and non-Natives mixed as workers within the regional order mostly when it was to the latter's advantage, and largely on the latter's terms. In the fur trade sector, which dominated the Mackenzie region but took second place in the Yukon and Alaska, traders, missionaries, and the Mounted Police worked closely with the aboriginal people. But in the mining camps and other communities, particularly Yellowknife, Whitehorse, Dawson City, and Fairbanks, the races remained largely separate. In these non-Native enclaves, discrimination and segregation worked to keep Indians and mixed bloods outside the community, welcome as occasional visitors, consumers, and seasonal or casual workers, but not as fellow citizens and neighbors. For the most part, Native people remained in the bush, continuing to hunt, trap, fish, and to gather the resources of the land as need dictated and season permitted.

The social structure of the Northwest—small in human scale, vulnerable to the economic dictates of outside forces—had grown out of the meeting of a permanent aboriginal population and a number of transient non-Natives. By the late 1930s, when the rumblings of an escalating international conflict reached the northland, the region had achieved a steady, though fragile, equilibrium. The Klondike gold rush appeared to have been an aberration, a promise of dynamic growth and prosperity that now seemed like a cruel joke. The decay of Dawson City, once a thriving metropolis and now almost a ghost town, bore mute and decaying testimony to the transitory expectations of the gold rush era. The reality was to be found in the hard-rock mines of Yellowknife and Keno Hill, and the dredges of the Dawson and Fairbanks region—not boomtowns or Eldorados, but examples of the slow, steady exploitation of the region's spotty, but occasionally rich, resources. Now, as World War II drew near, the region had settled into a new economic balance, one which had abandoned the gaudy dreams of the past and found survival despite the abandonment of the North by governments, businessmen, and purveyors of false hope.

The uneven, episodic nature of the development of the Northwest was due in part to the role of the United States and Canadian governments. In the Yukon and Northwest Territories, the federal government was notable before 1940 primarily for its absence. The Canadian government relied heavily on the Royal Canadian Mounted Police (RCMP) to enforce the criminal law and to take the place of civil servants in administering a wide range of regulations and providing services. The government of the Northwest Territory was even more remote—until 1967 it was centered in Ottawa, two thousand miles away from the Mackenzie River. The Yukon fared a bit better, though its government had fallen on evil days since the gold rush. Over twenty years its ten-member elected Territorial Council was slowly whittled away to three, dominated by a federally appointed commissioner. It was Ottawa's distant poor relation, perennially strapped for cash, relying on liquor and hunting license revenues to fund a meager range of services. The federal government saw no reason to spend money in either territory; both, it believed, had a limited and static future. Its priorities were to avoid costly commitments, provide a bare minimum of services to the Native people, and to rely on the RCMP to show the flag, demonstrating Canadian sovereignty at bargain basement rates.[9]

The situation in Alaska was remarkably different. Despite the fact that most Alaskans believe that they have always been shamefully neglected by Washington, the United States government had a surprisingly strong presence in Alaska, particularly when compared with the Canadian government presence east of the 141st meridian. The American military establishment, small in relation to the size of Alaska, was significant in terms of the size of the local population.[10] In contrast, there was no permanent Canadian military presence in the Yukon or Northwest Territories before 1940. Washington's influence was evident at many levels in Alaska, from a strongly interventionist and protective policy on timber and other natural resources to massive government investment in the Alaska railway which links Fairbanks with the sea. It is one of the ironies of life in Alaska that its residents in this period complained of excessive federal government interference in their affairs; some envied the *laissez-faire* attitude of the Canadian government towards the Yukon.[11]

Unlike the Canadian government, Washington had ambitions for its northern possessions, reflecting the still-powerful American belief in the mystique of the frontier. By the 1930s, Alaska had long since shed the "ice-box" image, and was now the last frontier, a resource-rich land of opportunity. During the depression, the Roosevelt administration supported an agricultural resettlement scheme in the Matanuska Valley, importing the model of westward expansion to the northwest.

But in Alaska, as in the Canadian north, the gospel of progress and the popular belief in frontier riches had not, by 1940, brought prosperity, nor a stability based on anything more than the lowest common denominator. In the 1930s there had been a debate over American and British Columbian proposals to build a highway from the Pacific Northwest states to Alaska, but the schemes foundered on Canadian suspicions of American motives and Ottawa's unwillingness to support British Columbia Premier T. D. Pattullo's dream of northern development.[12] On the eve of World War II, the Northwest remained geographically, politically and psychologically isolated from the rest of the continent. It was difficult to entice people to come north, and even more difficult to persuade them to stay. Given the limited interest of the American and Canadian governments in integrating the region into their continental empires, this was not surprising.

The men and women who did come north to work carried with them the attitudes and values of the United States and southern Canada, particularly a belief in the exotic nature of the region—that the North was different from the rest of the continent, a land of peril, hardship, and adventure. Those who came north to work also fell quickly into the exceptionally mobile pattern of labor on the periphery. Captivated and conditioned by images of the frontier, workers came to the region, in the words of Tony Penikett, former Yukon government leader, "to make a killing, not a living." From the days of the gold rush to the Arctic oil boom of the 1970s, few workers intended to settle permanently in the region. Drawn north by opportunities, real and perceived, they seldom stayed long. Many did not even bring their families with them.

In the early years of the century, most of the employees of the White Pass and Yukon Railway, the dominant transportation company in the Yukon basin,[13] came north for the short summer navigation season and returned to spend the winter in British Columbia or Washington State. The same appears to be true of the men working on the gold mining dredges—the largest employer of labor in Alaska and the Yukon. Efforts were made to extend the mining season into early winter, but with the dredges and hydraulic workers dependent on the flow of water, freeze-up inevitably forced a halt to operations.[14] Those working in the hard-rock mines worked year round, but life in the isolated company towns could be harsh, and most remained only a short time (though during the depression, they tended to stay longer for want of alternative opportunities). This pattern did not hold along the coast of Alaska, where the fishing and lumber industries provided a more stable foundation for the local economy, and where a milder climate partly compensated for the isolation. In much of the North, however, workers and owners alike looked on the region as a place to make money and leave. A major reason for this impermanence was the seasonal nature of the northern economy, created by the limitations imposed by winter and the uncertainties of a resource-based economy.

Northern workers were, as a rule, paid more than their southern counterparts. Other benefits provided in an attempt to compensate for climate and location were recreational activities, room and board, and subsidized transportation. There was little labor radicalism and few strikes in the North, partly because of the comparatively high wages and partly because of the mobility of the workers; if they felt they were getting a raw deal, they tended to leave rather than go on strike. The few labor disputes that did occur, particularly in the Klondike dredges, were usually quickly settled; the short work season and the high capitalization of the industry compelled management to respond quickly and reasonably to workers' demands. For these reasons, trade unionism made little headway in the far northwest. In any case, collectivism ran counter to the deeply ingrained sense of individualism that was an important part of the northern mystique. Thus the radical unions of the Pacific Northwest, particularly the miners' unions, seem to have made little effort to organize in the Northwest.[15]

Well before World War II, a distinctively northern pattern of labor had developed in the region. Large pools of labor existed in Seattle, Vancouver, and Edmonton, with smaller secondary pools in Juneau, Anchorage, Fairbanks, Whitehorse, and Dawson City. Workers typically came north on a seasonal basis, spending the summer on riverboats or dredges, then leaving for the south to find work before winter set in. The employers who operated year-round, such as the silver-lead mines at Elsa and Keno, were small, isolated properties. The fur traders also operated throughout the year, hiring a small number of clerks and managers to run their posts, but these were exceptions to the rule.

PONTOON BRIDGE OVER THE DONJEK RIVER, YUKON, SUMMER 1942.
YTA, MacBride Museum collection, 3554.

FRED FORD OF STRATHMORE, CALIFORNIA, HANDYMAN WITH
HEADQUARTERS AND SERVICE COMPANY, 18TH ENGINEERS,
BESIDE HIS TOOLS, HOLDING A PINE BURL, JULY 1942.
YTA, Robert Hays collection, 5671.

The Northwest had always offered more than dreams of wealth. Since the days of the gold rush, the Yukon and Alaska had been cultural symbols—the home of the last true North American frontier. Alaska was more successful at cultivating this image than was the Yukon, but a flow of fiction, poetry, and movies (such as Charlie Chaplin's *The Gold Rush*) kept alive the mystery and attraction of the northern frontier in both territories. The propaganda issued after 1942 to justify the decision to build the Alaska Highway capitalized on this public fascination with the northland—the project was touted as a battle of North American technology and manpower against a harsh and unforgiving wilderness. The size of the challenge, so the rhetoric went, proved the Allies' determination to protect North America. The images of adventure proved powerful, and in combination with good wages ensured a steady flow of civilian workers to the northern defense projects.[16]

Everyone, from government to managers to workers, knew and expected that these projects would provide only temporary employment. Like all the great construction enterprises, from the transcontinental railways of the nineteenth century to the northern pipelines of recent years, little thought was given to post-construction opportunities for the workers attracted to the North.[17] Managers expected that they might have trouble getting workers to come to the region, but they anticipated no difficulties in getting them to leave after the jobs ended.

In February 1942, only two months after the Japanese attack on Pearl Harbor, the United States government announced sweeping measures for the defense of the far northwest. Alaska had always been highly vulnerable to attack, but the absence of any threat before 1940, and the difficulty (and expense) of defending many hundreds of miles of coastline and vast tracts of land in the interior had prevented any real attempt to protect the region. Still, a military presence did exist in Alaska; a string of small military bases manned by 500 servicemen was scattered throughout the territory, in contrast to the total absence of a Canadian military presence northwest of Edmonton. The events at Pearl Harbor jolted Americans out of their slumber and forced consideration of the strategic and military needs of Alaska. No such concern affected Canada, due to a lesser sense of

ROAD CONDITIONS AFTER A RAINSTORM, SUMMER 1942.
YTA, MacBride Museum collection, 3552.

MEMBERS OF THE 18TH ENGINEERS MOTOR POOL
REPAIRING A JEEP, NORTHWEST OF WHITEHORSE, 1942.
YTA, Robert Hays collection, 5676.

military vulnerability, preoccupation with other defense issues, and the traditional neglect of the North.

The United States had a huge area to protect in Alaska,[18] and no immediate idea of how to prevent the Japanese army from invading it or harassing its coastline. Most of Alaska's population lived in a series of isolated coastal and island communities, including the Aleutian Islands archipelago, which at its western end was much closer to Tokyo than to Washington, D.C., or even to San Francisco. On a map, the Aleutians looked like a series of stepping stones, which the Japanese could use as a pathway to the North American continent, just as American military planners hoped to use the southern Pacific islands as a highway leading in the other direction. The Japanese invasion of Kiska and Attu in June 1942 showed that this fear was not entirely born of hysteria. Defending and supplying these Alaskan settlements would remain a military priority throughout the war.

Historians would later scoff at the hysteria which swept the United States in the early stages of the Pacific war.[19] Indeed, some of the military decisions taken in those days of near-panic were later seen to have been hasty and ill-conceived. Yet with the Japanese rolling across the Far East in the dark days of 1942 and their Nazi allies heading triumphantly for Moscow, the Allied forces had reason to be concerned. This fear, added to the racism endemic to North American society, led to shameful episodes such as the internment of Japanese-American and Japanese-Canadian citizens. It also led to the building of the Alaska Highway.

Even in 1942 some members of the American military establishment and Canadian officials openly questioned the military and strategic value of the plans drawn up for the defense of the Northwest. Some of the defense proposals were poorly conceived, showing the difficulty of making rational decisions in the face of military emergency, misdirected enthusiasm, well-meaning but ill-informed advice, and a bottomless well of public money. By 1944, with the Aleutians cleared of the enemy and the possibility of further Japanese attacks remote, some of the military projects seemed highly questionable. But such a perspective did not exist in 1942. Speed and a response of whatever kind were considered essential; thus American planners moved with haste, though with little knowledge of what

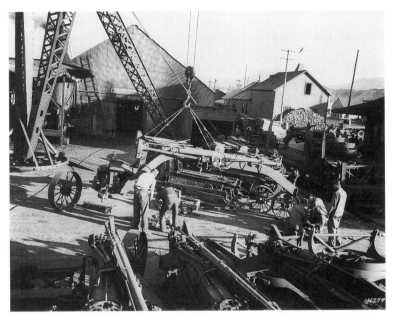

ROAD-BUILDING EQUIPMENT AT DAWSON CREEK RAILHEAD, SUMMER 1942.
NA, 111-SC 146279.

they were getting into. The decisions taken in the first frantic weeks of 1942 resulted in a series of northwest defense projects, the military occupation of the Canadian northwest, and the rapid militarization of Alaska.

The results of these decisions were sweeping in scale. The Northwest Staging Route, a series of airfields connecting Edmonton with the Yukon, had been largely completed by the Canadian government in 1941. Under the new agreements, this route was greatly expanded and upgraded. In 1942 the United States signed a lend-lease agreement with the USSR under which the Americans ferried hundreds of aircraft and other military supplies along the route. The exchange from American to Soviet pilots took place at Ladd Airfield in Fairbanks, making this old gold-mining community the cornerstone for the lend-lease program in western North America.[20]

As the conflict in the Pacific escalated, the supply and defense of this lend-lease route assumed greater importance.

One of the highest military priorities was the Alaska Highway, originally called the Alcan Highway, which was to be built by the American army from the railhead at Dawson Creek, British Columbia, to Big Delta, Alaska. The purpose of the road was to ensure unimpeded land access to the interior of Alaska, and to permit supply and servicing of the Northwest Staging Route airfields. An unhappy combination of legitimate concern about petroleum supplies in the Northwest and exceptionally bad technical advice convinced the U.S. government to build a pipeline between the Mackenzie River oil field at Norman Wells and Whitehorse. There, Standard Oil of California was to build a refinery. From Whitehorse, which was also the construction headquarters for the Alaska Highway, other pipelines would carry petroleum products north and south along the road, and to tidewater at Skagway, Alaska. The U.S. Army was also ordered to complete a number of smaller projects: a connecting road called the Haines Lateral, which joined the Alaska Highway to the port of Haines, Alaska, on the Lynn Canal; a regional telephone and telegraph system to link the many bases, airfields, and construction camps; and numerous other buildings, services, and access roads. Not since the Klondike gold rush had the Northwest experienced so massive an invasion.

The militarization of the Northwest during World War II which resulted from the construction of the Alaska Highway and its satellite projects raises numerous important issues, from the environmental impact of hastily planned and largely unsupervised construction projects to the implications of the absence of Canadian concern about the massive American invasion. Here, however, the focus is on the workers, a group generally ignored in historical writing on the wartime projects, the story of their experiences kept alive mostly by themselves, in anecdotes, photograph albums, and periodic re-unions. The successful and rapid completion of the projects relied on the recruitment, mobilization, and ultimately the work of thousands of military and civilian employees. These people, mostly southerners, were part of a unique exercise in Canadian-American cooperation, working under the exigencies of war in subarctic conditions—an experience that for many shaped their lives as surely as it reshaped the Northwest.

NOTES

1. A. J. Ray, *The Canadian Fur Trade in the Industrial Age* (Toronto: University of Toronto Press, 1990).

2. A notorious example of a bushman was the "Mad Trapper of Rat River." See Dick North, *The Mad Trapper of Rat River* (Toronto: Macmillan, 1972).

3. Source: *Canada Year Book*, 1932, 1938, 1950, 1952-53.

4. Source: *Canada Year Book*, 1937, 1938, 1947, 1952-53.

5. Source: *Census of Canada*, 1901, 1911, 1921, 1931, 1941, 1951.

6. Source: *Historical Statistics of the United States, Colonial Times to 1970, Part 1* (Washington, D.C.: U.S. Bureau of the Census, 1975).

7. Source: *Census of Canada*, 1941. Indians and half-breeds are included in the category "Native." The population of the Northwest Territories had a much greater proportion of Native people, and was thus more evenly balanced by age and sex; the same was true of Alaska. See George Rogers and Richard Cooley, *Alaska's Population and Economy: Regional Growth, Development, and Future Outlook, vol. 1* (Fairbanks: University of Alaska Institute of Business, Economic and Government Research, 1963), p. 66.

8. On the subject of northern transiency, see K. S. Coates and W. R. Morrison, *The Sinking of the Princess Sophia: Taking the North Down With Her* (Toronto: Oxford University Press, 1990), and K. S. Coates and W. R. Morrison, "Transiency in the Far Northwest After the Gold Rush: The Case of the Princess Sophia," in *Interpreting Canada's North*, ed. K. S. Coates and W. R. Morrison (Toronto: Copp Clark Pitman, 1989).

9. On this theme see W. R. Morrison, *Showing the Flag: the Mounted Police and Canadian Sovereignty in the North, 1894–1925* (Vancouver: University of British Columbia Press, 1985).

10. Of the 500 service personnel stationed in Alaska in 1940, 475 were in the southeastern part of the Territory. *Historical Statistics of the United States, Colonial Times to 1970, Part 1* (Washington: U.S. Bureau of the Census, 1975).

11. See Kenneth S. Coates, "Controlling the Periphery: A Comparison of the Territorial Administrations of Alaska and the Yukon Territory," *Pacific Northwest Quarterly* 78, no. 4 (October 1987).

12. Robin Fisher, "T. D. Pattullo and the British Columbia to Alaska Highway," in *The Alaska Highway: Papers of the 40th Anniversary Symposium*, ed. K. S. Coates (Vancouver: University of British Columbia Press, 1985).

13. Gordon Bennett, *Yukon Transportation: A History*, Canadian Historic Sites Occasional Papers in Archaeology and History, no. 19 (Ottawa: Supply and Services Canada, 1978).

14. The industry, with little reference to working people, is described in Lewis Green, *The Gold Hustlers* (Vancouver: J. J. Douglas, 1972).

15. The history of this process remains to be written.

16. This study draws heavily on a large number of interviews with men and women who worked in the northwest during this period. Almost without exception, they highlight the sense of adventure that accompanied their work. Clearly, this was more than just another job.

17. Though recently the managers of these mega-projects have been compelled to give at least some attention to what will happen once the construction is finished.

18. The state is 570,000 square miles in area, a little smaller than Quebec, at 594,000 square miles.

19. J. Dower, *War Without Mercy: Race and Power in the Pacific War* (New York: Pantheon, 1987).

20. The United States also shipped massive quantities of military hardware to the USSR by ship. To reach the port of Vladivostok, these ships had to pass close to Japan, easily within range of Japanese aircraft and submarines. Because the Japanese were anxious to avoid military confrontation with the Soviet Union, these American ships were not attacked until the very end of the war.

2 SOLDIERS AS WORKERS

Early in 1942 a decision was made in Washington, D.C., to use military personnel to do the preliminary work on the northwest defense projects, thus foreshadowing a massive mobilization of troops for northern service. The American military had little experience in Alaska, or in northern areas generally, and did not have the equipment or training necessary for easy adaptation to the region. Nor had it much information about the region it was heading for. It could, however, draw on the United States Army Corps of Engineers, which had generations of experience under all manner of difficult conditions.

The U.S. Army Corps of Engineers was established in 1779, disbanded at the end of the Revolutionary War, and reestablished in 1802. In time of peace, the engineers built fortifications, canals, dams, water control projects, government buildings, particularly in the District of Columbia—the Capitol dome and the Washington Monument were two of their projects—and helped with emergency disaster relief. In wartime, the corps built bridges, camps, airfields, and other military facilities. The modernization and mechanization of war in the twentieth century placed increasing demands on the Corps of Engineers. During World War I, for example, it staffed the engineer regiments that were part of all combat divisions, drafted military maps, built hospitals and the port facilities, roads, and railways needed to bring war material to the front, harvested timber for military construction, operated searchlights for antiaircraft defense, organized the first U.S. tank units, and developed offensive and defensive chemical warfare equipment.[1] Only occasionally did the engineers engage in actual combat, but the men were often at or close to the front lines. Their work seldom enjoyed much publicity, but it was essential to the war effort. For thousands of men who served in the corps during World War I, their work was more like that of a civilian worker than a combat soldier, despite its occasional dangers, although they were paid, organized, and directed under military law and in line with military priorities.

The size of the Corps of Engineers, like that of the entire American military, shrank rapidly after the end of World War I. By 1939, it had only 800 officers and 6,000 enlisted men on active service, a far cry from the force at the height of the war, and a reflection of the isolationism and general antimilitarism of the period. Most of its work between the wars was of a civilian nature; in 1938, for instance, its budget for civilian projects was 400 times that for military projects. Expansion and mobilization began with the switch to a policy of preparedness in 1940, with the engineers assigned to construction of military facilities in the United States, particularly airfields. After December 1941 the corps grew rapidly. Because it had a large number of construction units, it took in a large number of black workers, whose second-class status in American society was reflected in the belief that they were unfit for combat battalions. Twenty percent of those who served in the engineers were black, twice the proportion of blacks in the general population.[2]

While the primary responsibility of the corps was to provide support for combat troops in Europe and the Pacific, considerable work was done away from the theaters of war. It was the engineers, for example, who designed and built many of the buildings used in the Manhattan Project. They also undertook construction projects in such widely separated areas as Iceland, Australia, Tonga, and the Caribbean. It was only natural, therefore, that they should be charged with the responsibility for the initial design and construction of the Alaska Highway and providing logistical support for the CANOL

TRUCKS CROSSING THE TESLIN RIVER AT
JOHNSON'S CROSSING, USING A PONTOON FERRY, SUMMER 1942.
U.S. Army photograph, Anchorage Museum, B62.X15.3.

pipeline. The project was military in origin and purpose, the war made its construction urgent, and the Corps of Engineers had the manpower, expertise, and equipment necessary to do the job.

Typically, the military is excluded from considerations of the working class experience. It appears in histories of labor only when governments turn to the military for assistance in regulating or controlling workers, particularly during strikes—soldiers in such cases have traditionally been pictured not as workers, but as tools of class and management. But there are similarities between the industrial worker and the noncombatant soldier, just as there are similarities between the aims and activities of government and management and those of the upper-level military bureaucracy. In Canada, the cooperation between many soldiers and workers in the aftermath of World War I, particularly during the Winnipeg general strike of 1919, suggests that there may be more common ground than is generally assumed.[3]

That the military is an instrument of the state is obvious. Soldiers are the guardians of the state. Their task, in a general sense, is to defend the political and sometimes the ideological boundaries of a nation-state, to assist its allies, and to extend its influence into hostile territory. This side of the armed forces is time-tested and traditional. But there is another side to the armed forces that is often ignored. Soldiers, be they regular troops, militia, or National Guard, have long undertaken a wide variety of civilian work on behalf of the state. At one extreme are activities like strike-breaking that appear to be a logical extension of the military function. Here the soldiers' training with weapons and the use of force are simply applied to domestic rather than international threats to the state. At the other extreme, soldiers have been used for some quite nonmilitary tasks, ranging from acting as human guinea pigs in nuclear tests to service as emergency crews in catastrophes to cleaning up after oil spills, and to a surprising extent, as workers. This is, in part, a reflection of the complexity of the modern military, in which soldiers are trained for a wide variety of tasks, many of which are only distantly related to combat.[4] Soldiers who may be expected to build roads, bridges, camps, communications systems, and to perform other noncombat duties will obviously require previous training in such duties, and civilian work performed in time of peace provides excellent training for wartime tasks.[5]

Soldiers are valuable as workers in a number of ways. Because the military code stresses unquestioning obedience to lawful commands and requires soldiers to accept hard work under harsh conditions, soldiers make excellent workers in unfavorable settings. Military pay is set by fiat, not by collective bargaining. Soldiers are liable for duty twenty-four hours a day and are forbidden to air complaints in groups. They are expected to tolerate crowded quarters, poor food, isolation and other hardships as part of their patriotic duty. The reality sometimes differed from the ideal, particularly in the United States, where congressmen routinely received letters from servicemen full of complaints about pay, working conditions, or bad treatment; sometimes these letters were acted upon. Still, the soldiers as workers provided excellent value for the taxpayer's dollar, particularly compared to unionized workers, who

BUILDING A TIMBER BRIDGE OVER EDITH CREEK, SUMMER 1942.
YTA, MacBride Museum collection, 3557.

were far more demanding and likely to protest their grievances, war or no war.

The threat of court martial provided a measure of control of the military work force of which civilian employers could only dream. Twelve members of the 18th Engineers, one of the units that served in the Northwest, were tried on different occasions by court martial between April 1943 and January 1944; the most serious charge was willful disobedience to a lawful order—no rare offense among civilian workers—but the maximum sentence was six months at hard labor and loss of two-thirds of pay for that period.[6]

During World War II, the question of race also affected the use of soldiers as workers. The most overt forms of race prejudice, still endemic in the United States in 1940, restricted the use of black troops in combat roles throughout the war. The prevailing belief that blacks and whites could and would not fight alongside each other kept black troops out of the front lines. But blacks were volunteering in large

BRIDGING THE DONJEK RIVER, SUMMER 1942.
YTA, R. A. Carter collection, 1477.

numbers for military service, anxious, like other minorities, to
demonstrate their loyalty, and eager, at the end of the depression, to
secure the regular pay, clothing, housing, and meals that the army
provided. The peacetime draft which began in 1940 brought even
more black servicemen into the armed forces.

Though blacks, like everyone else, came to the military for a
variety of reasons, the government had little difficulty deciding what
to do with them. Denied the right (with some exceptions) to fight for
their country, they were assigned in large numbers to engineering
battalions, where they provided much of the logistical support
necessary to win the war. Hundreds of thousands of black servicemen were stationed in areas as diverse as the Northwest and the
Philippines, providing the U.S. government with a huge, mobile work
force.[7]

The main reason for considering soldiers in the Northwest as
workers is, simply, that they performed work—the same jobs as

civilian workers in the region—though they got lower pay, had fewer rights and avenues of complaint, were provided with fewer services and amenities, and operated under stricter forms of control and discipline. Like the civilians, they surveyed, cut trees, handled bulldozers, drove trucks, built camps, and otherwise worked for the completion of the northwest defense projects. They were "workers minus," doing everything civilian workers did, but with fewer rights, privileges, and lower pay.

In a sense, soldiers and civilian workers were in competition with each other. Where the cost of using civilian labor, or the difficulties anticipated in recruiting, controlling, or retaining civilian workers exceeded that of using soldiers, the government was tempted to employ the military option—a notable Canadian example is the use of the Royal Engineers to build the Cariboo Road in British Columbia during the 1860s. This was particularly true in frontier areas and foreign territories. Military engineering battalions, for example, built roads, ports, airfields, canals, camps, and other military facilities round the Allied world during World War II.[8] The use of soldiers to perform this work, only a small percentage of which was carried out in the face of the enemy, saved the American government countless millions of dollars and provided for the ready management and control of the work force.

The same was true in Canada, though on a smaller scale. The Canadian Army Corps of Engineers, or "Sappers," undertook a variety of civilian tasks in wartime and peacetime, notably responsibility for the maintenance of the Alaska Highway after 1946. They got the job more for reasons of cost and logistics than because of any strategic or defense policy.[9] The army retained this responsibility until 1964, when it was passed to the Department of Public Works.[10] During the construction of the Dempster Highway between Dawson City and the Mackenzie Delta town of Inuvik in the 1970s, engineering troops were called in to build bailey bridges across several rivers; the work was called a training exercise, but it also saved the federal government hundreds of thousands of dollars over having the same job done by civilian contractors.

In a practical sense, soldiers were perfectly suited for northern work. The standard process of organizing a northern work force—recruitment, enticing workers north, keeping them on the job by a combination of attractive pay and good fringe benefits, and doing everything possible to help them adjust to subarctic conditions, in the hope of reducing the turnover of labor as much as possible—did not apply to soldiers. The right to refuse work, choose employment, and demand better conditions was not in their contract; they went and did where and what they were told to. There was no haggling over wages and working conditions, and the soldiers, whose mail was censored,[11] and who were ordered not to discuss their northern work, had little public outlet for complaint.[12] Moreover, their bosses had an argument for hard, unquestioning work that was difficult to answer: how could anyone gripe about working conditions on the Alaska Highway when their counterparts in Europe or the Pacific were facing death under worse conditions?

The United States Army sent over 11,000 officers and men to work on the Alaska Highway. Most of these stayed in the region for less than a year, completing their assignments and then being reassigned to other tasks. Some of the men stayed in the North, moving to other construction projects in Alaska; others were sent to Europe or the southern Pacific. They were not all construction workers; a number of signal, quartermaster, medical and finance units accompanied the main force.[13] Further thousands of troops came north to assist with the construction of the CANOL pipeline and related facilities. Nearly 40,000 civilians worked on the northwest projects at the height of construction work in 1943.[14] The military also manned the Grimshaw Road, a winter tractor-train road that served the CANOL operations. Twenty-five hundred troops, with civilian assistance, ran the Mackenzie River transportation system that was the life-line for the Norman Wells oil field and pipeline project. Three hundred and sixty officers and men of the 9646A Engineer Railway Detachment[15] arrived in Skagway in September 1942 to take control of the White Pass and Yukon Route, and with the help of 120 civilians, they ran the railway for the next two years.

In January 1943, the 477th Quartermaster Regiment, over 4,000 strong, arrived in Dawson Creek, British Columbia, to begin operations. For almost a year, these troops were responsible for maintaining thousands of vehicles in operation along the highway, distributing oil and gas supplies, and patrolling the highway corridor. The original plan had been to send ten quartermaster regiments to the region, but

MEN OF THE 18TH ENGINEERS, SOME WEARING MOSQUITO NETTING,
BUILDING A BRIDGE OVER CRACKER CREEK, 8 JUNE 1942.
YTA, Robert Hays collection, 5702.

the downgrading of the military function of the highway, and the
realization that Alaska could, and had to be, supplied by sea, meant
that this plan had to be scaled down. In December 1943, the 477th
Quartermaster Regiment was disbanded, with some troops assigned
outside the North, and others remaining as part of a greatly reduced
work force.

Thus there were thousands of American soldiers directly and
indirectly involved with the construction and maintenance of the
northwest defense projects. Most of the engineer troops came north
in the spring and summer of 1942 and completed the initial work on
the highway, pipeline, and related projects. By December 1943, the
number of engineer units in the region had dropped substantially,
leaving the remaining work largely to quartermaster troops and
civilian contractors. The U.S. Army, however, would maintain a
presence in the Northwest until six months after the end of the war,
when official responsibility was passed to the Canadian Department
of National Defence.

While there was no question that the U.S. Army Corps of Engineers had the manpower and the technical expertise to tackle its northern assignments, there were doubts as to how the men would react to their northern posting. Thomas Riggs, governor of Alaska during World War I, who had worked with the Alaska International Highway Commission, cautioned the military to prepare properly for northern work. He warned the workers, with a touch of northern hyperbole, to prepare for the worst: "Please do not underestimate the mosquito plague. I have had horses killed by mosquitoes in the country into which you must go." He also urged that close attention be given to questions of morale:

> Supply each camp with papers, magazines, and a radio, if possible. Radio reception will be poor except with the most favorable weather conditions. Bootleggers will be found. They should be kept away if possible. Many of the men going to a town on a pass will get drunk, but if liquor is kept out of a camp, they will soon forget all about it when back to work.[16]

There were signs from the beginning that the army had underestimated the logistical and human difficulties of transferring thousands of soldiers, many of them from the American south, to the Northwest. Though the soldiers were seemingly well-provisioned for the subarctic conditions,[17] little had been done to prepare them psychologically for their northern experience. Few officers or men knew anything about the North, local surveys were sketchy, and the supplies were not always on hand.[18] Troops arriving in Fort St. John in the spring of 1942 faced a forced march north to Fort Nelson in preparation for their summer's work. A senior officer observed that

> The bitter cold and bitter wind combined with the difficulty of the "road" (winter trail) to work painful hardships on many men. There were many cases of badly frozen feet since the shoe pac is not a satisfactory piece of footgear when temperatures reach 35 degrees below. Tractor operators were found along the road sitting beside their parked equipment and crying violently so great was the cold.
>
> Men transported in trucks could scarcely walk upon arrival at destination. Once dragged inside a tent and piled near a fire, they fell quickly asleep. Some of the officers and noncommissioned, who were determined

MEN OF THE 18TH ENGINEERS REGIMENT
BOGGED DOWN IN MUD, SUMMER 1942.
YTA, MacBride Museum collection, 3557.

to keep going whether or no, soon learned to keep away from fires. Truck drivers who had not earned their pay since maneuvers began to earn it again; countless are the stories of drivers who went for days without stopping and almost without food.[19]

Even after the work settled into a routine, soldiers found things to complain about. They constantly criticized working conditions, mud, bugs, boredom, and bad food. Bob Seaton, who worked with the 18th Engineers in the Kluane region, recalled "the other famous three *M*s: mud, muskeg, and mosquitoes" with little fondness.[20] Tall tales about cold and insects were, of course, common in the North, and went over well with southern audiences.[21] One often-repeated joke went as follows: A GI at Whitehorse was awakened by two mosquitoes flying above his bunk. Said one mosquito: "Shall we eat him here, or shall we take him down to the river?" His companion wisely advised, "No, we'd better eat him here, or the big ones down there will take him away from us." There were the usual logistical snafus (an acronym—situation normal all fouled up—coined in this period) which sent vital equipment to the wrong camps. Few recreational facilities were provided the first year, and the men complained bitterly about boredom.[22] Behind the heroic rhetoric of man against nature lay the reality of months of tedious, hard, isolated, repetitive work, with poor living conditions and few distractions.

The soldiers complained endlessly about the poor food, especially the twin staples of the army mess hall—the notorious and ubiquitous "Yukon shrimp" (canned Vienna sausage), and the detested Spam. Corporal G. S. James wrote: "I am so hungry I can hardly stand it. We are now having hash allmost [sic] every meal and none of us can eat it, so all of us in my squad decided to send home and have packages sent to us. One boy has been doing this for a while and all of us have been eating it." Sergeant H. Kuihen of the 35th Engineers echoed these sentiments:

> Its [sic] 9:45 and we just had supper. It wasn't much and we went back for more but the cooks ran out of chow. Dotte this is the truth. We stood around the kitchen tent like a bunch of beggars. It was a site [sic] to see but what could we do, we being still hungry. The Lt. made the cooks fix something else for us and they ran out of that too. Talk about gripping [sic] you should have heard us. I had my fill of coffee bread and peanut butter. The peanut butter came from home. I don't know what I'd do if my Ma didn't send me thing like that. Starve I guess. I don't want my Ma to know just how things are up here and therefore can't ask her for things to eat. I wouldn't ask you either Dotte if I didn't get so damn hungry. So can you send me some jam, jelly, peanut butter, canned fruit or anything you think I'd like.[23]

Another soldier observed, "I think we survived only because of the moose, mountain sheep and goats we were able to shoot. Powdered milk and eggs, corned beef, Vienna sausages, has[h], etc., we were thoroughly sick of as well."[24]

HEADQUARTERS AND SERVICE COMPANY, 18TH ENGINEERS, AT LUNCH, JUNE 1942. DON FLICKWIR OF BALBOA ISLAND, CALIFORNIA, IS AT LEFT. YTA, Robert Hays collection, 5685.

18TH ENGINEERS WASHING DISHES, CRACKER CREEK, JUNE 1942. YTA, Robert Hays collection, 5686.

TRUCK ABOUT TO DESCEND ONE OF THE
STEEPEST GRADES ON THE HIGHWAY.
Public Works Administration photograph,
NAC, Donald Simms collection, C43511.

The weather presented a particular challenge, especially for
American servicemen unaccustomed to subarctic conditions. Cold,
the basis of the northern mystique that was supposed to bring out the
spirit of adventure among the troops, resulted instead in a blizzard
of complaints. There were hundreds of cases of frostbite, many
resulting from inadequate clothing or individual carelessness and
stupidity. During the winter months, temperatures dipping under
-40°F created havoc among men and equipment. Even at headquarters in Whitehorse conditions were unpleasant. In 1942 to 1943
Whitehorse was reported to be the "coldest post under the American
Flag." The buildings had been designed and constructed to southern
standards, and were barely usable in the subarctic climate.[25] Conditions in some of the camps were even worse. Some units, like the 29th
Engineers, lived in tents through November 1942, despite temperatures of -10°F. The men had no shower facilities and had difficulty
securing enough water even for cooking and washing.[26]

The length of the winter season only made things worse. The initial excitement and challenge of road building did not last. Once the pioneer road was finished in November 1942, the men who were not assigned out of the North faced a boring routine, broken only by bouts of viciously bad weather. Mail call, "beer busts," hunting, and other occasional distractions provided only slight relief from camp life, a routine that numbed both mind and body. While journalists extolled the challenge of northern life—man against wilderness at its toughest—the troops on the spot were considerably less enthusiastic.[27]

Efforts were made to protect the men against the dangers of winter. Unit commanders were given detailed instructions on winter precautions and the treatment of frostbite. Soldiers were advised on how to dress and sleep, how to prevent over-heating and hypothermia. The climate caused a delicate problem for camps using latrines. Sector Surgeon Walter Tatum noted, "In deep snow men are inclined not to use the latrines, particularly if they are out of doors. It will be necessary for all commanders to take appropriate measures to see that the ground is not polluted. Extra precautions now will pay dividends in the spring."[28] Press reports tended to treat winter as a kind of sporting challenge, stressing in a cheerful tone the adventure that accompanied the construction projects,[29] but the military authorities knew that winter represented their greatest physical and psychological challenge.

The work could be dangerous, too, sometimes because of the climate, or because of the haste with which the work was pushed and the fatigue experienced by the men. Accidents resulting in loss of time away from work ran ten percent above the average for the Corps of Engineers generally. Most of these occurred among carpenters, equipment operators and laborers, and eighty percent involved bruises, fractures, and strains. Five fatal accidents occurred in the Northwest Service Command (NWSC) in the month of October 1943 alone, "at least three. . . the result of laxity."[30] A typical accident was one that occurred on 10 November 1943 near Whitehorse, when a foreman driving a pickup truck lost control of it on a ten percent grade, rolled down a hill, and was crushed under the wreckage.[31] The history of one regiment alone—the 18th Engineers—recorded the accidental deaths of one officer and four enlisted men between April

1942 and January 1943. The officer broke his spine when his jeep overturned; one man was crushed when his power shovel fell on him; one when his truck went out of control on an icy road; one drowned while fishing; one died of a heart attack.[32]

One point of contention among the military was that men often worked side by side with civilians who were doing the same job as they were, but were being paid a great deal more. Cpl. Janex Rebouche, a welder on army pay of about $18 per week, found himself working alongside civilian welders making over $100 per week. He was cheerful about the situation: "We have to get this over and everybody's got the right to have a good job if they can, I guess. We need all the help we can get here, too," he said, though perhaps the fact that he was talking to a news reporter influenced his mood.[33] Others noticed this inequality. An American newspaper wondered why civilian highway workers were getting up to $30 per day "for doing work identical to that performed by enlisted men at a private's pay."[34] "It's too damn bad the government has to have civilians doing the same jobs as the soldiers," one officer complained. "The civilians make as much in two days as the soldiers do in a month. I wonder what type of suckers they think we are."[35] This situation was the cause of frequent complaints, but given the rigidity of the military structure, and the fact that the low rate of military pay was one reason that soldiers had been used on the projects in the first place, there was nothing to be done.[36]

The soldiers' resentment of better-off civilians was reflected in their letters home. Some of these letters reflect a deep and intense antipathy towards workers in the lower forty-eight states, and particularly towards organized labor. Soldiers may have been workers, but they felt no sense of solidarity with the American Federation of Labor. The censor's report from the Alaskan department for the period 29 January to 5 February 1944 contained thirty-four excerpts from letters expressing this hostility—considerably more than on any other topic, including food. Of these, twenty-six were from letters written by commissioned officers. A few examples reflected class bias:

> ...labor is beginning to worry about the retribution that guys in the armed forces may seek on their return. No press agentry will make these kids forget the racketeers who called strikes when we were wet, cold, hungry, and in

fear of our lives. These boys are coming home tough enough to slug it out with the bastards who have been forcing honest Americans to pay tribute to a union before they were permitted to work, even in war plants.

...I know next to the Japs and the Germans all us soldiers look at strikers as the second enemy of our cause.

...If I had John L. Lewis and a Jap in front of me it would be easy to shoot the one who is our worst enemy, and you can bet the Jap would still be alive.

...What I cannot understand is how labor can be so selfish by demanding so damn many rights when we out here have none at all, and the boys in the South Pacific and Europe haven't even the right to live. What is this—our war to fight and theirs to profit by?[37]

Some letters expressed resentment towards the civilians working in the Northwest. Though the tone was not as bitter as in the letters about organized labor, the comments were scathing about the civilians' lack of efficiency and high pay:

I work in an office with a crowd of civilian (male) employees.... They exaggerate that which is most awful within themselves. They do not know their jobs, probably are just in this line for convenience, and are producing nothing during their 70 hour week—for which they are being paid. We certainly earned what money we were paid. My conscious [sic] will certainly never bother me on that score.

...We have a very nice married lady in the office also. More people doing less work.

... $1400 per month. Wow—what a salary for being a Chief Chef. And when I think that we [military] doctors don't even hit $400.[38]

Not surprisingly, some of the troops directed their resentment towards their officers, following a tradition as old as organized military forces. A lieutenant with the 95th Engineers commented caustically on his brother officers, complaining about their laziness and their refusal to eat the same food as the enlisted men. They were, he said, "a disgrace to the service":

Strange as it seems these dastardly punks are southerners. The Army works for them, and the colored man is still his slave. I'd like to line them against a stone wall and then convert them into fertilizer. God have mercy on the

American people if we get too many of this type. If this despicable corruption was in the enlisted ranks, they'd spend their life on the "bull gang."[39]

The senior officers were, of course, no more pleased with conditions, though they had to defend army policy to their men. Privately, however, they complained bitterly about conditions that represented "a most deplorable waste of highly skilled men and special equipment."[40]

For many of the officers, certainly those responsible for overseeing the projects, the fact that a large number of the military work force was black complicated matters considerably. These troops were sent north despite specific directives against using black troops in cold climates. These regulations reflected deeply entrenched racial stereotypes—basically, the belief that black people, presumably descended from jungle-dwellers, were more sensitive to cold than were white people, and that they were too lethargic and childlike to adapt to northern conditions. As one officer put it, "Our colored boys especially are allergic to cold weather, and it's going to be a problem to keep them well and happy I fear."[41] What truth there was in this belief was not due to genetics—a number of blacks had joined the gold rush of 1898 and had fared no worse than white miners—but to the fact that black troops on average were more likely to be from Mississippi than from Minnesota. Some had never seen snow, and when it was announced late in 1942 that several black units were to remain in the North over the winter, their morale sank perceptibly.[42] One result of low morale was incidents like the following, related by a Canadian civilian construction worker:

> I was going to Fort Nelson from Dawson Creek…and these two fellows [black soldiers] were stopped at the top of a hill, in a transport truck, and they stopped me and they said "We're freezing to death, we've got no heaters." And it was cold, about 35 below or 40 below. "Can we get a ride to Fort Nelson?" And I said "Sure." They said "Just a minute." And they ran back and I turned around to look and here the trucks were going over a 500 foot bank. "It's too cold for us, mister." I never did report it because they shouldn't have been there. They should have had heaters, and they'd come from Alabama, those two soldiers…[43]

There are many similar stories, many second-hand, but enough eye-witness accounts to give them credibility:

> I felt sorry for those guys [black men]...they became completely irresponsible. Survival was their only aim. On one occasion I got a ride a few miles back the road for a repair. I knew better but was desperate. On the way going down a very steep hill and onto a narrow crooked bridge at a near uncontrollable speed, sensing I was well frightened, he said, "Don't worry, Boss, Uncle Sam has lots more trucks and lots more nigga boys to drive 'em."...that was typical of the whole attitude. The cost to the American government would be far above the wildest estimation.[44]

Another story makes the same point:

> ...there were some coloured people sitting there and they had a load of eiderdowns, either going to the cleaners or coming back, whichever...They were cold.... So when we made it to the top they decided to try it. So they took a run at it...it didn't work and it spun out on him and it started out backwards. They just jumped out and let her go. It went over the hill, down to the bottom, and caught fire . . . They just bailed out and they walked up, and they were cold, and they wanted a ride up to the Stikine camp which would be the next one. I said "how come you just bailed out and let that go? Didn't you think you could hold it?" "Man," he said "we weren't just about to try. Uncle Sam got lots of them God damn trucks, but," he said, "he's only got one coloured boy like me. Going to live a long time."[45]

Another man who felt sorry for the black troops remembered that the government

> brought them right up from the south and put them in Dawson Creek in bell tents when it was 40 and 50 below and those poor devils.... Now, the story is that—and then I saw—they all had good eiderdown sleeping bags, army issue sleeping bags; and they'd cut the bottom out—put holes in the bottom and they'd wear them. Of course, the feathers kept dribbling out.[46]

The assignments given black troops provides clear evidence of racism. Doubts about their value as combat troops, and the particular reluctance to place arms in the hands of black soldiers, led the government to assign most black servicemen to construction and supply battalions. Given the urgent need for workers in the Northwest, it was not surprising that several thousand blacks found themselves in subarctic regions, the accepted wisdom about their suitability for such service notwithstanding.

What difficulties black military workers encountered were due less to the weather than to the attitudes of their white superiors. From the beginning, senior officers worried about sending black troops to foreign countries, fearful about how they would be received, and were preoccupied with controlling their behavior. The general staff of the War Department, for example, commissioned a report on the "Utilization of Negro Troops in Friendly Foreign Territory," discussing the likely reception of black soldiers, the "local political, economic, or psychological disadvantages for the United Nations," and other problems that might arise. It was assumed that the black troops would be "subjected to a rigid discipline" under the guidance of white officers, have portions of their pay "withheld in the form of allotments" if their salaries threatened to cause problems with local citizens, and that they would be garrisoned with larger numbers of white troops. It was further assumed that "there were a few important areas of the world where the Negro troops should be used only in an extreme emergency." Canada and Newfoundland, the report observed, "recognize the necessity for us to send United States troops, regardless of color, to their territory. No serious difficulties are anticipated with regard to the presence of Negro troops."[47]

Where possible, black troops were assigned tasks in regions remote from large population centers. Many, for example, were employed transporting supplies from Edmonton to Norman Wells. In June 1942, the U.S. Army had over 2,000 troops stationed between Chipewyan, Alberta, and Norman Wells. Of these, over 1,200 were black, all stationed at remote communities—Chipewyan and Fitzgerald in Alberta, and Fort Smith and Norman Wells in the Northwest Territories.[48] All these units were commanded by white officers; B Company, 288th Engineers, which arrived at Fort Smith in June 1942, consisted of 316 black and seven white officers. In some places, black soldiers were restricted to manual labor, while white soldiers drove the trucks and operated heavy equipment.[49] Official propaganda naturally suggested that the black troops coped well with the rigors of work on the CANOL project:

BLACK TROOPS BUILDING A BRIDGE
OVER GOOSE CREEK, NEAR TESLIN, YUKON, 1942.
U.S. Army photograph, Anchorage Museum, B62.X.15.6.

Nothing could quite overcome the natural gaiety and love of song inherent in the Negro soldiers. They had several favorite songs which they sang as they wrestled with the heavy steel pipe. One was "Biscuits in the morning, biscuits at night, here comes the Athabaska with another load of pipe." Another was "Crackers in the morning, crackers at night, here comes the Athabaska with more damned pipe." A third favorite was "the night is light, the mosquitoes sho' do bite, look up de river and see mo' damn pipe."[50]

No one, unfortunately, recorded what the black troops sang when the officers were out of earshot.

In cases where black troops were stationed near larger communities, different problems arose. When large numbers of black soldiers arrived at Fairbanks, some of the town's citizens began a petition for their removal to a "country and climate more closely resembling their natural habitat."[51] Near Canadian communities it was the American military rather than the local population who worried about the influx of black troops. When a group of black troops arrived at Whitehorse, for instance, they were quickly removed to a camp several miles to the west. The people of Fitzgerald, Alberta, were warned not to get too friendly or talkative with the colored troops to discourage "a possible too intimate situation" between them.[52] At Fort Smith, the RCMP was pleased to find that there was "no mixing in any way with the local natives [i.e., the Indians]."[53] These limits on their freedom added to tensions between black troops and their officers and to the difficulties of the job.

White officers who commanded black troops varied considerably in their attitude towards them. Some were overtly racist, such as the officer who wrote

> Had trouble with a couple of the colored officers who were sent up to help me. First they wanted to live in the same barracks with us. That was too much so I told them that as long as they were working up above here with me no colored officers would live with any whites. Have trouble getting them to work and get up on time so just like Simon Legree I ride them.... Pretty soon I expect to be called before the Colonel but I'll be damned if I am going to live with any niggers. It's bad enough having to serve with them and wash and use the same toilets.[54]

A censored letter from a black noncommissioned officer shows the tensions that could arise when black troops had to serve under a racist officer:

> In this unit we have a new major, from Texas. The boys really almost got out of control. They disobeyed, object[ed] and showed what would happen if he kept saying and acting as he did. Any day I'm looking for a report to come in stating the major had been killed. The boys really hate him and he knows it. When the major was at Belvoir he was a Lt. Col. One day Gen. Davis [black] visited the post and the major wouldn't salute him. Because of this incident he was reduced to major and he has hated colored every sence [sic]. Then, we have captain just the same. One day he told a boy if he didn't be quite [sic], he make him. The boy told him that the first time

he tryed [sic] to close his mouth he would cut his throat. The boy really meant it.[55]

Other officers assigned to black units—happily, the majority—seem to have appreciated their men, though a tone of surprise in their positive comments suggests that they had little contact with black people before the war. One declared, "Service with colored troops is very pleasant. They are so polite, and so pathetically eager not to be found wanting, that it is really a splendid opportunity."[56] One Lt. Colonel observed, "Got some new non-coms and these new boys are Negroes. I've never been around them much and I'm finding these non-coms capable. When they're told to do something it is done."[57]

The final report on the northern operations of the 93rd Engineer Battalion provided a representative assessment of the performance of black troops in the Northwest. While the report was generally positive, it was filled with racial and paternalistic stereotypes. The officer compiling the report noted with approval that "During the most severe weather encountered, it is believed that Negro troops, properly led, have accomplished more physical labor than other troops in the same area engaged in similar work." But he recommended that black troops were best commanded bearing in mind their mental limitations:

> Routine tasks that might tend to become monotonous, and operations that can be conducted with the precision of a drill can be attractive to Negro troops provided that the results of their work are impressive and apparent from day to day. Instructions should always be given in simple language and should never be complicated.

The report continued in this vein, complaining about the high number of "illiterates and mentally handicapped enlisted men assignment [sic] to this regiment,"[58] and observing that black troops had to overcome "inertia" before becoming involved in recreational activities. It strongly supported segregation of black and white troops, recommended that white officers command black units, and observed that civilians have "generally been antagonistic and quick to exaggerate offences committed by Negro soldiers."[59]

Some efforts were made to react to complaints from the black troops, if only in the interests of military efficiency. On the national level genuine concern existed. There were numerous protests and "riots of a racial character" at bases across the United States in the early years of the war, and serious race riots in cities such as Detroit. Considerable War Department effort was expended on addressing the control of black troops; there was, however, little apparent awareness of the cumulative impact of institutionalized racism on the behavior of the black soldiers.[60] In the Northwest, troublesome white officers were reassigned, though apparently with no bad effect on their record, food allocations were improved, and special efforts were made to recruit black officers to help with the control of black troops. Such efforts, it was felt, would alert commanding officers to "the pulse, temper and morale of the Negro troops."[61] They also showed that the black troops did have the power to improve their lot by forcing the removal of unpopular superiors, but there was little change in their basic conditions.

It fell to an outsider, Ruth Gruber, field representative for the Department of the Interior, to provide a general account of the experience of black soldiers during the construction phase. She claimed that the men attacked their early assignments with enthusiasm:

> Even the southern officers spoke of them with praise. "The Negroes were better solders and builders than the whites. They put our gold-bricks to shame. We never had a bit of trouble with them; they policed themselves. If one of the Negroes got out of line about 10 others would get around him right away and yell: Everybody's been good to us. We don't want no bad nigger spoiling things for us."

The black troops, Gruber claimed, had been promised that they could go home after the Alaska Highway was completed; when their orders were changed, the soldiers were furious. "Tension ran so high," she wrote, "that some of the white officers slept fearfully with guns at their sides." Gruber reported that black soldiers faced discrimination throughout the Northwest, particularly in Alaska, where common sentiments included the refrain: The flower of American womanhood is in danger; white girls aren't safe on the street; the niggers are getting out of hand." Conditions were somewhat better in Whitehorse, where particularly offensive white officers had been removed and the quality of the food improved. The sad fact was that "the Negroes know the grim truth that they are unwanted and openly ostracized." She concluded her report,

> The War has awakened the aspirations of the Negroes. They are eager to fight; they have proved along the Alaska Highway how capable they are. But we are corroding their faith in us, ripening them for Nazi propagandists, and preparing the soil for more race riots, by willfully spreading race hatred wherever we go, whether it be England, Australia or north of the 60th parallel, in the frontiers where men are supposed to be free.[62]

Not surprisingly, the army paid little attention to this assessment by a civilian, and a woman at that, who sounded like a liberal trouble-maker; they knew how to handle their own "colored boys." The fact that she also swallowed and reported tall tales fed to her to the effect that "there were three dozen amputations of frost-bitten arms and legs," and "twelve Negroes are said to be still in chains in Whitehorse" may have lessened her credibility. "Employment of colored troops in Alaska and in the NWSC has been contingent upon the military situation," the army explained, "and not upon race or color. Admittedly, some hardships have been undergone, but by both white and colored troops alike." More specific observations were dismissed as "purely hearsay."[63] With army policy regulating their activities, benevolent white officers to lead them, and the military police on call in case they got out of line, there was little to fear from the black troops working on the northwest defense projects.

Many of the problems encountered in the North were shared by soldier-workers of all races. As the winter months passed, and one year in the Northwest grew into two, particularly for those troops stationed in Alaska, the leading complaint had to do with leave. After the pioneer road was finished, many of the men who had built it were posted elsewhere in the North—to serve in the Aleutian Islands, or on other northern defense projects. Many men sent north in the early summer of 1942 found themselves still north of the 60th parallel in 1944, not having once returned south. If such a system had been tried with civilian labor, it would have resulted in massive departures. The soldiers had no such option, and by 1944 the absence of a regular system of rotation had become the chief cause of complaint among

Alaska-based soldiers.[64] Under the 1944 regulations—drawn up after much urging from field officers inundated with complaints about the seemingly capricious administration of furloughs—soldiers were limited to twenty-one days of leave per year, not counting travel time to their homes. No more than fifteen percent of the complement of officers and men could be furloughed at any one time; regulations also made it clear that "In no event will the percentage of leaves [and] furloughs be so as to affect the normal functioning of an organization."[65]

Long periods away from the south—and from women—engendered considerable hostility and some radical changes in behavior. A psychiatrist's assessment of a young man stationed on the Aleutian Islands illustrates the "changes for the worse" that came after prolonged isolation:

> This is a striking instance of the impact of isolation upon a previously jovial, well integrated personality. As time went on and as he passed successively more isolated posts, his joviality was dropped and replaced with irritability. This probably represents a weak and inefficient show of effort against the surrounding frustrating circumstances.[66]

Complaints about the consequences of prolonged northern service were legion in the military ranks. One report noted that

> Men have been interviewed who have not seen a woman for a year. Many have wives and children—one man, a child sixteen months old he had never seen. These men seem to feel that from a standpoint of prosecution of the war and to maintain a man as a fighting soldiers, he cannot be kept in complete isolation too long in an environment that at best is taxing.[67]

Soldiers serving in the Northwest carried the added burden of being noncombatants during time of war. Those stationed in Alaska, particularly in the Aleutian Islands, were closer to the front, and lived with the immediacy of war; for others, based along the Mackenzie River or in Whitehorse, the war was distant and sometimes unreal. For some, the main grievance was not the food or the climate, but the sense of being far from the fighting, engaged not in front-line duties but in boring, civilian work in the middle of nowhere.[68] The race against time to complete the Alaska Highway and CANOL project had provided sufficient drama and challenge to occupy the soldiers in the first year of construction. As most of the troops were released for overseas service, and as a certain dullness crept over the maintenance and reconstruction duties associated with the highway and related projects, however, the soldiers became increasingly anxious about the lack of action. Buoyed by wartime fears and propaganda, the soldiers were particularly anxious to be perceived as doing their share. Military authorities, backed by the extensive publicity given the initial construction of the Alaska Highway, did their best to sustain morale among their soldiers. Patriotic pronouncements, public letters of commendation and repeated statements as to the importance assigned to the defense of the Northwest took on an increasingly hollow sound as the months progressed and, after 1943, the army down-graded the strategic importance of the highway and pipeline projects.[69] By 1944, even the commanders had difficulty promoting the northwest defense projects:

> The mission of the Northwest Service Command to maintain and operate a supply line for the defense of Alaska against the Japanese is no longer of prime importance, so we find ourselves today serving as a "standby unit," but we are nevertheless an integral part of the war effort and it is out duty to carry out the instructions of the War Department to the fullest extent of our abilities and I call on you all to continue to give your very best to your job while in this Command.[70]

Honest sentiments no doubt, but far from Churchillian.

After the completion of the pioneer road, morale began to slip badly. Managers complained of excessive slackness and an evident lack of commitment to the work at hand; clearly, the sense of urgency that had pervaded the Northwest in 1942 had disappeared by the following year. Preserving normal military discipline on the northwestern frontier proved increasingly difficult. Thousands of miles from home bases and just as far from the major battle lines, soldiers often became apathetic. As complaints against incompetent officers mounted, and as criticisms of their northern posting increased, so did reports of insubordination. The standard military courtesies, such as saluting, were noticeably absent. The NWSC issued orders demanding attendance to the formalities. New regulations were issued, involving a system of bells and whistles to announce the start and the end of each working day. Failure to heed them resulted in the docking of annual leave time.[71]

Service in the Canadian northwest was safe, even comfortable compared to the South Pacific, but uninspiring. And the problem was not limited to soldiers based in Canada: as one psychological report on soldiers in Alaska summarized, the American soldier "is sometimes confused and unable to figure out an ultimate aim. Also he sometimes lets slip a grouchy expression about 'not getting anywhere in helping to win the war.' But he does want to help win it."[72]

It was understandable if by 1944 soldiers had difficulty seeing the relationship between their work and the battles being waged around the world. By this time few military personnel remained in the Northwest Service Command. With the exception of office staff, some technical supervisors and quartermaster troops, the soldiers had been removed to more active fields. After initial construction—the high profile and exciting times—the Alaska Highway, CANOL pipeline and other projects were turned over to civilian workers, who would labor through the last half of the war under a military umbrella but typically with civilian superiors.

Nearly fifty years after the projects were completed, the American soldier-workers involved in them retain intense pride in the work they completed in the Northwest. They point, particularly, to the major obstacles to be overcome—the speed of construction, the difficult conditions under which they operated, their lack of experience in the Northwest, the absence of a suitable body of northern-based engineering upon which the project managers could draw, and their isolation. For many American soldiers, work on the Alaska Highway and CANOL project remains a highlight of what were often full and interesting lives.

Ironically, there are few signs of their wartime activities remaining in the Northwest. Even as the soldiers completed the pioneer road, civilian contractors had begun work on a relocated and improved highway, which often ran some distance away from the initial route. The soldiers' work was not designed to last, and most of it did not. Large sections of the pioneer road disappeared in the spring of 1943, victim of thawing muskeg, seventy-three overflowing rivers, and mudslides. Many of the hastily built bridges were similarly washed out by summer rains and much of the physical evidence of

MEMBERS OF THE 31ST ENGINEERS
BUILDING CAMP AT DAWSON CREEK, 1 MAY 1942.
NA, 111-SC 322877.

the CANOL project has disappeared. Their job was to work fast and hard; this they did, under difficult circumstances. Their tasks, including the pioneer road, and preliminary work on the Haines Lateral and CANOL pipeline, were completed on time; the men of the United States Army Corps of Engineers at least had this much to take with them when they left the North: they had, to use the rhetoric of that day, tackled the subarctic wilderness and won.

Clearly, the problems faced by the Americans troops in the Northwest were dealt with as military matters. The standard responses to workers' complaints in such frontier circumstances—raising wage rates, improving living conditions, or otherwise making life better for the men and women—were neither practical nor even considered. Because they were soldiers, their problems were perceived in the standard light of leadership, morale, loyalty, and discipline. Major efforts, to be discussed in a later chapter, were

BRIDGE UNDER CONSTRUCTION ABOUT FIFTY MILES
FROM LOWER LIARD, 1942.
U.S. Army photograph, Anchorage Musem B62.X.18.7.

devoted to improving recreational opportunities, but most efforts to control the military workers, or to deal with their complaints, were confined to standard military responses. Although the United States Army readily used soldiers as workers, it was not yet prepared to treat them as industrial employees. Uniform, not function, would be the primary determinant of how the men and women of the United States Army were treated during their time in Alaska and the Canadian northwest in World War II. Nonetheless, these soldier-workers managed, even under the duress of military law and regulations, to effect some amelioration of their working conditions. The job in the North had to be done, and no one in authority wanted to antagonize the work force unduly, since an unhappy worker was an unproductive worker.

NOTES

1. For a general history of the branch of the military, see U.S. Army Corps of Engineers, *The History of the US Army Corps of Engineers* (Washington, Corps of Engineers, 1986).

2. See L. D. Reddicks, "Negro Policy in the United States Army, 1775-1945," *Journal of Negro History* 34 (1949).

3. See Desmond Morton and Glenn Wright, *Winning the Second Battle: Canadian Veterans and the Return to Civilian Life, 1915-1930* (Toronto: University of Toronto Press, 1987); Desmond Morton, "Aid to the Civil Power; The Canadian Militia in Support of Social Order, 1867-1914," *Canadian Historical Review* 51, no. 4 (1970).

4. During the Vietnam War, for example, only fourteen percent of all U.S. service personnel in Vietnam actually engaged in combat; the remaining eighty-six percent worked in support and rear-echelon duties.

5. As this relates to Alaska and the U.S. Corps of Engineers, see W. A. Jacobs, *The Alaska District: United States Army Corps of Engineers, 1946-1974* (Alaska: U.S. Army Corps of Engineers, 1976).

6. Glenbow-Alberta Institute, Seaton Papers, A. S441 Log Book 18th Engineers, Alaska Highway (April 1942-January 1943): 13.

7. See Annette Palmer, "The Politics of Race and War: Black Soldiers in the Caribbean Theatre During the Second World War," *Military Affairs* XLVII (April 1983).

8. Joseph Bykofsky and Harold Larson, *The Transportation Corps: Operations Overseas* (Washington: Department of the Army, 1957) provides a detailed overview of this work.

9. Steve Harris, "Really a Defile Throughout Its Length," in *The Alaska Highway*, ed. K. S. Coates.

10. Ken Coates, "The Civilian Highway: Public Works Canada and the Alaska Highway," in *The Alaska Highway*, ed. Coates.

11. United States National Archives (NA), RG 338, NWSC, Box 10, Office Memos, Memorandum re: Establishment of Military Censorship, Northwest Service Command, 11 April 1943. Military and civilian employees of the army were forbidden to discuss the location of units, movements of troops, supplies or vessels, forecasts or plans, use of transportation facilities, or location of camps. Special instructions were given about the use of cameras. Canadian authorities had similar regulations. See National Archives of

Canada (NAC), RG 85, vol. 306, file 1009-9(1), *Press Censorship Directives* August 1942, no. 30A, Subject: Alaskan Highway; and other U.S. Activities in Canada.

12. The soldiers were not as close-mouthed as their superiors demanded, leading to specific orders not to discuss "the nature of the operations of our forces in the northwest." Col. J. J. Schmidt to Commanding General, Seventh Service Command, SOS, 16 March 1943, NA, RG 338, Box 6, file 350.05, Intelligence Branch.

13. American Troops Engaged on Alaska Highway Construction

UNIT	ARRIVAL	DEPARTURE	OFFICERS	MEN
18th Engineer	Apr. 42	Jan. 43	55	1,459
Co. D, 29th Engin	Apr. 42	Feb. 43	5	186
39th Engineer	Mar. 42	Feb. 43	46	1,230
Co. D, 58th Med.	Mar. 42	Feb. 43	5	54
73rd Engineer	Apr. 42	Feb. 43	6	215
74th Engineer	Mar. 42	June 43	10	328
93rd Engineer	Apr. 42	Jan. 43	46	1.250
95th Engineer	June 42	Jan. 43	48	1.228
97th Engineer	Apr. 42	Jan. 43	51	1,227
340 Engineer	Apr. 42	May 43	46	1,260
341 Engineer	May 42	July 43	43	1,146
438 Engineer	July 42	Jan. 43	4	118
Co. A, 648 Engin	Mar. 42	Nov. 42	8	270
Signal Det. B.	May 42	Feb. 43		16
Signal Det. H.	Apr. 42	Feb. 43		4
Signal Det. D.	May 42	Feb. 43		15
Signal Det. I	June 42	Feb. 43		16
Signal Det. I.	Apr. 42	Feb. 43		16
Finance Dept.	Mar. 42	-----	1	10
Finance Dept.	Apr. 42	-----	1	10
Quartermaster	-----	-----	5	127
Quartermaster	Apr. 42	-----	2	86
Quartermaster	Apr. 42	-----	1	5
133 Quarter. Truck	Aug. 42	May 43	4	120
134 Quarter. Truck	July 42	May 43	4	120
140 Quarter. Truck	Apr. 42	May 43	3	126
141 Quarter Truck	July 42	May 43	3	114
Total			394	10,756

The Alaska Highway: Interim Report from the Committee on Roads, House of Representatives (Washington, D.C.: Government Printing Office, 1946), 104-105.

14. 39,606 civilians worked on the northwest projects at their height in 1943, but given the turnover of labor, the number of civilians who actually spent some time on the projects was considerably higher. Special Commissioner's 11th Report, Part 16, Contracts and Employment, 30 April 1944, NAC, RG 22, vol. 107, file 84-32-6, pt.1.

15. Later designated the 770th Railway Operating Detachment.

16. Thomas Riggs to Sturdevant, 21 March 1942, U.S. Army Corps of Engineers (ACE), 72-A-3173, file 50-39.

17. Heath Twichell, letter of 4 March 1942, YTA, 82/546, Misc. Manuscripts. Standard issue, according to Twichell, included a sheep-lined coat, reversible parka, fur helmet, sweater, scarf, gloves, wool pants, heavy shoes, socks, wool underwear, goggles and a sleeping bag.

18. C. L. Sturdevant Memorandum for Commanding General, Services of Supply, Enclosure to Memo, 2 May 1942, ACE, Fort Belvoir, 72-A-3173, Box 15, Documents May-June 1942.

19. Heath Twichell, letter of 3 March 1943, YTA, 82/546.

20. Memories of Building the Alaska Highway-As Recalled by a U.S. Engineer. Yukon Territorial Archives, Seaton Scrapbook, Accession 82/146.

21. See *North Star Magazine* (November 1944), "Bush Bunk."

22. Ibid., (November 1944), "And at 60 below."

23. Excerpt from letter of Sgt. H. Kuihen, Co. D., 35th Engineers, 10 July 1942, ACE, 72-A-3173, Box 15, 50-15.

24. YTA, Seaton Scrapbook.

25. "Master Sgt. R. F. Doolan Presented with U. S. Army Legion of Merit," *Whitehorse Star* 15 (October 1942).

26. Albert Allen to Major Raymond Moore, 8 November 1942, NAC, RG 407, box 18583, ENBN-29-0.1.

27. Company diary, author unknown, 26 March 1943 to 5 July 1943, NAC, RG 407, Box 22331, ORCO-3470-0.1.

28. Walter Tatum to All Unit Commanders, Whitehorse Sector, Alcan Highway, 7 November 1942, NC, RG 112, Entry 54B, Box 15A, HD 350.05, NWSC.

29. *Edmonton Journal,* 29 August 1942.

30. "Conferences" Office of the Division Engineer, Edmonton, 1 November 1943, NA, RG 338, NWSC, reel 10.

31. "Conferences" Office of the Division Engineer, Staff Meeting, 1 November 1943, NA, RG 338, NWSC, reel 10.

32. Log Book 18th Engineers, Alaska Highway, April 1942 January 1943, pp. 11-14, Glenbow-Alberta Institute, Seaton Papers, A. S441.

33. Clipping from *Seattle Post-Intelligencer*, 23 September 1943, ACE, Main Collection, X-1-4.

34. *The Greenville Piedmont*, 7 January 1943, clipping in ACE, 72-A03173, Box 16, file 50-33.

35. NA, RG 407, Box 32, file 91-DPI-2.1, Annex No. 3 to G-2 Periodic Report No. 104, p. 10.

36. NA, RG 407, Box 32, file 91-DPI-2.1, Annex No. 3 to G-2, Periodic Report No. 108, p. 9. It is difficult to be precise about the question of military pay. American service personnel were paid according to rank, but also according to length of service and for certain special skills. There was also extra pay for overseas service. An army corporal with no special skill, not long in the service, posted to Great Britain, made $18.28 per week in the summer of 1942, according to Norman Longmate, *The G.I.'s: The Americans in Britain, 1942-1945* (London, 1975), far more than British soldiers—here the shoe was on the other foot.

37. NA, RG 407, Box 32, file 91-DP1-2.1, Annex No. 3 to G-2 Periodic Reports No. 89 and 104. Another lively grievance was the fact that *Esquire* magazine had been banned from the mails by civilians concerned about its corrupting influence on military morals.

38. NA, RG 407, Box 32, file 91-DP1-2.1, Annex No. 3 to G-2 Periodic Report No. 112, continued. Comments from the civilians about the military, on the other hand, were almost uniformly positive—a typical civilian comment was "The Army here is a lot better to civilians than any place else I've been."

39. The comments were contained in a letter from Lt. Joseph Sincavage to his wife, 15 July 1942 that was intercepted by military censors. C.L. Sturdevant, Brigadier General to Commanding Officer, Southern Sector, Alcan Highway, 3. August 1942, ACE, 72-A-3173, Box 16, file 50-26.

40. Albert Allen to Major Raymond Moore, 8 November 1942, NAC, RG 407, Box 18583, file ENBN-29-0.1.

41. Heath Twichell, H. to My dear One All, 26 July 1942, YTA, Accession 82/546, Misc. Manuscripts.

42. Const. R. H. Swift, RCMP report re: Construction of Oil Pipeline, 30 August 1942, NAC, RG 85, vol. 865, file 8327.

43. Interview with Harry George, June 1988.

44. Questionnaire answered by Cyril Griffith, Naicam, Saskatchewan.

45. Interview with Lake Southwick, Taylor B.C., July 1988.

46. Interview with Gordon and Lorna Gibbs, Tsewassen, B.C., July 1988.

47. Major General Geo. Strong Memorandum for the Assistant Chief of Staff, 17 June 1942, NA, RG 165, OPD291.21 (Section I), Cases 1-20. See also Kay Saunders, "Conflict Between the American and Australian Governments over the Introduction of Black American Servicemen into Australia During World War Two," *Australian Journal of Politics and History* 33, no. 2 (1987); Kay Saunders and Helen Taylor, "The Reception of American Servicemen in Australia During Word War 2: The Resilience of 'White Australia,'" *Journal of Black Studies* (June 1988).

48. Corporal R. W. Thompson, Royal Canadian Mounted Police report re: Proposed Pipeline from Norman Wells, NWT to Whitehorse, 22 June 1942, National Archives of Canada (NAC), RG 85, vol. 865, file 8327.

49. Corporal Gray, RCMP, report re: Construction of Oil Pipeline, 26 June 1942, Ibid.

50. ACE, x-2-10, Public Relations Branch, Northwest Service Command, *Canol*, nd (c. mid 1944), p. 13.

51. NAC, RG 407, vol. 7, file 91-OC1-2.1, Annex No. 3 to G-2 Periodic Report No. 48, 17-24 April 1942. A brighter note is that fact that only 14 people signed the petition.

52. Constable G. W. Allen, Royal Canadian Mounted Police, report re: Piping of oil from Norman Wells, NWT to Whitehorse, Y.T. NAC, RG 85, vol. 865, file 8327. It is not made explicit whether the warning came from the police or army officials. In Britain, too, it was the Americans rather than the British who worried about the presence of blacks. Britain in those days was relatively free of color prejudice, and some Americans were horrified at the way British girls befriended black troops. See Longmate, *The G.I.'s.*

53. Ibid., Corporal Gray, Royal Canadian Mounted Police report re: Construction of Oil Pipe Line From Norman Wells, 26 June 1942.

54. NA, RG 407, Box 32, file 91-DPI-2.1, Annex to G-2 Periodic Report no. 94, 4 March 1944 to 11 March 1944.

55. Paul Thompson to Commanding Officer, Southern Sector, Alcan Highway, 18 August 1942, ACE, 72-1-3173, Box 15, file 50-15.

56. Heath Twichell, H. to My dear Ones All, 26 July 1942, YTA, Accession 82/546, Misc. Manuscripts.

57. NA, RG 407, Box 32, file 91-DP1-2.1, Annex No. 3 to G-2 Periodic Report No. 99, p. 11.

58. There was some truth to this harsh assessment. American blacks had few educational opportunities in the 1930s and often lived on a substandard diet. A sad commentary on the education of blacks in the United States was the comment that "Training of negro units would be greatly simplified if illiterates were given an elementary course in reading and writing before being assigned to duty for basic training."

59. History of the Alaskan Operations Ninety-Third Engineer Regiment (GS), NA, RG 407 Box 19550, file Engr-93-3.0, p. 2, 8.

60. War Department Memorandum to Commanding Generals, Army Air Forces, Army Ground Forces, Army Service Forces, NA, RG 338, Box 2, file 291.2 (Race).

61. Adjunct General to Commanding Generals, All Service Commands, including the Northwest Service Command, 21 August 1943, NA, RG 338, Box 2, file 291.2 (Race).

62. Ruth Gruber to Secretary, U.S. Department of the Interior, 11 June 1943, NA, RG 165, OPD291.21 (Section II), Cases 21-52 (Negroes and Negro Race).

63. Ibid., Memo to the Record, Negro Discrimination in Alaska and Along the Alaskan Highway, 17 June 1943.

64. NA, RG 407, file 91-DPI-2.1, G-2 reports for 1944 from Alaska contain dozens of references relating to leaves or rotation. A rotation system was implemented early in 1944, leading to yet another set of complaints about favoritism and inequities. In the Canadian northwest, with the projects finished by 1944, there was less urgency, and leaves were granted more regularly.

65. William Booth to All Unit Commanders, re: Leaves of Absence and Furloughs, 29 June 1944, NA, RG 338, Box 42, USED, No. Memos.

66. Military Information, Report on the Psychiatric Problems of the Aleutian Area, p. 4, NA, RG 338, NWSC, Box 7, file 350.5.

67. NA, RG 407-7-91-DCI-2.1 Annex No. 3 to G-2 Periodic Report No, 51, 8 May 1943 to 15 May 1943, p. 5.

68. The play and movie "Mr. Roberts" are based on this theme.

69. See, to provide but one example, the memorandum B. Somervell, Commanding General, Army Service Forces, 4 July 1943, NA, RG 338, NWSC, Box 10, Office Memos,

70. Army Day Message from Brig. General F. S. Strong, Commanding General, Northwest Service Command, NA, RG 338, Box 10, NWSC, Office Memoranda, 1944.

71. Office Memo, Office Memorandum No. 177, Subject: Tardiness and Absence Without Leave, 18 September 1943, NA, RG 338, NWSC, Box 10. Ibid., Office Memorandum No, 189, Subject: Observance of Office Hours, 8 October 1943.

72. NC, RG 407-7-91-DC-2.1, Annex No. 3 to G-2 Periodic Report No. 33, 2 January 1943 to 9 January 1943. The sense of ennui noted at this early date only increased over the following three years.

73. An explanation for southern readers—muskeg is a kind of northern bog, which in areas of permafrost is frozen hard as iron, and if left undisturbed makes a fine roadbed. If the few inches of overburden that usually rests on top of muskeg is removed, however, the muskeg will thaw in the spring and turn into a thick swamp, unable to support any kind of vehicle. The proper road-building technique is to lay gravel on top of muskeg to keep it from thawing.

3 REGULATING THE CIVILIAN WORK FORCE

North American governments, though historically more than willing to hamstring and harass trade unions, have been reluctant to regulate the movement and freedom of workers as individuals. Though employers and civilian authorities looked upon organized labor as a threat, they felt that individual workers would follow the dictates of Adam Smith's "invisible hand," and would gravitate away from regions of job scarcity towards areas of high employment. This *laissez-faire* policy enabled employers to rid themselves of surplus workers in times of economic hardship, yet rapidly rebuild their pool of labor when prosperity returned. Governments, believing that social and economic stability rested more in the contentment of employers than employees, smiled on this arrangement. Only in the 1930s, when economic chaos threatened the fabric of North American life, did governments introduce policies which had massive effects on labor markets. The classic American example was the National Recovery Administration (NRA), which largely suspended the operation of the free market in the interests of economic recovery. Most employers reluctantly went along with the NRA, but more from a desire to head off radicalism than out of genuine concern for the plight of the unemployed.[1]

During wartime, however, many of the ordinary rules of labor economics were suspended. In both world wars, governments moved quickly to control and regulate the work force[2] with a view to ensuring the most efficient and productive use of labor resources.[3] By 1943 unemployment in both Canada and the United States was practically zero. In order to regulate the labor market, both governments established regulations and controls over the pay, mobility, and working conditions of labor to ensure that the war effort would not be impeded, and that workers would not be able to take advantage of their scarcity to bargain for high wages and increased benefits.

World War II created an unnatural combination of economic circumstances. Insatiable military demands, supported by governments willing to tax and borrow endlessly to finance them, combined to end unemployment, gave industry a tremendous shot of adrenaline, and raised national debts to undreamed-of levels. The contrast with the early years of the depression, when governments worried more about the national debt than national misery, was striking and provided an argument for those few who had the temerity to suggest publicly that capitalism thrived on war. At the same time, however, national policy required that workers keep their wage demands within acceptable limits, for full employment raised the specter of inflation. This danger was averted partly by wage and price controls, and partly by propaganda that portrayed radicalism and labor demands as unpatriotic and reminded workers of the greater sacrifices being made by the fighting men—an argument that was hard to answer. The Second World War, like all wars of this century, ensured full employment and a measure of economic security for workers, but it limited their freedom and the options open to them.

During the First World War, many of the measures taken to ensure labor peace had been taken at the expense of working people and had resulted in a post-war burst of political radicalism and intense labor unrest. Anxious to avoid a repetition of these episodes, and aware of the fact that organized labor remained strong in 1940, governments approached labor relations with greater astuteness, if not greater sympathy.

In recent years, historians in Canada and the United States have begun to evaluate efforts by governments, unions, and employers to regulate the labor marketplace during World War II. In Canada, Laurel Sefton MacDowell has led the way, analyzing the imposition of national controls and legislation. In a study of Kirkland Lake gold miners, she has examined the local forces and controversies that contributed to the creation of national policy. In America, work on this theme has been more diverse. U.S. labor historians have focused on the major trade unions, particularly the American Federation of Labor and the Committee for Industrial Organization (AFL-CIO), as they negotiated with government and business leaders in an effort to protect their members' rights. The accommodation reached in the United States, unlike its Canadian counterpart, placed few restrictions on the freedom of American workers.

The northwest defense projects brought two national systems of labor regulation into contact and sometimes into conflict. Canadian and American workers, recruited for northern projects, were asked to do similar work under similar conditions—but the rates of pay, conditions of employment, and freedom of movement varied considerably, depending on the worker's nationality. During the war, the northwest defense projects employed as many as 40,000 civilian workers of both sexes and all ages and skills, from highly specialized petroleum engineers to unskilled laborers, from stenographers to bulldozer operators. Hiring these men and women and getting them to the job site posed a formidable challenge, particularly since the rapid expansion of North American industry to meet the production demands of war was rapidly drying up the pool of available labor left over from the depression.

The initial hiring process often posed problems of bureaucracy and red tape. An employer in Edmonton hiring labor for work on the U.S. airport there reported the rigmarole that faced applicants:

> When a worker was given a permit by us he was required to travel a distance of seventeen city blocks to the contractor's personnel office and take his turn in a queue for interview. Yesterday morning Major Thurston and I saw at least fifty men milling around the company's office (waiting to be dealt with). If the man appeared satisfactory to the company's officer he was then required to go to the United States Dispensary which is twelve city blocks (for medical examination). At this point he may have had to wait a day for medical examination. If found medically fit he returned to the Personnel

office and after another wait was required to complete certain application forms. He was then sent about three miles to United States headquarters for finger printing before he could proceed to the project and become enrolled. One can well image the effect this would have on artisans and labourers who have been accustomed to commencing work immediately after one interview.[4]

The major project tackled by civilians was the reconstruction of the Alaska Highway. Beginning in 1942, the U.S. Army turned over responsibility for the improvement of the army's pioneer road to civilian standards to the Public Roads Administration, which in turn delegated it to four management companies: R. Melville Smith Construction of Toronto, Dowell Construction of Seattle, Okes Construction of St. Paul, and Lytle and Green from Des Moines. These contractors all worked under "cost-plus" contracts, an arrangement, common during the war, by which companies were paid the actual cost of doing the work, plus a small profit. The opportunities for abuse were obvious and frequently exploited, but the system ensured that the job got done in the least possible time. The principal contractors then employed subcontractors to carry out specific tasks. The CANOL pipeline, for instance, was built by the consortium of W. A. Bechtel, W. E. Callahan, and H. C. Price. Imperial Oil of Canada got the job of expanding the Normal Wells oil field, while the Whitehorse refinery was built and operated by Standard Oil of California. The recruitment of civilian labor for the Northwest was largely left to the private companies, although both the Canadian and American governments gave what assistance they could.

From the moment that the civilian contractors and the Public Roads Administration began to plan for their work in the Northwest, problems with the recruiting of labor began to emerge. By 1942, the North American economy was increasingly occupied with war production, hundreds of thousands of men and women had gone into the armed forces, and unemployment had almost disappeared. With work readily available in southern centers, convincing workers to volunteer for hard, isolated jobs in the Northwest, land of legendary climatic extremes, was no easy task. An additional complication was that this hiring was done in a time when governments were moving to regulate the pay and distribution of the work force by means of national registration schemes. Canada in addition had established special boards to rule on the distribution, pay, and conditions of workers. The purpose of the Canadian regulations was to avoid exploitation of workers and, in particular, to ensure that specific industries or areas, rich with wartime work and cost-plus contracts, did not distort standards of work and pay. It would have been easy under a cost-plus contract to pay sky-high wages and pass the cost on to the government, and the regulations were designed to ensure this would not happen.

In the spring of 1942, with construction projects beginning simultaneously all over the Northwest and the Mackenzie valley, the civilian employment situation was very much in a state of flux. Exaggerated rumors were circulating that 15,000 workers were urgently needed for a single sixty-five-mile stretch of the Alaska Highway.[5] More realistically, Richard Finnie, liaison officer between the Canadian government and American contractors, announced in May 1942 that 1,200 men were immediately required for road construction, and another 1,200 would soon be needed for the pipeline.[6] To solve the labor shortage a number of schemes were suggested, both by Americans and Canadians. Lt. Col. Paul Thompson of the Office of the Chief of Engineers, U.S. War Department, complained of "the lack of positive control over the workers" and suggested that consideration be given to "militarizing, by some special form of selective service, all construction forces employed in areas outside our continental limits."[7] But alas for military fantasies, the conscription of civilian labor into the military was politically inconceivable, even in time of dire necessity. The Canadian deputy minister of labour suggested in July 1943 that German prisoners of war be used as construction workers. Major General W. W. Foster, Canadian special commissioner for northwest defence projects, dismissed the proposal as unworkable, noting that

> The stringing out of men over a distance of 1,200 miles, one or two men to each mile, would require an extraordinary outlay for supervision, both of their work and for guards. I am quite sure the U.S. authorities would not be favourable to such a proposal, as the cost of supervision would far exceed the value of any work obtained.[8]

Presumably the idea was to ask for volunteers among the prisoners, as had been done for some who worked during the war on prairie farms, since the use of involuntary labor of prisoners was, as the general doubtless knew, against the Geneva Convention. Since both these suggestions were impractical, civilian labor had to be used.

The United States government had put the nation on a wartime footing very quickly after Pearl Harbor; indeed, the country was well on the way even before the attack. With the introduction of lend-lease, of the first peace-time draft in the country's history, and of an undeclared war on German submarines, the country was already half at war before the Japanese attack. On the labor front, the war effort took top priority, yet Washington made few direct efforts to control American workers. The traditional dislike and distrust of government control remained strongly imbedded in the American psyche, despite the interventionist innovations of the New Deal, and the wartime crisis.

In the early 1940s, with unemployment ebbing and renewed concerns about inflation, battles broke out in the United States over the control of labor, many of them provoked by management's demand for an open shop and a no-strike policy.[9] After Pearl Harbor, the Roosevelt administration moved quickly to bring both labor and management in line with national war policy. In January 1942 a National War Labor Board was established, replacing the National Defense Mediation Board created the year before,[10] with representation from both the American Federation of Labor and the Congress of Industrial Organizations.[11] The board functioned at the management level, setting wages on an industry by industry basis, providing a mechanism for settling industrial disputes through mediation and arbitration. In return for a ban on lockouts, the two labor organizations agreed to a no-strike pledge for the duration of the war.[12] Later that year Congress passed the Economic Stabilization Act, designed to hold down wage and price increases. The National War Labor Board was given the power to regulate wages.

By the end of 1942, the depression days of unemployment were a fading memory, and actual shortages of labor were beginning to appear in areas of the United States. This situation provided opportunities for people—particularly women and those who were black—who had been so far out of the labor picture that they had not even been counted among the unemployed of the 1930s. The war clouds had silver linings for the thousands of black workers from the rural south who found good jobs in defense plants in Detroit, California, and the Pacific Northwest at wages that would have seemed impossible a decade earlier. In April 1942 a War Manpower Commission was created, with the power to ensure that critical industries obtained the necessary workers. The commission made one attempt, in 1943, to control essential workers, but in general its operations were hampered by vigorous opposition from organized labor and the political sensitivities of the administration. Military officials, like their Canadian counterparts, dreamed of a "labor draft," which would give the government the authority to assign workers as national needs dictated, but this was even less likely in the U.S. than in Canada. Towards the end of the war, the government toyed with the idea, but the war ended before any legislation could be passed.[13]

Thus American workers did not face particularly onerous controls and regulations on their mobility during the war. All workers of military age had to register with the Selective Service Commission; some received exemptions because of their skills, the nature of their work, or their physical condition. Those exempted from the draft because they were engaged in essential work had to get the permission of their local draft board before changing jobs, but those otherwise ineligible for the draft were generally free to take whatever work they wished.

This was the limit of official attempts to control the American labor market during the war. The participation of the AFL-CIO on the National War Labor Board did serve to co-opt unions to a degree into the management process and "did much to spread the responsibility for even unpopular decisions to the trade union leadership itself."[14] Organized labor gained much after 1940: increased representation on national boards, an erosion (which proved to be only temporary) of anti-union feeling in the country, increased membership, and an increased standard of living for workers generally.[15] But there was a price: a certain loss of union independence, and a co-option of union leadership to implement government policy.

In Canada, workers were more closely regulated in the interests of the national war effort. Early in the war, fearing a repetition of the inflation of World War I, the federal government moved to control wages, prices, and corporate profits. Ottawa had an efficient tool with which to accomplish these goals—the War Measures Act. This law, passed on the eve of World War I, permitted the federal government to govern by decree during time of war or insurrection.[16] A flood of Privy Council orders (that is, government decrees) were issued during the war, with the force of law. In June 1940, under Order 2685, the government urged employers to negotiate in good faith with unions and called for restraint in wages. Later orders simply set wage levels; beginning in 1941, they were to be "the highest wage rates generally prevailing and normally established for the different occupations in any given establishment during the period 1926–1929 or any higher rates established thereafter but before December 16, 1940." There was provision for cost of living bonuses to compensate for changing circumstances; special adjustments were permitted in exceptional cases.[17]

There was little evidence of sympathy on the part of the Canadian government for the difficulties of working people during the war. "Canadian labour policy throughout the war was concerned only with eliminating industrial unrest," argued Laurel Sefton MacDowell. "For political reasons, the government felt it necessary to conciliate business, its wartime ally in developing the war economy. It was therefore unprepared to establish collective bargaining as a 'right' or grant labour an important role in running the war."[18]

The Canadian government moved on a number of fronts to regulate the distribution, pay, and status of Canadian workers. A National War Labour Board, consisting of a chairman, two members from employer and two from employee groups, was set up to establish and supervise national employment policy. In addition, a number of Regional War Labour Boards were created,[19] with provincial ministers of labour as chairmen and employer and employee representation. The regional boards were given sweeping power to determine wage rates and working conditions and to allocate labor to specific projects.[20]

During 1942, wage and work classification disputes arising out of the northwest defense projects were arbitrated by the Regional War

Labour Board for Alberta and British Columbia, a system that soon proved unmanageable.[21] The size and number of the projects swamped the board. Overlapping jurisdictions, administrative rivalries, and the fact that both Canadians and Americans were working on the same job sites complicated efforts to regulate the labor force. Some workers came under the aegis of the British Columbia board, some under the Alberta, and some under neither. The system also complicated the efforts of American firms to hire Canadian workers. Construction officials were pleased, therefore, to learn in 1943 that a new committee was to be set up, "one which would have sufficient control of Canadian labour to adjust all of the major problems now prevalent."[22]

Believing that a consolidation of authority would "facilitate the completion of such projects, would reduce uncertainties of jurisdiction and would tend to stabilize wage and employment conditions in the area," the federal government created a single Western Labour Board. The new authority had one representative selected in consultation with Alberta, one from British Columbia, one representing workers, one the employers, and one National Selective Service Officer. The board included Mr. Justice O'Connor of the Alberta Supreme Court (chair), Col. John Keen (British Columbia), George Henwood (Alberta), Malcolm Ainslie (workers' representative), H. G. Macdonald (employers' representative) and William Carnill from the National Selective Service. An American representative, Major Henry Thurston, was appointed to the board as a "special consultant."[23] On the Canadian side, the Western Labour Board was ordered to confer with Major General W. W. Foster, the newly appointed special commissioner for defence projects in northwest Canada, in establishing suitable policy. The board, like its provincial counterparts, was empowered to regulate wage rates, establish occupational classification, and set hours of work and cost of living bonuses on all American-financed western defense projects.[24] It represented a specific response to the particular needs of the Alaska Highway and CANOL projects, and an effort to separate the unique circumstances facing workers in the northwest from the general Canadian situation. The board had its headquarters in Edmonton, and held most of its 280 meetings there, between July 12, 1943, and April 11, 1946. Few attempts were made to travel to the actual work sites; the board traveled to Vancouver, Victoria, and Whitehorse twice and Prince Rupert once.

The Western Labour Board went quickly to work, holding open meetings that allowed workers (or their representatives) to air their grievances and managers to state their case.[25] Employers submitted proposed wage schedules to the board, where they were discussed, sometimes amended, and eventually approved. Appeals, both general and specific, were routinely heard. While the many problems tackled by the board were not all easily resolved, the separate handling of defense project issues suited all parties concerned.

From the beginning, the board took note of the higher cost of living in the Northwest and the need to compensate workers for the long periods of isolation in frontier camps. To assist construction companies in their attempts to lure workers north, a zone system was established, permitting companies operating farther north to pay higher wages. Zone I covered the region south of a line joining Dawson Creek, British Columbia, and Fort McMurray, Alberta. Zone II took in the Yukon and parts of British Columbia. and Alberta north of zone I and "west of the Yukon-N.W.T. boundary extended." Zone III included the remaining parts of Alberta, and the Northwest Territories. A forty-four-hour work week was the norm in zone I, but forty-eight hours was the rule in the other two zones. Workers in zones I and II were charged $1.25 per day for subsistence; room and board were free in zone III. Wage rates varied by zone; carpenters earned ninety-five cents an hour in zone I, but $1.20 in zones II and III. Laborers got fifty-five cents in zone I, seventy to seventy-five cents in zone II, and seventy-five cents in zone III.[26] In June 1944 the system was altered to six zones instead of three for the purpose of establishing wage rates and conditions of employment; the new areas were Edmonton, Grand Prairie, Dawson Creek, Fort St. John to Watson Lake, Whitehorse (which included Norman Wells), and Waterways-Simpson.[27] This arrangement caused some administrative confusion, but it did recognize employers' needs to offer better wages and working conditions to attract workers to isolated and undesirable locales.

Wage rates were adjusted many times during the war, and companies or government agencies often requested redesignation of individual workers or of job classifications. The board dealt with numerous requests from workers for increased wages or for cost of living bonuses for northern workers. On some occasions adjustments were made, but time and time again the board pointed to the prevailing wage structure in western Canada as justification for refusing these requests.[28]

The existence of the National War Labour Board tended to make redundant the trade unions, who were most active on behalf of workers working outside the defense projects—in the restaurants, hotels, and other businesses—in the communities subjected to the American invasion. The board usurped the role played by the collective bargaining process and served as a final court of arbitration in labor disputes; there were no appeals from its decisions. On the other hand, it could be used as a scapegoat by the construction companies, who did not much care what they paid in wages, since wage costs could be passed on to the government under a cost-plus contract. Contractors cared only about securing enough workers to get the job done. Often, the companies and the workers' representatives presented joint requests to the board for higher wages, or at least the companies did not oppose such requests. There were therefore few wage disputes in the workplaces themselves. Though organized labor was weak in the Canadian northwest during this period, two unions that did remain active during the war were Local 815 of the Whitehorse and District Workers' Union and Local 884 (Whitehorse) of the Hotel and Restaurant Employees' Union. Their leaders assiduously petitioned the Western Labour Board for better wages and working conditions, and their reports to the board give a revealing picture of the strain placed upon people in less skilled occupations. Towards the end of 1944, a complaint went to the board about working conditions for waitresses in Whitehorse:

> ...working conditions of waitresses employed by the Standard Oil Co. in Mess Hall B where waitresses are working on a split shift basis the situation is one that has no parallel anywhere. They must put in a full 8-hour [sic] on the job stretched out over a period of 14 hours. It is the general custom anywhere where the split shift is in existence that as soon as the work of the three meals are over they are off the job. The system used here is based on the long abolished sweat shop system of many years ago. We request that your Board make it compulsory for any one employing any classifica-

tion of labour on the split shift basis be compelled to have the shift worked within the already established 11 1/2 hour period. Further, the split shift has been abolished in most large industries and most of the catering industry, in fact it has been made illegal in the Province of Ontario . . . the most unheard of sweat shop methods have been adopted by the Northwest Service Command in the operation of its Mess Halls, methods that we vehemently condemn....[29]

Employers of civilian labor had much to offer prospective workers: comparatively high wages, a chance for adventure, and an opportunity to perform vital wartime service. They also had to overcome considerable resistance and prejudice against the North, based on ignorance, a well founded fear of the winter, job opportunities in more salubrious climates, tough working conditions, and a disinclination to be separated from family and home for a prolonged period. Despite good pay, finding workers was not easy; keeping them in the Northwest was even more difficult.

There were several options for civilians who wished to work on these projects. Depending on their training, skill, and inclination, they could hire on with the Public Roads Administration, which had the administrative responsibility for the Alaska Highway, with the United States Engineering Department (USED), which had a large establishment in the Northwest, or with one of the many contractors and subcontractors. They could hire on in the lower forty-eight states. Canadian workers had the additional alternative of applying at company offices at Edmonton or elsewhere or simply showing up at the job site to ask for work. In the hectic days of 1942 and 1943, when construction activity was at its peak and labor shortages endemic, this technique often worked. Other Canadians, brought north by employers on nondefense jobs, quit and hired on at higher wages with the defense construction companies.

There is a pattern evident in the first year's hirings. The companies that won the big contracts brought many of their engineers, equipment operators, and support staff with them. As a result, there were sizable concentrations of workers from the states where the companies had their headquarters: Iowa (Lytle and Green), Ontario (R. Melville Smith), Washington (Dowell Construction), and Minnesota (Oakes Construction). The selection of subcontractors followed a similar pattern; of the fifteen companies hired for Alaska Highway work by Oakes Construction, all but one were from Minnesota (the other was from Wisconsin). The same was true of the other major contractors and subcontractors. These connections lasted throughout the war as personal contacts, word of mouth, and specific recruiting efforts brought a stream of workers from the home base to the Northwest.

But these local connections did not answer all the labor needs. Skilled workers and professionals, especially those with experience in the oil industry, were in very short supply. Most companies were perennially short of workers and were constantly trying to recruit them wherever they were to be found. In finding workers, the civilian contractors made an effort to be honest about northern working conditions. The poster in the Bechtel-Price-Callahan hiring hall pulled no punches:

> This is No Picnic. Working and living conditions on this job are as difficult as those encountered on any construction job ever done in the United States or foreign territory. Men hired for this job will be required to work and live under the most extreme conditions imaginable. Temperatures will range from 90° above zero to 70° below zero. Men will have to fight swamps, rivers, ice and cold. Mosquitoes, flies and gnats will not only be annoying but will cause bodily harm. If you are not prepared to work under these and similar conditions, DO NOT APPLY![30]

Such warnings deterred the halfhearted, but many workers reacted enthusiastically to the prospect of northern employment. The wide publicity given the projects led to a flood of volunteers—men and women eager to help with the war effort, to make money, or just to participate in a great adventure. An example was a man named Ralph Spear, who, returning to Connecticut after fifteen months in Bermuda, applied for a northern position. Exempt from the draft and a skilled truck and "cat" driver, Spear felt well qualified for highway work. He was also anxious "to do my share as close to the 'firing line' as possible."[31] For many workers the northern projects were a kind of vicarious war, providing a tough and useful alternative to military service for those who could not bear to take a cushy job in Toronto or Detroit while their neighbors or relatives were fighting overseas.

JUNE IS 42

THIS IS NO PICNIC

WORKING AND LIVING CONDITIONS ON
THIS JOB ARE AS DIFFICULT AS THOSE
ENCOUNTERED ON ANY CONSTRUCTION
JOB EVER DONE IN THE UNITED STATES OR
FOREIGN TERRITORY. MEN HIRED FOR
THIS JOB WILL BE REQUIRED TO WORK
AND LIVE UNDER THE MOST EXTREME CON-
DITIONS IMAGINABLE. TEMPERATURE WILL
RANGE FROM 90° ABOVE ZERO TO 70° BELOW
ZERO. MEN WILL HAVE TO FIGHT SWAMPS
RIVERS, ICE AND COLD. MOSQUITOS, FLIES,
AND GNATS WILL NOT ONLY BE ANNOYING
BUT WILL CAUSE BODILY HARM.
IF YOU ARE NOT PREPARED TO WORK
UNDER THESE AND SIMILAR CONDITIONS
DO NOT APPLY

Bechtel-Price-Callahan

THREE TEXANS HEADING FOR THE NORTH COUNTRY
IN FRONT OF BECHTEL-PRICE-CALLAHAN'S WARNING SIGN.
NAC, PA110859.

In the months following the announcement of the projects, scores of applications came in from across the United States, mostly directed to the U.S. Army Corps of Engineers. Some came from professionals—engineers, draftsmen, architects, and geologists—but most came from construction workers, eager to participate in one of the largest highway and pipeline projects ever undertaken. The engineers compiled lists of applicants and forwarded them to the Public Roads Administration. The list covering March to May 1942 contained the names of 149 applicants for jobs.[32]

The Alaska Highway and the CANOL pipeline were what would today be called "megaprojects," and like the great construction projects of the 1930s—the Hoover Dam, for example—they exerted a strong pull on engineering professionals anxious to participate in one of the really important projects of their generation. When Brigadier General Sturdevant described the highway project to a meeting of American military engineers, for instance, there was an immediate response. Calvin Cook, a mechanical engineer with the Corps of Engineers, immediately requested a transfer to military or civilian work on the highway. His work in Washington, D.C., was deemed more important, and his request was denied.[33] There were many like him in 1942, but even then, project managers were constantly short of skilled professionals.

Because of the glamour associated with the northern projects, and because professionals did not face the same work regulations as semiskilled employees, the contractors were able to hire men well-known in their fields to supervise the CANOL pipeline. The Corps of Engineers put together a Who's Who of the oil industry to administer the CANOL project. Paul Lambright, project manager, was a prominent petroleum engineer, formerly in charge of Standard Oil's operations in Rumania. A team of geologists brought years of international experience to Norman Wells. Among them were O. Boggs, a subsurface geologist who had spent twenty-three years in oil exploration in Canada, Peru, and Equador. Lloyd Noble, of Noble Drilling Corporation, was "probably the best known oil drilling contractor in [the] United States." J. S. Walton, of Turnbull-Sverdrup-Parcel, was a professor of chemical engineering at the University of Oklahoma, and was "recognized in the petroleum profession as an authority of refinery design."[34]

The initial enthusiasm for the northern projects did not, however, guarantee a steady supply of professional help in the later construction stages. The Whitehorse refinery was chronically short, due to the high priority assigned to oil refining in the lower forty-eight states. CANOL was also perennially short of field professionals. One official observed

[T]here are none available. Every available geophysical man is busy looking for oil here in the United States. Every effort is being put forth to locate new reserves. The only way we could supply you these men would be to stop some of our operations, when we are doing everything we can to increase our operations. This manpower shortage is not just something that you read about in the newspapers; it exists.[35]

In June 1944, with work on the Whitehorse refinery well advanced, Standard Oil began a continent-wide search for employees. Two hundred and thirty-one positions were posted with the War Manpower Commission and Selective Service for clearance. Within a month over one hundred people were hired, including forty-four from the Whitehorse area, forty from Edmonton, sixteen from San Francisco, six from Redding, California, and two from Texas.[36]

Employers could not rely on volunteers for work on these projects, and they located American workers for northern service in a number of ways. Southern employees could be transferred north; newspaper advertisements were extensively used, as were government recruiting offices. The United States Employment Service acted as a hiring office for several of the large American contractors active in the North. The U.S. Army Corps of Engineers also used its network of offices to identify surplus labor available for northern service.[37] This arrangement worked well; the engineers were able to advise the firm of Bechtel-Price Callahan to recruit in the Los Angeles area, while the Metcalfe-Hamilton, Kansas City Bridge consortium was told to look in upper New York State and in Pennsylvania. Employers also worked through the Employment Service of Canada and the U.S. Employment Division to find workers, hoping to free themselves from the burden and cost of direct recruiting.[38]

Despite all this assistance, the construction companies' need for labor was so great that they had to send agents to recruit likely workers. In 1944, for example, Marine Operators Company hired two men to travel throughout the Missouri River valley, "contacting prospective employees, either at their home or places of work."[39] At times, the needs of the companies gave the process a modern flair; like college basketball coaches recruiting star high school athletes, the agents flouted the rules and poached on forbidden territory. The government had to order Okes Construction to stop "proselytizing" laborers and commissary workers in the Sioux Falls district and to obey the directives of the U.S. War Manpower Commission to target their efforts in areas of labor surplus.[40]

Finding willing workers was only half the battle, however—more difficult were the administrative and logistical difficulties involved in getting the workers to the northern job sites. In the spring of 1944, Pomeroy Erectors, contractors for bridges on the Alaska Highway, hired a man named John Edwards, a Canadian citizen living in Seattle. In order to get to his new job in Alaska, Edwards needed an alien departure permit in order to be able to re-enter the United States. Before such a permit could be issued, he needed clearance from the secretary of war and the local draft board. He also had to go through Alaska Travel Control, which also needed clearance from his draft board.[41] Napoleon said that an army marches on its belly; twentieth century armies often march on typewriters. Nonetheless, appeals to the proper military authorities could often do wonders in cutting through red tape.

Recruiting difficulties got worse after the winter of 1942 to 1943 when horror stories about northern working conditions and the dreadful climate began to reach the south. With the pioneer road completed and the race to Alaska over, fewer workers wished to risk frostbite for what increasingly seemed an ordinary unglamorous construction job. It became increasingly difficult to recruit enough men to keep the projects proceeding on schedule. After a visit to St. Paul, R. B. Shackleford told a staff meeting that information received by prospective employees "did not give the people the proper picture of the conditions in the Northwest Division." He was convinced that "there are many persons in the higher paid brackets who would possibly be interested if they knew the conditions; many of them are old employees with families in the States and they hesitate to leave their families in view of uncertain conditions in the North."[42] But recruiting continued to be an uphill struggle.

Because of the urgency of filling the jobs in the construction camps, officials worried that draft dodgers and other undesirables might use the hiring procedures to escape military service by hiding in the Northwest.[43] But this fear, on the whole, seems to have been groundless. A police review of Canadians working at Norman Wells in May 1944 reported that while some "may be remaining here with the intention of evading Military Service, this percentage is extremely small."[44] Later in 1944, when the Canadian government introduced conscription for overseas service, it found that of the 3,639 Canadians employed in the Northwest Service Command, only eighty-six were callable for military service, with five others potentially callable.[45] Of these men, only 405 were under the age of forty; most young men by that time had enlisted or had been drafted for home service.[46]

Taking the entire 1944 population of the Yukon and Northwest Territories, it was found that there were 2,347 Canadian men available (callable and fit and callable subject to fitness), of whom 1,100 were expected to receive medical deferments, and an additional 373 deemed essential. The total yield from a call-up from both territories would yield under 850 men. Canadian officials questioned the quality of the men who would be called up:

> It is considered likely that the best material will be found amongst those classified as essential, i.e., foremen, engineers, surveyors, mechanics, etc. Amongst the balance will be found trappers, half breeds, Indians, delinquents and possible deserters. The quality of volunteers would probably be good but the numbers might be small.[47]

Another official said of the trappers, mixed bloods, and Natives that "the majority...would not be up to standards, particularly mental, of that desired for the Service."[48] On the other hand, while the results would hardly make the effort worthwhile, the "psychological and political results might justify some action," particularly in the larger communities.[49] Eventually, the National Selective Service decided the likely returns did not justify the bother.[50] Some men were called up,[51] but the war ended before the full effect of the Canadian draft reached the Northwest.

The American workers were also subject to the same rumors. RCMP Constable T. J. Keefe, reporting from Camp Canol, rejected a rumor that the camp was full of Canadian draft-dodgers, but mentioned "reports of boasts made by a number of these Americans with regards to their being up here to evade the draft in the U.S."[52] D. T. Bath, a Canadian heavy equipment operator working on the Alaska Highway in 1942, remembered that "On the highway, though not particularly in our camp, there were quite a few men with shaven

INSPECTOR CRONKITE AND MEMBERS OF THE
RCMP DETACHMENT, WHITEHORSE.
NA, 111-SC 323152.

heads and big, bushy beards. It was generally accepted that they were
more or less in disguise (draft dodging?)."[53] An American spokesman,
on the other hand, stated that "Every American citizen we bring north
is 4F or over 30 years of age."[54] On the whole the evidence indicates

that only a few workers on the northwest projects were draft evaders; the large majority of Canadian workers were over military age, and of the younger men there, it seems likely that the majority had been rejected for service on medical grounds.

The urgency of the northern work and the difficulty of finding workers led inevitably to a number of bad characters being recruited by the construction companies. While most of the workers were reliable, honest, and hard-working, observers reported a larger than normal number of malcontents and troublemakers among their ranks. The military police complained in October 1942 of "the drifting [men], asserting that the men were highly paid, created a serious problem because of liquor, and usually came out without the funds for passage home."[55] "Many of these employees have serious prison records or undesirable backgrounds," reported a military intelligence officer. "Many stay only for a short time and become dissatisfied with their living conditions and recreation facilities, or the rigors of the climate." To control "this type of personnel," a system of controls was implemented, including fingerprinting of all civilian employees.[56]

Despite these efforts, "undesirables" sometimes slipped through the official net. One man, a carpenter for Bechtel-Price-Callahan at Skagway, accused the company of mismanagement and corruption. On investigation, it turned out that the Alaska Travel Control had tried to prevent his entry into the territory. The reason was clear in a letter provided by the sheriff of the man's hometown: "This man is considered the worst character we have had in the Country.... Take no chances on this man as he is bad medicine, and can't be trusted with anything that can be moved, burned or destroyed."[57] That a few such men would get to the North was inevitable; the security network was designed to keep the number under control.[58]

Not all northern workers were reliable, or even honest. A few were probably fleeing the draft—though there were many military postings far more pleasant than civilian work on the Alaska Highway or the CANOL project. No doubt a few were thieves—and these projects provided rich pickings for them. But the frontier has always been, in legend if not in fact, a place where people could go to escape their past and be judged on what they were, not on what they had been. The northwest construction projects continued this tradition; so long as a worker did a good day's work and did not prove disruptive, the authorities were not inclined to identify or prosecute those who had slipped through the cracks in the hiring process or those whose past was blemished.

From the beginning, American employers were eager to sign up Canadian workers, even in the face of Canadian regulations and diplomatic agreements. There were thousands of workers in the region northwest of Edmonton and thousands more throughout western Canada, many of whom could be enticed away from their farms, classrooms, mines, traplines, or city jobs—if the price was right. In the first hectic year of construction, employers often ignored local labor conditions and regulations. RCMP S/Sgt. Bryan described the situation at Fort McMurray and Waterways:

> Labour conditions may become aggravated. Already there is a bottle-neck in the movement of supplies, with insufficient river equipment to move it. The U.S. are paying big wages $1.10 & $1.25 per hour and found, working 10 and 17 hours per day. Natives are being hired as river pilots at $8.00 per day and found. As a consequence, men are eager to leave other employers to engage with the U.S. who will take them upon presentation of a written release from previous employers.[59]

Local employers, who paid far lower wages, were angered by the sudden competition. General C. L. Sturdevant reported that they were "very unhappy over what you [the CANOL employers] are doing to their labor by offering employment at higher than local rates, thus causing men to leave their jobs and accept employment on your project." He ordered project managers to honor Canadian regulations and wage rates in order "to avoid constant friction with the Canadians,"[60] a policy which was difficult to enforce.

The problem soon became endemic to the Canadian west. Early work on the CANOL project drained much of the work force from logging camps in Alberta and British Columbia. By July 1942, over 300 Canadians had been employed at rates considerably higher than national standards.[61] An urgent need for shipwrights led an American contractor to place advertisements in Vancouver papers; the offer of $1.25 per hour, plus free room and board and transportation found many takers. The departure of twenty-five skilled workmen, however, created an immediate shortage in the Vancouver shipyards and led to panicked calls for federal intervention.[62] Two workers on an airport project in Edmonton requested an increase in wages. Their employer concurred and prepared a submission to the National War Labour Board. Before a decision was rendered, the men quit, saying they had been offered better jobs on the Alaska Highway. Another man also accepted a much better paying position with a highway contractor, but turned it down when he found he would be away from his family for nine months. There was also a tremendous American demand for female employees, particularly stenographers; within weeks there were noticeable shortages throughout the region.[63] Two telephone operators at the Macdonald Hotel in Edmonton who made $75 per month were offered $125 to work for an American contracting firm.[64] Canadians charged that the United States was "only interested in its own project and is not concerned as to how this work affects the stability of the local labour market." It was a matter of some urgency, for "the transportation and mining services which are vital to the welfare of the people in the Northwest Territories will break down as a result of a loss of personnel attracted by higher wages to the pipeline project."[65]

Given the leisurely pace of the bureaucracy, and bewildering thicket of Canadian regulations, it is easy to understand why the American companies, fired with the can-do spirit and the stimulus of cost-plus contracts,[66] were willing to circumvent them. The goal was to complete the projects on time; failure to do so might lead to financial penalties or cancellation of the contract. In the summer of 1942, Coast Construction Company, a Canadian firm working on the Edmonton airport, found itself several hundred workers short, a situation that was partly its own fault, since its president was strongly anti-union, and the company could not use union hiring halls as a source of employees. To attract workers, it unilaterally announced that it would pay the higher British Columbia wage rates.[67] The Western Labour Board quickly stepped in and forced the company to adhere to Alberta's wage schedule; 120 men immediately quit rather than accept the lower wage rate.[68] Despite patriotic appeals to Canadian authorities—if the company could not complete its work, the president claimed, "our national prestige is definitely sabotaged"—there was no movement on the question of wages.[69]

Brigadier General L. D. Worsham, in charge of construction in the Edmonton region, worried that manpower shortages were slowing the work. He threatened that "unless there is prompt action by Selective Service and the War Labour Board in manning the job, I propose to ask that the contract with the Canadian contractor be withdrawn and that the United States be permitted to use American contractors on the Edmonton Airport."[70] Coast Construction supported the American position: "This work is either a war emergency or it is not a war emergency—and if it is a war emergency, it requires the maximum scale of wages as prevails on other war contracts under your jurisdiction." That the company was a cost-plus contractor no doubt made it easier to be magnanimous.[71] The persistence paid off: in early September, Major General W. W. Foster, special commissioner for northwest defence projects, recommended that efforts be made to assist Coast Construction with recruitment.[72] Negotiations with the Saskatchewan Farm Labour Service and employment offices in Saskatchewan and Manitoba resulted in the selection of 300 laborers and fifty carpenters to work on the project.[73] There was less movement on wage schedules, however, which remained lower than Coast Construction had hoped for, leading to yet another round of negotiations.[74] Ultimately, Coast Construction was unable to complete its contract on schedule. The contract was let out for tenders and Coast Construction was unsuccessful in its effort to retain the work.[75]

American companies, too, despite statements to the contrary,[76] were oblivious to or prone to ignore Canadian wage and labor regulations.[77] The Canadian government later admitted "The fact is that we have probably not 'policed' the job sufficiently well to guarantee compliance."[78] From time to time there were attempts at enforcement. Several American companies working on the CANOL project had to agree to release their Canadian employees, who were to be hired by Canadian highway contractors or reassigned through the Employment Service of Canada, and replace them with American workers.[79] Canadian workers protested their treatment, demanding that they be permitted to remain where they were. A meeting on the issue resulted in an informal agreement to permit the workers to complete their contracts.[80] The CANOL project seemed particularly prone to confusion of this sort, probably because it had been conceived in such haste.[81] Eventually the Americans, both the military and civilian contractors, declared their intention to avoid further controversy simply by not hiring any more Canadians.[82]

The initial agreements on the highway and pipeline projects had given priority to the hiring of American personnel. As a result of the debate over labor and hiring, it was eventually decided that American contractors would hire only American, and Canadian contractors Canadians.[83] Such regulations were often ignored, however, and scores of Canadians worked for American companies throughout the life of the projects. The Public Roads Administration, for example, hired numerous Canadian workers, particularly in secretarial and professional positions. On the other hand, at least some Americans were reluctant to hire Canadian labor. The Dawson Creek Diary of the NWSC reported,

> Mr. Hill called Captain Lamar, at his request, who advised that a young Canadian was available for a timechecker. At this time Mr. Hill informed Capt. Lamar that we had not employed any Canadians and that he understood the policy of this office was to avoid employing them unless necessary. He asked the reason and Mr. Hill told him that we didn't feel they worked like our people, or thought like our people, and that this experience had come to us from the experience of other activities here where Canadians had been employed… it created a lack of harmony in an office to have two different scales of wages for people doing the same work.[84]

Canadian authorities were unhappy with the arrangement which limited Canadians' access to work and tried to increase local participation in the projects. As early as May 1942 it was suggested in Canada that the Canadian sections of the Alaska Highway should employ only Canadians and that all work done south of the 60th parallel should be done by Canadians. A number of critics suggested that labor shortages would disappear overnight if greater efforts were made to recruit workers from the prairie provinces and northern Ontario, which had still not entirely recovered from the depression.[85]

The Canadian government attempted to increase the participation of Canadian nationals in the construction work. American companies promised to do their best; Standard Oil of California,

WAITING FOR SUPPER.
YTA, Robert Hays collection, 5682.

anxious to escape Canadian regulations on foreign companies, promised to hire as many Canadian workers as possible. It cautioned that "our experience so far indicates that only a small percentage, if any, of the total number required will be available."[86] In 1943, at the height of civilian construction work, 39,606 workers were active in the Northwest. Of these, 30,702 were American, over three-quarters of the total.[87] In May of 1943, the Canadian Employment and Selective Service reported over 6,200 Canadians working in the areas administered by their Edmonton and Dawson Creek offices. Of this number, 1,628 worked for U.S. employers; Canadian contractors accounted for the remaining 4,671. (Females, employed primarily in office positions, accounted for 532 of the Canadian total.[88])

The difficulty of recruiting Canadian workers rested in large measure in the restrictions placed on wage rates and other benefits. Canadian nationals, including those who lived in the Northwest, faced higher costs of living than did their American counterparts,

CIVILIAN WORKERS ON BOARD
A TRANSPORT SHIP HEADING FOR SKAGWAY.
Note the four-tiered bunks.
U.S. Army Corps of Engineers photograph.

most of whom left their families in the south, enjoyed access to a subsidized canteen (a low-cost snack bar) and received free room and board. In November 1944, engineers and firemen in Prince Rupert had their wages rolled back by several cents per hour, bringing their rate in line with Vancouver wages. As John Mulroney, Local 115, Operating Engineers, quickly pointed out, Prince Rupert workers faced prices twenty to thirty-eight percent higher than Vancouver, had to put up with an acute shortage of housing, and lived in a place where it rained even more than in Vancouver. No wonder, he pointed out, employers had difficulty finding suitable workers for Prince Rupert projects.[89]

At the same time, however, businessmen were concerned that such a hiring rush would distort the labor picture through all of western Canada:

> a drastic increase in the wage rate to Canadian workmen employed on the Alaska Highway would be reflected in labour demands upon Canadian industry and probably create a stampede to higher paid jobs on this project.[90]

Local residents in the Northwest reacted angrily to the agreement which barred Canadians from lucrative wartime work. The Edmonton branch of the Canadian Legion protested the policy directly to Humphrey Mitchell, the federal minister of labour.[91] Carl Berg of the Labourers' International Union wired Ottawa, charging that the policy made it "most evident that the intent and purpose of Canadian employing interests, is to create a reservoir of unemployed Canadian labour to the end that they will continue to maintain economic control over the unskilled workers and maintain unlimited numbers of low paid workers at their command."[92] In a newspaper interview he charged that "the low wage structure for common labour in Canada under the present high cost of living equals peonage and should not be tolerated in any democracy. It is a dangerous practice which undermines the whole fabric of our social system."[93] Canadian employers resisted the demand of Berg and others[94] for higher pay fearing that "any interference by the Labour Unions [would] be dangerous, create sectional and selfish motives and resentment by those who are endeavouring to maintain stability in costs and wages."[95]

The minister of labour replied by reminding Berg that the Americans were paying for the projects, and that Canadians could find plenty of work with Canadian contractors. The higher American wages were due to the fact that U.S. law required payment of a bonus, in this case twenty-five percent, to American civilians working outside the USA.[96] He also observed that Americans were likely being paid no more than if they had remained in the United States, a view disputed by American officials.[97]

Labor representatives in northern Canada complained on several occasions about the hiring priority given Americans. G. P. Belanger, general secretary of the Yukon Trade Union Co-ordinating Council, alleged that the Northwest Service Command was clearly discriminating in its hiring practices against Yukon residents. Several local men had been cleared for work by the National Selective Service but had failed a physical examination conducted by a U.S. Army doctor. Since they had passed similar tests in the past, this was, Belanger charged, "a pretext to discriminate against local labour."[98] American authorities denied the charge, but the suspicion lingered in the region.[99] Eventually the policy was changed; now, "all local men wishing employment will be accepted if they sign a waiver in regard to medical examination."[100]

Even the federal government was compelled to take extraordinary measures to keep the northern civil service up to strength. In 1944, R. A. Gibson, director of the Department of Mines and Resources, reported that a living allowance of $100 per month had to be offered to entice employees to Dawson City:

> Tall stories have been circulated about the rates of remuneration of those engaged on defence projects and about the cost of living in the north, and there is sufficient truth in both these statements to make outsiders unwilling to go to Dawson unless the total remuneration looked adequate.

The problem, Gibson claimed, was endemic within the federal civil service, locked into a classification and pay schedule that had not changed since the beginning of the war.[101] In Alaska, where work could be found on the highway, pipeline and a number of local defense projects, local employers experienced trouble securing enough workers. The collapse of the Alaska gold mining industry during World War II (a crisis not duplicated in Canada), however, had turned many local workers out of their jobs and created an unusual labor surplus in Fairbanks and the interior of Alaska. These workers were only too happy to find employment with military contractors, although like their counterparts in northern Canada, they discovered a strong bias in favor of imported employees.

The strong pro-American hiring practices of the first eighteen months of construction did not persist throughout the war. Labor shortages forced a reconsideration of policy, and in July 1943 new rules were announced. Now, U.S. contractors were permitted to hire either Canadians or Americans, but they were urged to separate nationalities on a work site. Wage rates and benefits were to be determined by the nationality of the work force.[102] American officials were also given permission to employ Canadians in Alaska, usually on an emergency, short-term basis.[103] In December 1944, for example, the U.S. government applied to Canadian authorities for permission to recruit 200 civilian maintenance workers for work on Alaskan airfields.[104] Of course, the workers themselves were not given much more freedom under these new arrangements and were barred from seeking work except as determined by governments.[105]

Even this did not solve the problem, and by the summer of 1943, the larger American companies were circumventing the regulations designed to stop the pirating of labor by subcontracting out major portions of the work. These subcontracts, many of which went to Canadian firms, permitted employing local workers on projects managed by American companies. As a result, local employers once again found themselves unable to find sufficient labor for their own activities and again petitioned the Canadian government for assistance:

> Our Labour and Wage situation is all snarled up here on account of the arrival of American contractors who are competing for local labour and paying a wage scale away in excess of that prevailing for any similar kind of work such as on [an] airfield here. The E. W. Elliott Construction Company …are paying ninety six and a half cents per hour for common labour plus ten per cent against our controlled rate of seventy five cents…If this scale for local labour is maintained it is going to disorganize all work in the territory, government or private, and we submit that pressure should be brought to bear to compel these contractors to adhere to the regular scale.[106]

By late 1943 there were still local shortages of labor, but the boom in the North was beginning to fade, and the sellers' market for labor had ended. Thomas Broderick, discharged from the American army, discovered this to his cost. He was hired in 1943 by the Kansas City Bridge Construction Company to work in the Whitehorse area, but arrived there only to learn that he was no longer needed. He worked for a few weeks on a different job, got part payment of his wages, and was sent back home. The company promised to forward the rest of his salary and traveling costs to his home address. Two months later, in financial difficulties, he had not received his pay. His vision of wealth through high northern wages had turned sour.[107]

By the end of the war, participation of Canadian workers in the northwest work force had increased as a percentage of the total. A survey conducted at the end of February 1944 showed the following figures given in Table 3.1, [below]:

Table 3.1
CIVILIAN EMPLOYMENT IN THE CANADIAN NORTHWEST, 1944[108]

	American	Canadian	Total
Canol	6,088	1,484	7,572
Airfields	2,709	2,609	5,318
Highway Construction	184	8	192
Highway Maintenance	1,437	821	2,258
Mackenzie River	100	20	120
HQ, Civilian Staff	2,685	1,141	3,829
Total	13,203	6,083	19,286
(Peak Employment 1943)	30,702	8,904	39,606

A different set of statistics from July 1944 that omit the CANOL project show the ratio between military and civilian workers, given in Table 3.2 [see next page].[109]

In August 1944 the Western Labour Board reported that "there is no cause for anxiety regarding supply of men for Northwest projects."[110] Further changes in Canadian regulations governing the use of Canadian labor on American projects also helped. By the spring of 1944, the government waived many of the outstanding restrictions on the hiring of Canadian workers by U.S. companies.[111] By August 1944, the work force had shrunk to 10,068 people, including 6,001 Canadians and 4,067 Americans. Almost a third of these workers, 3,200 including 1,863 Americans, were associated

Table 3.2
WORKERS IN THE NORTHWEST, JULY 1944

	Military	Civilian	Air Force	Total
Headquarters	100	885	0	985
Edmonton	650	900	2,658	4,208
Dawson Creek	1,188	1,488	841	3,517
Whitehorse	1,775	1,290	1,160	4,225
Skagway	1,590	300	0	1,890
Fairbanks	324	585	525	1,434
Prince Rupert	2,997	300	0	3,297
Total	8,624	5,748	5,184	19,556

with the CANOL project. Alaska Highway construction had fallen off considerably. Just over 2,100 men and women worked on the highway, divided between maintenance, construction (mainly bridges), operations, and airport and access roads.[112] The U.S. Army estimated in September 1944 that they had 4,700 Canadians in their employ, with major concentrations in Edmonton (1,100), Dawson Creek (600) and Whitehorse (1,800).[113] According to Major Henry Thurston, Northwest Service Command, over half of these employees were female, handling the bulk of the administrative and clerical duties associated with the northwest defense projects.[114] In January 1945, the Northwest Service Command had 2,100 Canadians on staff, 400 of them women. The Air Corps had 1,500 Canadian employees, including 425 women; seventy-seven of the Transportation Corps' 941 Canadian workers on staff were women.

By the end of 1943, the United States government had begun to down-scale its northern defense projects. Nearly 40,000 civilians had worked in the Northwest earlier that year; by March 1944 that number had fallen to just under 17,000.[115] As part of an overall attempt to disengage itself from northern commitments, the American government tried to recruit Canadians to take over maintenance responsibilities for airfields and the Alaska Highway. The goal was to replace maintenance contracts, many of them held by American companies, with "hire and purchase" or day labor, using local Canadian workers.[116] After an initial controversy, complete with allegations that American officials still resisted the hiring of local workers, the United States government implemented a policy designed to reduce the level of American staffing to the lowest possible level.

With the urgency of construction behind it, the government altered its regulations on the hours of work. Road maintenance workers were limited to eight hours per day, six days per week, far short of the previously authorized seventy-hour work weeks. Similar reductions were imposed for other classes of workers.[117] Wage rates established for maintenance workers fell considerably below those of construction employees who preceded them; according to one estimate, National War Labour Board decisions called for payments "about one-third of the American rates and very nearly half of what is now being paid the Canadian employees on the highway." The decision, Major Henry Thurston argued, compelled employers to "salvage as much of the American personnel as we can, establish Canadian recruitment centers and see what we can do with these new wage rates."[118] Also, the U.S. government moved to lower wage rates generally in the last year of the war, a sign of changing priorities and steadily decreasing interest in northwest defense projects.[119]

The Canadian government had its own reasons for supporting the move towards local staffing. Camps filled with single men, while necessary during the construction phase, were too transient for the government's postwar policy. Now, employees were encouraged to bring their families north with them; they were housed in small maintenance camps spaced along the highway.[120] As part of the change, the U.S. Army discontinued its practice of providing food and supplies to workers along the highway. The employees petitioned the Western Labour Board for special dispensation, given the excessive cost of food in the maintenance camps. The board accepted the request, authorizing the payment of $7.50 per month to each employee located between Mile 0 and Mile 456; other highway employees were to receive $50 per month.[121] The transition to a peacetime labor force was underway.

By the summer of 1945, recruiting workers for northern service was no longer a major problem. As the North American industrial plant, geared up for military production, began to slow down, and as thousands of men were demobilized, many more workers became available. Americans were no longer part of the picture, save for a small complement, mostly composed of Alaskans, working on the U.S. portions of the defense projects. By the end of the war—and six months before the Canadian government assumed responsibility for the highway—Canadian workers had assumed most of the duties associated with the Alaska Highway, Haines Road and CANOL pipeline (although the latter was already in the process of being shut down).

With the war nearly over, the long hours and high wages of the early years were no longer available as an enticement. Now the orientation of recruitment had changed. Project managers were concerned now with the stability of the work force; workers were encouraged to bring their wives and children to the Northwest, and governments moved with some speed to provide the schools and other facilities required at the widely dispersed maintenance camps. The problem was now a peacetime matter, and entirely new considerations took effect. Recognizing the likely difficulties in finding and retaining workers in the Northwest, the Canadian government turned over responsibility for the highway to the Department of National Defence and not, as many expected, to the Department of Public Works, the federal government's construction arm. It was expected that the army could do the job cheaply and efficiently, and that it would have few labor problems, since most of its employees could not easily quit. It also gave the army an important peacetime job, even if it was one that it tackled without much enthusiasm. For the next eighteen years, the Canadian military reluctantly maintained and repaired the Alaska Highway. As a military agency, and operating without the restrictions and limitations faced by a private sector employer, the Department of National Defence was able to employ a stable, comparatively low-cost civilian labor force along its sections of the Alaska Highway. Beginning on 1 April 1946, the wartime pattern of recruitment and management of the labor force had ended.

The experience of the men and women who worked on the northwest defense projects fits neatly into the traditional pattern of northern labor. Very few who worked in the Northwest in these years came with any experience in the region; even fewer stayed after the job was done or their contracts expired. The decision to go north was, for almost all the workers, a short-term commitment. The companies and government agencies recruiting men and women for these duties played on these elements—the frontier setting, the land of the Midnight Sun, the race to protect the continent from the Japanese—but realized from the beginning that this would not be enough. So they also offered what the workers really wanted—extremely high wages, coupled with free or heavily subsidized room and board, and long working days and weeks, which ensured exceptional earnings for those who landed a job in the North.

The enticements proved adequate for American workers, who came by the thousands, often recruited by project contractors from their home town or home state. It was not as easy for Canadians, who had to comply with various regulations before accepting work in the Northwest. The basic incompatibility of Canadian and American regulations, particularly those governing wages, led to efforts to separate the workers from the two countries. As the work progressed, and as it became increasingly difficult to secure enough American workers, the Canadian government relaxed its regulations somewhat and allowed greater hiring of its workers by U.S.-based companies. The revised approach increased Canadian participation on the projects but at a time when wage rates and hours of work were already declining. Improved opportunities for Canadians caused other problems, however, as northern employers encountered increasing difficulty holding onto or attracting workers for their companies.

The regulations facing American and Canadian workers interested in positions on the northwest defense projects seemed a microcosm of the differences between the two countries. Canadian workers faced myriad regulations and powerful labour boards. Wages, conditions and even the decision to accept a specific job were subject to ratification by a government-appointed board. American workers faced no such limitations on their freedoms. The National War Labor Board set country-wide wage policy and mediated labor disputes, but otherwise workers were free to move about as economic forces dictated. So long as the American and Canadian workers were separated by a border, the differences were of little importance. Once thousands of American workers, operating under U.S. regulations and wage scales, invaded the Canadian northwest after 1942, the contrast was immediately apparent. The difference became a major source of conflict and forced governments and project managers to take numerous steps to deal with the anomalies. Canadian workers were already angered by the many restrictions, corporate resistance to unionism, and federal government checks on their liberties; having Americans enjoying benefits that few of them enjoyed only added to the frustration of Canadian workers on the northwest defense projects.

Recruiting civilian workers proved to be a difficult challenge for the American and Canadian contractors and American government agencies active in the Northwest during World War II. The combination of military exigencies, northern location and the complications of Canadian-American relations dictated the tactics of recruitment and the limitations placed on the employers. American companies enjoyed much greater freedom than their Canadian counterparts, reflecting the more *laissez-faire* attitude prevailing in the United States. In both countries, however, the recruitment and management of labor clearly illustrates that governments considered working people to be national resources, to be used, particularly in times for war, for national purposes.

Workers were not without options in the wartime economies of the United States and Canada, however, and special enticements were required to draw them northward. Creating a northern labor force, therefore, required more than the commitment of two governments to the construction of the northwest defense projects. The workers had to be enticed into accepting northern work. The enticements—high wages, patriotic propaganda, and generous benefits—were often taken, attracting thousands of men and women into the Northwest who otherwise would not have considered for a moment spending months working on construction projects in the subarctic. The very process of recruitment helped create (and reinforce) workers' attitudes toward Alaska and the Canadian northwest. These attitudes, in turn, determined how the workers responded

U.S. ARMY HOSPITAL, WHITEHORSE.
YTA, Cust collection, 84/64 36.

to their work and to the North, and ensured that the historic pattern of northern labor would persist through the war years.

Construction workers have historically worked under the most difficult of conditions. Railway crews, canal workers and road builders have traditionally been the vanguard of the modern work force in frontier areas. They were often among the most exploited of all workers, drawn from the immigrant classes and controlled by tough-minded contractors. The combination of workers desperate to make a living and the hard hand of corporate capitalism ensured the successful completion of the continent's canals and transcontinental railways. The frontier construction setting had long been among the most exploitative workplaces in the North American economy, as employers drove their workers to keep projects on time and on budget.

This pattern persisted through the nineteenth century and into the early twentieth century, and was repeated in both the United States and Canada during the Great Depression. In the United States, the Public Roads Administration supervised a series of make-work highway projects, in which thousands of the unemployed were put to work building and improving rural roads. In Canada, the exploitation of workers during times of economic hardship was severe. Fearful that the unemployed might be infected by radical ideologies if left to their own devices, the Canadian government opened a series of frontier work camps, far from population centers, and filled them with relief workers. In return for a pittance and room and board, the men had to accept rigid discipline and work on a series of labor-intensive construction projects, such as airfields and the Big Bend Highway in eastern British Columbia. In both cases, frontier construction remained low paid and relatively low-skilled work.

In more recent times, that pattern has been turned on its head. Contemporary frontier construction projects, like the building of the Alyeska Pipeline across Alaska in the 1970s and many Canadian power projects, have been among the most lucrative opportunities available for working-class people anywhere on the continent. Exceptionally high wages and remarkably generous benefit packages have completely transformed the image of the construction worker from exploited immigrant to highly paid, unionized frontier aristocrat of labor.

The World War II northwest defense projects fall in the middle of these extremes. The employment of civilian workers in the subarctic during World War II did not create this post-war work environment, but it is an excellent illustration of the transition to a highly paid frontier work force. Faced with a general labor shortage during the war, flush with government cost-plus contracts that made wage scales substantially irrelevant, and knowing the North American workers' understandable reluctance for frontier labor, employers offered generous salaries and additional benefits in order to attract the necessary men northward. Thousands of men accepted the challenge—and the opportunity—presented by the northwest defense projects, came north, made their money and returned home.

NOTES

1. Alvin Finkel, *Business and Social Reform in the Thirties* (Toronto: James Lorimer, 1979), covers the Canadian situation.

2. And management too—the production of automobiles for civilian use and a wide range of consumer goods was suspended during the war.

3. See Robert Aieger, *American Workers, American Unions, 1920-1985* (Baltimore: Johns Hopkins University Press, 1986), chapter 3, "The Unions Go To War, 1939-1945"; Joshua Freeman, "Delivering the Goods: Industrial Unionism During World War II," *Labor History* (1978); James Green, "Fighting on Two Fronts: Working Class Militancy in the 1940s," *Radical America* 8 (1975).

4. Wm. Carnhill to A. MacNamara, 26 August 1943, NAC, RG 36/7, vol. 18, file 5-5, part 2.

5. *Whitehorse Star*, 12 June 1942: 3.

6. L. E. Drummond, Alberta and Northwest Chamber of Mines to R. A. Gibson, 29 May 1942, NAC, RG 27, vol. 676, file 6-5-755-1.

7. Thompson to Brig. Gen. C. L. Sturdevant, 18 September1942, ACE, 72-72-A-3173, Box 16, file 50-26.

8. Heeney to Foster, 27 July 1943. Ibid., Foster to Heeney, 30 July 1943, NAC, RG 36/7, vol. 36, file 11-4.

9. The following is drawn from Patrick Renshaw, "Organized Labor and the United States War Economy, 1939-1945," *The Journal of Contemporary History* 21, 1 (January 1986): 3-22.

10. The National Defense Mediation Board was created on 19 March 1941 to settle labor disputes in defense industries. Its powers were limited to consultation, mediation and voluntary arbitration. Richard Morris, ed., *A History of the American Worker* (Princeton, N.J.: Princeton University Press, 1983), 177.

11. On the CIO during the war, see Nelson Lichtenstein, *Labor's War at Home: The CIO in World War II* (New York: Cambridge University Press, 1982).

12. The Board's rigidity on the question of wages resulted in that pledge being broken on a number of occasions.

13. This survey is drawn from Irving Bernstein, "Americans in Depression and War," in Richard Morris, ed., *A History of the American Worker* (Princeton: Princeton University Press, 1983), 151-186.

14. Lichtenstein, *Labor's War at Home*, 151.

15. On the role of the war in increasing the power and accomplishments of mass-production unionism, see David Brody, *Workers in Industrial America: Essays on the Twentieth Century Struggle* (New York: Oxford University Press, 1980): Chapter 3, "The Emergence of Mass-Production Unionism."

16. The war or insurrection could be real or perceived, and since it was the government itself which determined whether such war or insurrection existed, the act gave it enormous powers.

17. Wartime Wages Policy, Suggestions for the Application of Order in Council PC 7440 by Boards of Conciliation and Investigation, 31 March 1941, Edmonton Municipal Archives, RG 11, Class 39, file 1.

18. Laurel Sefton MacDowell, "The Formation of the Canadian Industrial Relations System During World War Two," *Labour/Le Travailleur* (1978): 186.

19. Initial legislation called for five Regional Labour Boards; this was amended to nine in December 1941. See EMA, RG 11, Class 39, file 2, PC 9514, 5 December 1941.

20. EMA, RG 11, Class 39, file 1, Privy Council 8253, 24 October 1941; Ibid., Order in Council 9298, Wartime Salaries Order. See also *The Wartime Wages and Cost of Living Bonus Order* (PC 8253 of October 24, 1941, as Amended) (Ottawa, 1942).

21. E. V. Lane to Officer in Charge, Canol Project, 8 July 1942, NA, RG 338, Box 62, file 336.6, vol. 1.

22. Henry Thurston to Chief of Engineers, U.S. Army, 5 June 1943, NA, RG 338, NWSC, Box 32, 091.4 (NWD).

23. Major Thurston was later replaced by Colonel Largent. O'Connor resigned in March 1944 and was replaced as Chairman by Mr. Henwood. Macdonald resigned in August 1945 and was replaced by C.H. Whitham. Victor Macklin served as chief executive officer from 1943 to 1945, when he was replaced by H. E. Bendickson. Memo as to the organization and activities of the Western Labour Board, c. 1947, NAC, RG 36/4, vol. 114.

24. Order in Council Establishing a Western Labour Board, P.C. 3870, 17 May 1943, NAC, RG 36/7, vol. 18, file 5-1.

25. U.S. Engineers Office, Weekly Staff Meeting, 12 July 1943, NWSC microfilm collection, Reel 10, Conferences file.

26. Report on the Canol Project, Book 3, E. E. Kirkpatrick to District Engineers, Area Engineers, Contractors and Others Concerned, 14 December

1943, ACE, 72-A-3173, Box 18.

27. Circular Letter No. 135 (Personnel Branch No. 14), 14 June 1944, NAC, RG 338, Box 12, NWSC Circular Letters 1944.

28. Misc.-Wage Rates and Personnel, file 22-53, Division Circular Letter No. 246 (Industrial Personnel No. I), 10 February 1944, ACE, Main Collection, Box 419.

29. G. Belanger to V. J. Macklin, 16 December 1944, NAC, RG 36/4, vol 112, Agenda Book September 1944-May 1946. We have not located the records of the disposition of this complaint.

30. The sign appears in a photograph which was widely published during and after the war. See the Washington Post, 31 January 1943.

31. Ralph Spear to Department of Interior, n.d., ACE, Acc. 72A-3173, Box 15, file 50-15. There is no indication of whether Mr. Spear received the position he sought. See also Ibid., file 50-26 for more letters requesting work.

32. Applications for Employment, Canadian-Alaskan Highway, 1942, Ibid., Box 14.

33. Calvin Cook to Brig. Gen. C.L. Sturdevant, 12 December 1942; A.H. Burton to Calvin Cook, 9 January 1943, ACE, 72-A3173.

34. Oil Experts Concerned and/or employed by Corps of Engineers on Canol, n.d., ACE, Accession 72A-3173-2.

35. R. W. Gemmer to T. A. Link, 20 August 1943, ACE, Corps of Engineers Collection, Box 418, file 20-15.

36. Canol Refinery Operations, Activities of Personnel Department, June 1944, NA, RG 338, Box 64.

37. Office of Division Engineer, Edmonton Staff Meeting, 23 August 1943, NWSC, Reel 10, Conferences.

38. Paul Grafe, Bechtel-Price-Callahan: Meetings, Notes on employment of Canadian Labour on the Canol Project, 3 July 1942, NA, RG 338, Box 62, file 336, vol. 2.

39. J. L. Kear to District Engineer, U.S. Engineer Office, 17 December 1943, ACE, Corps of Engineers Main Collection, Box 418, file 20-15.

40. C. D. Barker, Corps of Engineers to T. H. MacDonald, Public Roads, 17 November 1942; Acting Commissioner, Public Roads Administration to Chief of Engineers, War Department, 19 November 1942, ACE, 29-52-A-434. The

army, itself a large employer of civilian labor, paid close attention to national regulations, hiring only those Canadian cleared by the National Selective Service, and Americans designated "4F" or over the age of 30. Statement made by Major Thurston, Northwest Service Command, 9 January 1945, NAC, RG 27, file 1488, file 2-171, pt. 2.

41. A. L. Mosier to Department of State, 11 March 1944, John Edwards to Secretary of War, 25 March 1944, ACE, 29-52-A434.

42. Staff Meeting, Edmonton, 31 May 1943, NA, RG 338, NWSC, Box 18, Staff Meetings, 1943-1944.

43. On this issue, see NAC, RG 27, vol. 1488, file 2-171, Part 1. See in particular the letter from J. P. McIsaac, divisional registrar, to Major G. R. Benoit, director of mobilization, 20 April 1942.

44. Constable R. C. Francis, National Selective Service Mobilization Regulations, 17 May 1944, NAC, RG 27, vol. 1488, file 2-171 Pt. 1.

45. Few Draft Evaders in the North, n.d. (c. 1945), NAC, RG 27, vol. 1488, file 2-171, pt. 2.

46. Ibid.

47. Lt. Col. A. L. Tosland Memorandum re: Potential Manpower N.W.T. and Yukon, 14 July 1944, NAC, RG 27, vol. 1488, file 2-171, pt. 1.

48. Potential Manpower Pool N.W.T. & Yukon, n.d. (c. 1944), Ibid.

49. Toland Memorandum, 14 July 1944, Ibid.

50. S. H. McLaren to A. MacNamara, 3 March 1945, NAC, RG 27, vol. 1488, file 2-171, pt. 2. The only arguments in favor were the need to find all the men possible for military service and "the publicity which could be obtained if it is found that there are very few men and the fact that the Department would then have taken every possible step to clarify this situation."

51. Charles Pennock to S. H. McLaren, 18 August 1944, NAC, RG 27, vol. 1488, file 2-171, pt. 1.

52. T. J. Keefe report re: National Selective Service Mobilization Regulations-Norman Wells and Camp Canol, N.W.T., 18 May 1944, NAC, RG 27, vol. 1488, file 2-171, pt.1.

53. Questionnaire answered by D. T. Bath, Peterborough, Ont.

54. Statement made by Major Thurston . . . re Total Number of Men Employed by U.S. Projects in the North Country, 9 January 1945, NAC, RG 27, vol. 1488,

file R-171 part 2.

55. Annex to G2 Report No. 20, 3 October 1942 to 10 October 1942, NA, RG 407, Box 6, 91-DCI-2.1, Part 2.

56. Report of Army Intelligence Officers' Conference, New Orleans, 17-19 November 1943, NA, RG 338, NWSC, Box 2.

57. Ned Price to Alfred Baker, 13 August 1942, ACE, 72-A3173/1.

58. Major Mage re: Mr. Hoffman, 28 January 1944, ACE, 72-A3173-2. The case of Mr. Hoffman, described by an investigator as "a congenital liar, no word that he says can be believed," was publicized in a Fulton Lewis broadcast. An intensive investigation tracked Hoffman from Canada, to the United States and to Mexico. It was decided that he was not a security risk.

59. Labour Conditions—Generally, Waterways and District, Alberta, 21 June 1942, NAC, RG 27, vol. 676, file 6-5-75-51.

60. C. L. Sturdevant to Colonel T. Wyman, 25 June 1942, NA, RG 338, Box 62, file 336, vol. 2.

61. E. R. Complin to Dr. Bryce-Stewart, 7 July 1942, NAC, RG 27, vol. 676, file 6-5-75-5-1.

62. MacNamara to N. A. Robertson, 22 June 1942, NAC, RG 27, vol. 676, file 6-5-75-5-1.

63. Reg Rose, executive secretary, Edmonton Chamber of Commerce, to Col. H. C. Craig, Treasury Department, 25 June 1942, NAC, RG 27, vol. 676, file 6-5-75-5-1.

64. H. C. Craig to R. A. Gibson, 25 June 1942, NAC, RG 27, vol. 676, file 6-5-75-5-1.

65. Ibid.

66. A cost-plus contract, also called a fixed-fee contract, is an arrangement by which a contractor agrees to do a job for the actual cost of doing it plus a fixed fee or a percentage, typically three to five per cent, of the estimated cost. For instance, in one case the cost of building a section of road was estimated to be $1 million, thus the contractor was to be paid the costs of building it plus $45,000. But cost overruns were permitted so long as they could be justified. It was fairly easy to count such things as the purchase of new machines, which would become the property of the contractor, or various extras, as "costs."

67. The contractor had to pay the difference between WLB rates and his own

standard. Coast Construction later applied to American authorities for reimbursement of the sum. See Foster to Heeney, 25 November 1944, NAC, RG 36/7, vol. 3, file 2-A.

68. L. D. Worsham to Major General W. W. Foster, 13 August 1943, NAC, RG 36/7, vol. 18, file 5-5, pt. 2.

69. J. L. MacDougall to Major General W. W. Foster, 26 July 1943, NAC, RG 36/7, vol. 18, file 5-5, pt. 2.

70. L. D. Worsham to Major General T. M. Robbins, 9 August 1943, ACE, 72-A-3173, 50-29, file 16/20.

71. J. A. Collins, Coast Construction Company to Western Labour Board, 17 August 1943, NAC, RG 36/4, vol. 111, vol. 1.

72. Foster to A. D. P. Heeney, 2 September 1943, NAC, RG 36/7. vol. 3, Reports.

73. W. Duncan, Regional Employment Officer to A. O. Maclachlan, Unemployment Insurance Commission, 25 November 1943, NAC, RG 36/7, vol. 18, file 5-5, pt. 1.

74. NWSC, Reel 10, Conferences, Office of the Division of Engineers, Edmonton, 1 November 1943.

75. Collins to W. W. Foster, 3 March 1944, NAC, RG 36/7, vol. 18, file 5-5, pt. 1.

76. Lewis Clark to H. L. Keenleyside, 13 July 1942, NAC, RG 36/7, vol. 44, file D-19-4-C pt. 1.

77. E. R. Complin to Dr. Bryce-Stewart, 7 July 1942, NAC, RG 27, vol. 676, file 6-5-75-5-1.

78. A. MacNamara to Mr. Mitchell, 5 March 1943, NAC, RG 27, vol. 676, file 6-5-75-1.

79. Memorandum of Meeting, Edmonton, Alberta, 6 July 1942, NA, RG 338, Box 62, file 336.6, vol. 2.

80. C. L. Sturdevant to Officer in Charge, Canol Project, 27 July 1942, NA, RG 338, Box 62, file 336, vol. 2. C. D. Barker to A. MacNamara, 16 July 1942, NAC, RG 27, vol. 676, file 6-5-75-5-1.

81. Memorandum of Meeting, 6 July 1942, NAC, RG 27, vol. 676, file 6-5-75-5-1. The members admitted the shortcomings with this project, noting that "operations had been commenced on the Pipe Line Project which were not

strictly in conformity with the basic understanding reached at Ottawa."

82. Report to Officer Commanding, RCMP, "G" Division, 31 July 1942, NAC, RG 85, vol. 865, file 8327.

83. Gibson to LeCapelain, 12 June 1942, plus enclosed minutes of meeting, 3-4 June 1942, NAC, RG 85, vol. 942, file 12641/1.

84. NAC, NWSC, Dawson Creek Diary, Reel 14, 19 December 1942.

85. A. MacNamara, associate deputy minister of labour, report on meeting on labour requirements in British Columbia, 18 May 1942, ACE, 72-A-3173, Box 15, file 52-1.

86. J. T. Hanna to chief of engineers, United States Army, 4 November 1942, ACE, 72-A-3173-2.

87. Authorities Granted by the Special Commissioner, Part 16, Contracts and Employment, NAC, RG 22, vol. 108, file 8432-6 pt. 2.

88. E&SS Office at Edmonton, 3 May 1943, E&SS Office at Dawson Creek, B.C., 1 May 1943, NAC, RG 27, vol. 676, file 6-5-75-1.

89. Mulroney to Macklin, 7 November 1944, NAC, RG 36/4, vol. 112, Agenda Book, Sept. 44-May 46.

90. Memorandum handed to Alfred Leikforth, American consul general-Winnipeg, 29 May 1942, NAC, RG 27, vol. 676, file 65-75-5-1.

91. *Whitehorse Star*, 24 July 1942.

92. Berg to Mitchell (telegram), 7 June 1942, NAC, RG 27, vol. 676, file 6-5-75-3. Berg offered a more detailed critique of the arrangement in Ibid., Berg to Mitchell, 9 July 1942. He was particularly perturbed that labor representatives were not consulted during a series of meetings between Canadian and American officials on the labor question.

93. *Whitehorse Star*, 19 June 1942. The Yukon's Conservative M.P., George Black, threw in with the unions, arguing that it is "manifestly unfair to Canadian labourers, who, by that agreement, are deprived of the opportunity of earning as high wages as American labourers." Black to Mitchell, 5 June 1942, NAC, RG 27, vol. 676, file 6-5-75-3. The editor of the *Whitehorse Star*, in a private letter to Mitchell, supported the arguments advanced by Black and Berg. Ibid., Horace Moore to Humphrey Mitchell, 4 July 1942.

94. One of the first cases heard by the newly established Western Labour Board was an appeal by Canadian employees of Bechtel-Price-Callahan for the same pay schedule as Americans. Minutes of meeting, 14 July 1943, NAC,

RG 36/4, vol. 110, vol. 9, Minute Book, June 43-April 44.

95. L. E. Drummond to R. A. Gibson, 14 July 1942, NAC, RG 27, vol. 676, file 6-5-75-5-1.

96. Mitchell to Berg, 9 June 1943, NAC, RG 27, vol. 676, file 6-5-75-3. This became his standard refrain. See Ibid., Mitchell to P. R. Bengough, Trades and Labour Council, Vancouver, 30 June 1942. See also parliamentary exchange between George Black and Humphrey Mitchell in the House of Commons, House of Commons Debates, pp. 3190-3191, June 8 1942.

97. Robert Lockridge to Imperial Oil Limited., 22 September 1943, ACE, Main Collection, Box 418, file 20-15.

98. Belanger to W. W. Foster, 25 April 1945, NAC, RG 36/7, vol. 18, file 5-2, pt. 1.

99. As Foster explained to Belanger, "At one time, due to the emergency conditions, medical examinations were waived. Once men, however, left the service, their re-employment would be conditional upon the medical examination now enforced." Foster to Belanger, 30 April 1945, NAC, RG 36/7, vol. 18, file 5-2, pt. 1.

100. W. McKinstry to A. MacNamara, 16 May 1945, NAC, RG 36/7, vol. 18, file 5-2, pt. 1.

101. R. A. Gibson to G. A. Jeckell, 12 June 1944, YRG 1, Series 1, vol. 55, file 33440-2.

102. Peter Goers to chief of engineers, U.S. Army War Department, 3 July 1943, NA, RG 338, Box 62, file 336.6, vol. 2.

103. NA, RG 338, Box 62, file 336.6, vol. 2, Report: "Employment of Canadian Nationals."

104. Lewis Clark to Hugh Keenleyside, 5 December 1944, NAC, RG 27, vol. 1488, file 2-171, pt. 2. S.H. McLaren, Associate Director of the National Selective Service, suggested that such workers could be found, most from civilian ranks with the rest being men discharged from the RCAF. McLaren to MacNamara, deputy minister of labour, 6 December 1944, Ibid.

105. A. MacNamara to W. H. McLeod, 27 March 1943, NAC, RG 27, vol. 676, file 6-5-75-3.

106. C. J. Rogers to George Black, 20 May 1942, ACE, 72-A3173, Box 15, 52. See also C. J. Rogers to Humphrey Mitchell, 3 March 1943 and Mitchell to Rogers, 5 March 1943, YTA, YRG 1, Series 1, vol. 61, file 35402.

107. Michael Longo, Army Emergency Relief to Division of Engineers, 20 December 1943, ACE, 29-52A434.

108. W. W. Foster, 9th Report, Contacts and Employment, Part 16, 29 February 1944, NAC, RG 22, vol. 107, file 84-32-6, pt. 1.

109. Army Exchange Conference, Edmonton, 1 and 2 March 1944, NA, RG 338, NWSC, box 35, 337, (NW Division) 395, 1944. The civilian total included about 3,600 Canadian citizens. By October of the same year the grand total had declined to 15,166.

110. Authorities Granted by the Special Commissioner, Part 16, Contracts and Employment, 31 August 1944, NA, RG 22, vol. 108, file 84-32-6 pt. 2.

111. Foster to Heeney, 13 March 1944, NAC, RG 36/7, vol. 3, Reports 2-B.

112. Authorities Granted by the Special Commissioner, Part 16, Contracts and Employment, NAC, RG 22, vol. 108, file 8432-6 pt. 2.

113. E. A. W. Miles to Registrar, Division "M," 9 September 1944, NAC, RG 27, vol. 1488, file 2-171, pt. 1.

114. Statement Made by Major Thurston, Northwest Service Command, 9 January 1945, NAC, RG 27, vol. 1488, file 2-171, part 2.

115. Of whom 8,059 were working on the CANOL project and the Whitehorse refinery, 4,098 on airports and allied works, 266 on bridges along the Alaska Highway, 1,792 on highway maintenance including flight strips, 55 on the Mackenzie River water route, and 2,668 at Prince Rupert, Edmonton, and at other stations. Special Commissioner's 11th Report, Part 16, Contracts and Employment, 30 April 1944, NAC, RG 22, vol. 107, file 84-32-6, pt. 1.

116. Inspectors Report, Period Ending 15 March 1944, T. S. Mills, Chief Engineer, YTA, YRG 1, Series 1, vol. 70, file 21, pt. 3, pt. 2.

117. Field Memo Book, W. H. Harvie to All Camp Foremen, Mile 0 to Border, 10 August 1944, NA, RG 338, Box 47.

118. "NWSC and District Staff Meetings," n.d. (c. Fall 1943), NA, RG 338, Box 17.

119. *Edmonton Journal*, 3 May 1944, "Alaska Road Pay is Cut, Charge" NAC, RG 27, vol. 676, file 6-5-75-3; B. Ballah, E.& S.S. to Clarence Gillies, 5 May 1944, Ibid.

120. Special Commissioner's 11th Report, Part 16 Contracts and Employment, 30 April 1944, NAC, RG 22, vol. 107, file 84-32-6, pt. 1.

121. Minutes of Meeting, 10 April 1945, NAC, RG 36/4, vol. 110, Minute Book, May 1944-Apr. 1946.

4 OUT OF THEIR ELEMENT: NATIVES AND WOMEN IN THE NORTHERN WORK FORCE

At the root of the mythology surrounding the northern defense projects is a legend which is essentially male, and white: a force of Americans and Canadians set aside their work in the south and came north to accept the challenge of conquering the subarctic in one of the greatest construction endeavors of the twentieth century. Like so many myths, it contains much truth, but ignores much of importance. In particular, it leaves out the contribution of Native people and women to the completion of the defense projects. Neither of these groups provided large numbers of workers, but their work in specific areas was of considerable importance.

Because the writing of Native history, particularly in the twentieth century, is still a new field, there are still many facets of the subject which are virtually untouched. There is, for instance, little work available on the role of Native people in the work force. Rolf Knight, in a study that anticipated the growth of interest in this area by more than a decade, has described the integration of Native people into the British Columbia work force, and shown that Indians were capable of, and interested in, a variety of work.[1] They were not, as conventional wisdom would have it, locked into a traditional mentality that limited them to hunting, trapping, fishing, and gathering.

The role of Native people in the northwest defense projects provides an opportunity to examine widely held attitudes towards Natives as workers and to assess the Native response to employment opportunities held out by a wider world. The wartime invasion of the Northwest also provides an interesting example of corridor development—the rapid unplanned opening of an isolated area by means of the construction of a transportation corridor. Corridor development has dominated the Canadian north since 1970: the Alyeska pipeline across Alaska, the opening of the Dempster highway between Dawson and Inuvik, and the hotly debated proposals for gas and oil pipelines from the Arctic coast to the south. A central question addressed during the discussion of these projects was whether Native people would share in the economic benefits they were expected to generate. The northwest defense projects, built with no debate at all thirty years before these other schemes, provide a historical opportunity to study the role of Native people in such corridor development.

World War II saw the largest mobilization of women for industrial work in the history of western society. Recently, Canadian and American historians have begun to study the war from this perspective, charting the rapid growth in employment opportunities for women, particularly in such nontraditional fields as factory and construction work, and transportation. In both countries, of course, working class women, as the term suggests, had a long tradition of working outside the home; the rapid growth in female employment during the war came largely through the recruitment of middle class women.[2]

The history of working women during World War II shows, however, that there was no change in official and generally held attitudes towards the proper role of women in society. Middle-class women worked because the country needed their labor; it was expected that when the war ended they would eagerly reassume their traditional role in the home. During the war years, governments encouraged women to leave the home and provided decent wages, child care, and other support to enable them to do so.

FOUR YOUNG NATIVE MEN
SOMEWHERE IN NORTHERN BRITISH COLUMBIA, C. 1944.
Anchorage Museum, B84.82.4.52.

North American women made economic gains during the war, but they were temporary ones. The accepted role of women had not expanded to include careers above the level of the service sector, at least not for married women, and government support for working women vanished soon after V-J day. Millions of returning servicemen looking for jobs pushed many women out of the work force, and a revitalized cult of domesticity encouraged them to return to the kitchen and the nursery, wiping out most of the integration of women into the labor force that had occurred during the war.

For northern Native people, too, the war brought changes in employment patterns. Before 1940, Natives in the Canadian and American north had remained heavily dependent on harvesting activities, gaining much of their sustenance from country food and much of their income from the fur trade.[3] They had not in any significant way been integrated into the resource-based economy of the region. Yet their traditional "Indian work" was not the whole of their activities. From the days of the early fur trade, Native people had sought and accepted work—usually temporary, unskilled and seasonal—whenever it presented itself, and whenever it suited their own routines and needs. They worked at a variety of tasks: guiding, packing, loading and unloading riverboats, prospecting, cutting wood for steamers. Occasionally they accepted greater economic integration through participation in business or mining. Of course there were never very many of these kinds of jobs in the North, and discriminatory hiring practices and Native nomadism limited opportunities for wage employment even more.[4]

On the eve of World War II, Native people in the North had developed what amounted to a mixed economy, a blend of harvesting activities and temporary employment in the wage sector. They needed some cash income, if only to purchase the guns, ammunition, clothing, boats, fuel, and other manufactured items that had become part of their lives. The fur trade provided most of this cash, particularly in the Mackenzie Valley and the more isolated areas of the Yukon and Alaska. Near settled areas such as Dawson, Whitehorse, and Fairbanks, however, there were other means of earning it. These means almost always consisted of unskilled casual labor, but such work meshed nicely with Native needs and routines. The Native people had no objection to wage labor, so long as they could hunt and trap as the seasons and the migration of animals dictated. When the North's economy faltered, as it did periodically, temporary work cutting firewood, unloading boats, working on a construction site, or a summer's work on a riverboat provided money to help support a family in the bush during the winter.

The onset of World War II, heralded by the construction of the Northwest Staging Route airfields, brought change to the employment patterns of Native people in the Northwest. In July 1941 Gordon Sinclair, then one of Canada's best known journalists, visited Whitehorse. In a story headlined "Money Makes Indian Squaws Klondyke Fashion Leaders," Sinclair wrote in his usual breezy style about the effect of wage income on Native workers. In the past, he wrote, "the Indian had less use for money than he had for a golf club," but now the Natives were spending large sums on finery imported from the south.[5] The article was typical of Sinclair's penchant for finding catchy, facile stories that would appeal to his Toronto readership. Indian women incongruously decked out in southern fashions was the kind of story that had made his reputation, but it was contradicted by observers who knew more about the Yukon. Clifford Rogers of the White Pass and Yukon Railway offered a different assessment: the Indians were not much interested in southern knick-knacks—they were "not a shiftless lot" but were "strong, able, and self-reliant. . . . the idea of working for a master made them turn up their snoots and drift into the bush."[6]

Rogers had a contract to build the Whitehorse airport and hired two contractors, Art Kennedy and Happy LaPage, who worked well with Indians. These men convinced a number of Indians to work on the project at the same wages paid to non-Native workers. Some whites complained that equal pay for Indians was "immoral, ridiculous, fantastic," while others suggested that their wages be held in trust for them so they would not squander them.[7] To Rogers' credit, he rejected the idea that Natives should be paid less: "Well, we won't have Jim Crow laws up here. If labour gets $7.50 and labour is Indian, then Indian gets $7.50." According to Gordon Sinclair, the Natives needed some guidance in how to spend money; their taciturn nature and limited needs made it difficult for them to see the link between wage labor and prosperity. He noted that the question of what to do with their earnings was quickly solved when Native women were introduced to silk stockings, girdles, and permanents, and their children to ice cream. More vintage Sinclair—the Natives in the Whitehorse region had in fact been in contact with the world of consumerism for forty years and knew all about stockings and ice cream. The Native workers generally demanded to be paid every week, a request Sinclair assumed came from their fear of dying while owed money. It was more likely a combination of unwillingness to commit themselves to working for long terms and distrust of employers who might cheat them.

This work, which was on a relatively small scale, did little to prepare the Native people of the Northwest for the massive invasion of southerners which engulfed them in the spring of 1942. In some isolated locations there was virtually no warning; the arrival of surveyors, closely followed by bulldozers, was the first indication that a huge construction project was underway. At no time was serious consideration given to using Native people as an important part of the

ELDERLY NATIVE WOMAN DRYING MEAT, C. 1944.
The caption reads, "Didn't know her age—well over 90."
Anchorage Museum, B84.82.4.53.

work force, though the Canadian government was not opposed on principle to the use of Native labor. One civil servant replied to a request to hire Native guides to help with reconnoitering the route for the CANOL project: "This Branch will be very pleased if you are able to give employment to Indians, either at Fort Norman or elsewhere as guides or in any other capacity in connection with the project."[8] But hiring Natives for casual labor and as guides was about as far as employers were prepared to go; deeply entrenched stereotypes of Native people, and particularly the idea that northern Natives were the continent's last nomads, meant that there was no thought of integrating the small and scattered Native population into the construction crews.

On the whole, these defense projects did more harm than good to the Native people of the Northwest. The arrival of thousands of American servicemen, followed shortly by even more civilian workers, turned the region upside down. In Alaska, several Native bands were pushed off their lands by the military. Remote areas from Northway, Alaska, to Fort Smith, Northwest Territories, hitherto largely isolated, now became temporary metropolises, sites of large construction camps with thousands of workers and ancillary personnel. Relations between the newcomers and the Native people were often strained; in most areas, relations between workers and Native women in particular caused individual and community problems. In addition, the workers hunted extensively for recreation along the highway, depleting game stocks and forcing the Natives into the back country for their supplies of country food.

Perhaps the worst effect of this invasion was the diseases which the soldiers and construction crews carried with them, illnesses for which the aboriginal people had little natural immunity. Despite the quarantines that were routinely imposed on Native settlements, the death rate, particularly among children, soared during the war. The small Native settlement of Teslin, in the Yukon, endured eight separate epidemics in 1942–43, and spent much of that winter in quarantine, enforced by the American army.[9]

Many Native people responded to the human, technological, and epidemiological onslaughts by withdrawing from the construction corridors. Since the harvesting life-style was still quite viable throughout the Northwest, sustained by a still-profitable fur trade, many

A NATIVE FAMILY CAMPED ALONG THE HIGHWAY.
There are no adult males in the photograph.
Anchorage Museum, B84.82.4.51.

Natives simply avoided the army and civilian contractors' camps. This was not the first time such a thing had happened, nor would it be the last.[10] Many of the southerners who came north to work on the projects commented on the limited contact they had with the Native people, particularly in northeastern British Columbia, though there was more contact further north. They remember the Natives as being amazed by the massive invasion of their territory and the baffling array of industrial technology. Stories, some probably apocryphal, others racist or at least highly ethnocentric, abound, recounting the Natives' surprise about everything from binoculars to photography to doorknobs:

> We ran across some that had never seen a motor vehicle or been in a town. They came wandering into camp and were trying to open the door to the mess hall. I guess they hadn't seen a door handle and didn't know you had to turn it.[11]

Julius Garbus, who spent eighteen months working on the south end of the Alaska Highway, reported only a single contact with local Native people:

This occurred at the Beaton River Bridge. A group of 12-15 natives, 2-3 males on horseback with the women, children and dogs following on foot, stopped at the bridge. The males dismounted and approached the concrete structure. They felt the concrete, tapped it and evidently discussed the product. After a short while they mounted and continued on southward.[12]

This limited contact did not mean that the Native people were shut out of the projects altogether. When the survey crews headed into the bush—terrain as unfamiliar to them as was the far side of the moon—they were eager to hire Native guides, depending on their knowledge of the country to help pick the best and shortest route for the highway and the pipeline. A number of well-known Yukoners served in this capacity. Johnny Johns, the famous guide, helped locate portions of the Alaska Highway and the Carcross Road. In later years, answering questions about the extremely crooked route of the road, Johns laughed and said that he deliberately led the surveyors along a path that passed close to his two favorite fishing lakes.[13] David Johnston, who performed a similar service for army surveyors at Teslin, recalled that the American soldiers assumed that the Indians knew "every tree in the country." Not wanting to shatter the illusions of the friendly and generous Americans, Johnston guided the surveyors to the southeast, even though he knew next to nothing about some of the country he was passing through.[14]

Heath Twichell, working on the southern part of the Alaska Highway, found that the Native guides did not always understand the magnitude of the project: "The Indian trappers' idea of what is needed for [a] road, for instance, is liable to be what is required for pack animals." He was, however, impressed with Charlie MacDonald, his guide, who had been discovered by the advance crew "living on the sap which you get by peeling the bark off the trees. We have his undying friendship at the cost of a sack of flour and a few supplies." MacDonald, like the other guides, was assumed to "know all our country like the back of his hand, having trapped it for 55 years."[15] Hampton Primeaux was less impressed with the wranglers who worked with his crew near Burwash: "These two Indians were something else. When they wanted to go to the nearest Indian village or whatnot, they would cut the horses loose and pretend they were rounding them up. They would always come back though."[16] Burwash also provided services for the men of the 18th Engineers:

> It boasted a cow and one of our homesick boys milked her one afternoon. For awhile we were able to get good meals for a dollar. When Mr. Jacquot needed moose or sheep he sent one of his half-Indian daughters out with a rifle and pack horses and it was just like sending her to the market. What we particularly enjoyed were the salads of fresh lettuce or cabbage and delicious whitefish, caught in Kluane Lake only in nets. Jacquot sold us food items at high but not unreasonable prices, coffee at 85 cents a can . . . after a while somebody goofed off and Burwash Landing was placed off limits.[17]

But such activities were about the extent of Native involvement with the highway, particularly in its southern section.

In other parts of the North there was, however, more contact with Natives. The Alaska Highway passed close to seasonal Native settlements in the southern Yukon and the interior of Alaska. In the spring of 1942 the residents of Lower Post, Teslin, Champagne, Burwash, and Northway found that their previous isolation had been broken. The Haines Lateral similarly affected Native people at Klukwan, Alaska, and Klukshu, Yukon. The CANOL pipeline, on the other hand, passed through territory which was much more sparsely inhabited, although the network that serviced it did tie the Natives in a number of communities in northern Alberta and along the Mackenzie River to the northwest transportation grid. Even the airfields, built at formerly remote places like Watson Lake, Aishihik, and Snag, had an immediate impact on nearby Native populations.

Just because a road or an airfield was being built near a Native settlement did not mean that Natives were offered jobs, nor that they would accept them if offered. There was considerable casual work for them—unloading supply trucks, burning slash along the roads, cutting firewood, providing meat, and doing odd jobs during construction of the camps—but there were few regular positions. Much the same was true of Native women, who found only part time and unskilled work in laundries, cafes, hotels, and camp cookhouses. This was not entirely due to racism or official insensitivity. Few if any Natives had the experience necessary to operate machinery or the heavy equipment used on the projects, and there was no program to train them, nor any thought of establishing one. They had in any case an alternative in the fur trade, which remained generally profitable throughout the war, though it declined catastrophically during the postwar period. John Honigman, an anthropologist who traveled along the highway in the war years, remarked of the Indians in northwestern British Columbia, "Economically the war has benefited the Indian. High prices for fur have increased his earnings to the point where a family may now come through the winter and spring with $2,000 to $3,000 worth of fur on the trader's books."[18] With such earnings, Indians avoided the disruptive influences of the construction projects, living in the bush during trapping seasons, yet returning to the camps to take seasonal work in the summer, as they had traditionally done on the riverboats and elsewhere. This pattern suited employers as well, since construction activity peaked during the short northern summer.

In more isolated areas, such as the Mackenzie valley, where it was more difficult to find replacement or casual workers, Native people actually found greater opportunity for employment. The Canadian government assisted by making special provisions for Native workers. When in August 1942 the hiring of Canadians on the CANOL project was restricted, it was decided that "those who reside in the vicinity of the work, such as Indians, halfbreeds and trappers will be kept on, if at all possible."[19] Employment prospects also improved along the highway when construction ended and the nature of the work shifted to rebuilding and maintenance. Since much of this work was done only in the summer, Native men were often hired to assist with it.[20] Frank Speer, who worked at Teslin during this period, wrote, "They had been trappers before the road started but quite a few worked with us as laborers or truck drivers. The Yukon Indians were very good people."[21]

The arrival of thousands of Americans with cash in their pockets also created economic opportunities of a more traditional nature, particularly for Native women. Hungry for souvenirs, the Americans fueled a booming market in Native crafts. One surveyor, working near Burwash Landing, noted: "Natives would make caribou coats, muklucks, moccasins, caps, etc. decorated with sequins with very reasonable prices as we went north. On the way back though, prices had gone way up. They learned fast."[22] There was money to be made; the women of Moosehide, near Dawson City, earned over $1,300 from the sale of one shipment to Whitehorse. J. E. Gibben, an Indian agent in the region, tried to interest the Native women in taking full advantage of these opportunities. The results were mixed: it was difficult to get the necessary supplies, particularly beads, during wartime, and Gibben found that it was difficult to get the younger women interested in making moccasins and other traditional goods. Nor were the older women keen on going into business full time.

The defense construction projects created other opportunities for Natives in areas far from the projects themselves. The highway and pipeline camps drew many workers away from other businesses in the Northwest. Small operators—retailers, hotels, dredge operators, transportation companies—lost many employees to the military contractors. This led some managers to consider hiring Native workers as replacements. Near Dawson, the Yukon Consolidated Gold Corporation, faced with a major labor shortage, hired Native workers for the first time in its forty-year history. The results were mixed. The Natives answered one of the company's concerns: they were not as mobile as non-Native workers and would not follow the job opportunities hundreds of miles to the southern Yukon. On the other hand, they were unaccustomed to the rigidity of the industrial workplace; management acknowledged that they could handle the work, but they were generally depicted as "undependable."[23]

Except for the ravages of disease, World War II had little immediate effect on the Indians of the Northwest. Some had worked as guides, some had taken part-time work. Others had avoided the projects altogether. Few sought, or found, full-time regular employ- ment with the construction crews. Since they could still live as harvesters, few saw any reason to look for jobs which in any case were often closed to them. Certainly the war had not integrated them into the wider Canadian society, nor into the wage economy. Summarizing the situation, J. E. Gibben observed, "A good many Indians earn substantial sums working on the various war projects, and all have benefited to some extent by the high fur prices of the last few years . . ."[24] Since harvesting still provided a good life, few Natives found full-time regular jobs with construction crews, nor did they seek them—they would not have been offered such jobs even if they had.

As was the case with the Native people, non-Native women played only a limited role in the northwest defense projects. Even more than the Natives, women were hampered by the prevailing stereotypes about their abilities and their proper role in society. Construction on the frontier has typically been a male preserve, a rough, hardworking, often hard-drinking, profane environment that was deemed unsuitable for ladies. Women who wished to break through this stereotype, either in search of a well-paid job or of adventure, had to contend with male concepts of their abilities and a paternalistic desire on the part of employers to protect them from the hardships and rough company to be found in the isolated construction camps.

Traditionally, women's opportunities for employment in the Northwest were strictly circumscribed. During the Klondike rush a few women had joined the stampede. Some of them found job opportunities in the North, particularly when they capitalized on their domestic skills—cooking, washing, sewing, operating boarding houses. A handful moved into nontraditional areas and worked as miners or entrepreneurs.[25] In the postrush era, very few women in the North found employment outside occupations such as cooking, cleaning, teaching, nursing, and prostitution. New settlements, such as mining camps in remote areas, were generally almost exclusively male preserves; the arrival of women (other than prostitutes) and children, as at Yellowknife in the late 1930s, was taken as a sign of the community's permanence.[26]

The relegation of women to traditional jobs was not unique to the North, of course; women across North America also faced limitations on their options. The difference was that while the war broke down the barriers of custom, if only temporarily, the same thing did not occur in the North. There, with only a very few exceptions, women remained within their traditional roles and spheres; there were no "Rosies" handling riveting guns in the Northwest. There were expanded opportunities for office work and cooking, but with a few exceptions women were barred from truck driving, construction, or any other form of "men's work."[27]

STAFF OFFICERS OF THE WHITEHORSE ARMY HOSPITAL, 1944.
NA, 111-SC 323188.

The reasons for this had more to do with the social structure of the North than with workplace or economic considerations. The northwest defense projects involved work in isolated subarctic camps with few amenities, little social life, and a tremendous imbalance of the sexes. In the south, Rosie the Riveter could fulfill traditional feminine roles after work, but this was not possible in the contractors' camps along the Alaska Highway and the CANOL pipeline. Their lack of recreational facilities and pervasive masculine atmosphere marked them in the eyes of authority as unsuitable places for women, and hiring practices reflected this assessment. There was some validity in the assumptions underlying the policy of not hiring women for camp work. The physical layout of the camp, with large, open dormitories, outdoor latrines and spartan facilities was not conducive to a mixed work force. The dominant characteristics of frontier labor—hard-working, hard-drinking, and boisterously masculine—created a social environment that was decidedly unfriendly towards women. Tasks such as cooking, laundry and cleaning were, in most camps, left to the men.

The result was that almost all the hundreds of women who worked on the northwest defense projects did so in urban centers, filling traditional female roles. Virtually all the prostitutes also worked in the urban centers. Civilian, army, and government offices in Edmonton, Dawson Creek, Fort St. John, Whitehorse, and Fairbanks hired scores of women for secretarial and administrative duties. Even here there was a sense of daring and adventure for women. Rosemary O'Byrne, about to take an army job in Whitehorse, was warned against going north: "You'll freeze—Girls can't stand the living conditions—You'll die of boredom." She went anyway, and later reported that Whitehorse was "a nice town;"[28] others, no doubt, were discouraged by such negative comments. Coreen Bafford, twenty-four years old and working at the Office of Price Administration in Denver, Colorado, and her friend Rita Freeley "decided we'd like to do something for the war effort," so they visited the Civil Service Commission. Learning of the urgent need for stenographers at the Public Roads Administration office at Fort St. John, they applied for release from their jobs. They traveled by train from Denver, through Wyoming, Montana, and on to Edmonton. From there, a Public Roads Administration driver picked them up and escorted them to Fort St. John. Connie Bafford's northern adventure began, although she soon discovered "I don't think we had much to do."[29]

Even in Whitehorse, conditions for women were fairly spartan. A newspaper account from the summer of 1943 which described the lives of nineteen female employees of the USED, complete with contemporary stereotypes (the women are referred to as "girls" throughout, and there is much emphasis on the shortage of bobby pins), gives a fairly accurate picture of conditions in the town:

> They lived first in a private home, in an unheated room, and the temperatures were already hitting 20 below. The house had no running water, no bath, and canvas cots for beds. They made a deal with a man at the public roads administration barracks to take a bath in his quarters while he was at work, and sneaked over there on their lunch hours... they did their laundry there too.... The only electric iron to be found in town belonged to the town laundryman, who was too busy to take on more customers. He agreed, however, to let them borrow his iron after 10:00 p.m....
>
> Their offices, for the first months, were in the U.S.E.D. headquarters in an abandoned parlor car of the White Pass and Yukon railroad, parked on a siding. Stoves were the only heat, and when the thermometer hit 50, 60,

and 70 below, the stoves fought a losing battle. The ink froze in their
fountain pens, too....

In February things took a turn for the better...They moved into their
present quarters, a barracks buildings labelled "Civilian Barracks—Female."
Here they live in luxury—comparatively speaking....

And if anybody thinks that life in the Yukon, where there are
approximately 100 men to every female under 85, is a round of gayety, he
can think again. So far, these girls have been to exactly three dances...the
third was the one the girls at the barracks gave themselves, a few nights ago.
It was a big success. "The only trouble," says Miss Boyd, "was that we all
had to wear ski boots to keep our heels out of the cracks in the floor.
Otherwise it was just wonderful—for the Yukon."[30]

The accounting and payroll offices in these urban centers
employed more women than men, although most supervisors were
male. These offices were located in places where there were separate
quarters for women as well as the other services. The women's
facilities were comfortable, but far from luxurious:

In the dorm where I lived we each had a little cubicle of a room, with a single
bed, dresser and maybe a chair. There was a "common room" where we
could meet and be together, and a long bathroom with a number of sinks
and showers. There was also a sewing machine, and we bought material and
made curtains for our room.[31]

Reflecting the northern bias towards traditional female roles, however, is the fact that even in centers like Whitehorse and Fairbanks
there was little evidence that women participated in the sort of men's
work that was assumed by women in the south during the war. The
large maintenance yards, supply depots and other support services
in these towns remained male preserves, with women restricted to
office and secretarial work. Late in 1943, the editor of *The Highway
Magazine* traveled the Alaska Highway and commented on the
employment of female workers:

A GROUP OF WOMEN GOING TO VISIT PATIENTS
AT THE FORT ST. JOHN ARMY HOSPITAL, SUMMER 1943.
Photograph courtesy of Margaret (Percival) Stuart.

Female help was confined largely to the engineering and contractors' offices at Edmonton, Dawson Creek, Fort St. John, Whitehorse and Fairbanks. There were nurses at hospitals at one or two other points along the line. Female kitchen help (and laundry) was found mainly in the Canadian contractors' camps west of Fort Nelson and at Fairbanks.[32]

Even with this definition of their role, not everyone was happy with the influx of women into the urban centers of the Northwest. A junior officer stationed at Fairbanks vigorously objected to the presence of women: "Back to women. The post is lousy with them. I'd like to present them as a great argument for a national service law. Can't see why they can't all be sworn in as WAC privates and herded into barracks."[33] In fairness, this perhaps reflected the animosity of the military towards civilian labor rather than sexual hostility, but it shows that women were not universally welcomed in the region.

Some women lived in the civilian construction camps, since they were not officially barred from them, but they were not recruited for

USAAF HALLOWEEN DANCE.
The men outnumber the women three to one.
Photograph courtesy of Marion (Ambrose) Clark.

work there, nor were any facilities provided for them. A number accompanied their husbands to the Northwest, some joining them in isolated camps. Vera Brown and her husband, for instance, had lived on a farm near Grande Prairie. Hearing of the high wages in the Northwest and needing money to improve their farm, they left home and signed on with Wilson Freightways in Dawson Creek, returning home on weekends to work their land.[34] Management felt no compulsion to provide quarters for families, and a number were compelled to build makeshift cabins out of scrap lumber. Once the women were there, however, they often found their labor in demand, family circumstances permitting, in the kitchen, laundry, or the camp office. And once a woman had moved into camp, it was deemed acceptable to recruit additional women for work there—but always in traditional female occupations.[35] Many camps had a woman like Dell Black, who joined her husband at the Campbell Construction camp at Muncho Lake, British Columbia. Robert Black had gone up the year before, spending a lonely but lucrative year in the Northwest.

Dell and their young son John came up to Dawson Creek to meet Robert. A thirty-hour drive, stopping only for gasoline and a snack, brought them back to the camp, where Dell got work in the warehouse office. She was not the only woman in camp; there were at least twelve others, including six waitresses and six office workers. The Blacks continued to work on the highway after Campbell's contract was completed, signing on with the USED at Mile 177, where Robert worked as an equipment operator and Dell as a waitress.[36]

Some women who lived and worked in these camps found that the stories they had heard about problems caused by an excess of men were true. One woman, a second cook employed by Melville Smith Construction Company in an isolated camp, recounted that she had been promised room and board in a supervised dormitory. The reality was quite different. She was harassed by drunken men, and by her superior, who insisted that she and the other cooks work fifteen-hour shifts, with two hours off, seven days a week. She lived in a small shack with nine other women, and was later moved to a warehouse where, in a partitioned space about ten by eighteen feet, she lived with eight women. She and several of the other women protested these conditions and demanded to be released from their jobs. They were told that they were "frozen for the duration" and could not leave.[37] This experience was apparently not common, for the majority of women worked in headquarters or division offices, and had relatively decent working conditions and accommodations. In the camps, however, this kind of thing could and did happen.

Most observers reported that the women employed in the Northwest performed their duties ably and conscientiously. In the Fairbanks area, some men claimed that there were too many women, while others commented that there were too few. Some said that their work was excellent; others said that their inefficiency slowed the entire operation. The thrust of the comments, however, suggested that they were hard workers.[38]

National and racial differences existed among these women, some American, some Canadian. Most were white, a few black, giving rise to some disharmony. A Canadian nurse recounted a story of the experience of one of the few black women working on the highway. The woman arrived at the nursing station, escorted by six or seven black soldiers, and asked to be "put up" for the night. She had apparently come north to find work but had been "made to feel so unwelcome was leaving." The nurse was not surprised by the black woman's reaction:

> In our barracks there were quite a few office-working girls from the American deep-south, specifically I remember Alabama, Mississippi, Georgia, Tennessee and possibly others, who actively verbalized their unwillingness to live with or work with black people. To our group of Canadian nurses this was an unfamiliar value system.[39]

Canadian and American women discovered other differences. Although there is little evidence of nationally based conflict, and most female workers reported that work relations between Canadians and Americans were cordial and professional, some observers noted a certain level of tension. Coreen Bafford wrote,

> There were some Canadian girls living in our dorm, but we didn't have much to do with them, they seemed to stick together and we did the same. There were five of us American secretaries who spent most of our time together.[40]

It is difficult to be exact about the number of women employed on the northwest defense projects, since employment figures were not consistently broken down by gender. In May 1943, near the peak of construction activity, the Selective Service Office identified 6,200 Canadian workers employed on defense projects in the Edmonton and Dawson Creek districts. Of these, 532, or about nine percent, were women.[41] This figure reflected the women employed in the main offices and at headquarters. In September 1944, the United States Army employed 4,700 Canadian civilians, of whom over half were female, handling the bulk of administrative and clerical duties connected with the projects.[42] In January 1945, the Northwest Service Command had 2,100 Canadians on staff, 400 of them women. The Air Corps had 1,500 Canadian employees, including 425 women; 77 of the Transportation Corps' 941 Canadian workers on staff were women.[43]

Women working in the Northwest, like women working elsewhere in that era, found that the exigencies of war had not liberated them from discrimination in the areas of wages and working conditions. There was no official policy of pay equity, and women doing the same work as men received significantly less money. Female laundry workers in Edmonton, for example, received $56 to $75 per month, while men doing the same job received $105 to $160.[44] Canadian women suffered the additional penalty of their citizenship. Like Canadian men, they were paid less than Americans doing the same jobs.[45] Under 1944 wage rates, for example, American waitresses received $175 per month while the top Canadian rate was only $108.50; the American women also paid less for room and board and received more generous benefits.[46]

Audrey Coey was a Canadian woman caught in the pattern of low pay and restricted work opportunities. Coey applied for work as a driver at the Edmonton Selective Service Office, but she was turned down flat. She was offered instead a position as a "cookie" in Dawson Creek at $90 per month. A bout with appendicitis forced her to look for alternative employment. After working as a waitress, she was hired by the USED in June 1943 as a driver at $120 per month—the first woman so employed on the highway. A year later, she discovered that other women in her position had been paid $150 per month, and that men were paid $180. Although she was careful not to harass her employers unduly, she noted that "I never received the difference in monthly pay nor overtime rate. Everytime I asked for it I got surplused."[47]

As the work progressed, and the camps were transformed from rough-hewn temporary establishments to more substantial ones, women were welcomed further north, particularly along the Alaska Highway—the CANOL project, except for the Whitehorse refinery and the base at Camp Canol, was virtually an all-male preserve throughout the war. By 1944, when Canadian and American authorities were planning a transition to peacetime operations, it became evident that the transient construction crews would be replaced by a more stable maintenance work force. Civilian contractors were encouraged to provide quarters for married men, in the hope that the presence of families would make the work force more stable. This policy, ironically, lessened women's already minor role as workers, signaling a return to post-war domesticity.

CAMP OF F COMPANY, 18TH ENGINEERS,
ON THE DONJEK RIVER, SEPTEMBER 1942.
YTA, Robert Hays collection, 5675.

Native and female workers filled small but crucial niches in the northwest labor force during World War II. In both cases, prevailing stereotypes and employment patterns proved difficult to break. Native people were reluctant to abandon their mixed economy and seek regular work with the construction crews. They took work on a seasonal and casual basis, showing interest in those tasks calling on their traditional skills and knowledge of the land. Women also found themselves limited to a narrow range of occupations, particularly compared to the many new opportunities opening up for other women elsewhere in the United States and Canada. They were not often recruited for work in isolated camps, and then only for traditional jobs; the vast majority remained in the major centers, and only a few found jobs in the kitchens, laundries and offices along the CANOL pipeline and Alaska Highway.

The wartime pattern of female and Native employment in the North highlights the durability of assumptions about frontier conditions, even under wartime emergency conditions. Negative stereo-

BRIDGE OVER THE SLIMS RIVER,
155 MILES WEST OF WHITEHORSE, OCTOBER 1943.
NA, 111-SC 322965.

types about the work habits and abilities of Native people lessened from the very beginning the possibility that Indians would be recruited for construction work. At the same time, the assumption that every Native knew the country "like the back of his hand" resulted in the ready acceptance of Native men as guides for survey and locating crews. Similar considerations governed the use of female labor. Women had seldom found isolated, frontier camps to be accommodating places; they were, it seems, a permanent bastion of rampant masculinity, where men were men and decent women stayed away. This ideology of the frontier—the idea that men in isolated settings would prey on women, who would be unable to cope with the social and work-related pressures of such an environment—persisted throughout the war years.

The reality, of course, was very different than these expectations. Women who worked with the army, government or civilian contractors were able, skilled, and flexible. Camp life was not as wild and uncontrolled as frontier folklore would have had it; those women who worked, with their husbands or by themselves, in isolated camps report with some exceptions that they were treated with respect. Native people were not as visible as women; many of those who went north to work had virtually no contact with them. Their relative absence among the construction work force did not reflect a fear of hard work, as many non-Natives assumed, but rather illustrated their primary interest in maintaining a harvesting life-style. Women and Natives made a significant contribution to the completion of the northwest defense projects but have remained largely invisible in its folklore and mythology.

NOTES

1. Rolf Knight, *Indians at Work: An Informal History of Native Indian Labour in British Columbia, 1858-1930* (Vancouver: New Star Books, 1978).

2. See Ruth Pierson, *They're Still Women After All: The Second World War and Canadian Womenhood* (Toronto: McClelland and Stewart, 1986); K. Anderson, *Wartime Women: Sex Role, Family Relations and the Status of Women* (Westport, Conn.: Greenwood Press, 1981); D. Montgomerie, "The Limitations of Wartime Change: Women War Workers in New Zealand," *New Zealand Journal of History* 23, no. 1 (April 1989); Margaret Allen, "The Domestic Ideal and the Mobilization of Womanpower in World War II," *Women's Studies International Forum* 6/4 (1983); Chester Gregory, *Women in Defense Work During World War II: An Analysis of the Labor Problem and Women's Rights* (New York: Exposition Press, 1974); Maureen Honey, "The Working Class Woman and Recruitment Propaganda During World War II: Class Differences in the Portrayal of War Work," *Signs* 8/4 (1983); Sheila Robias and L. Anderson, *What Really Happened to Rosie the Riveter: Demobilization and the Female Labor Force* (New York: Modular Publishing, 1974); D'Ann Campbell, *Women at War With America: Private Lives in a Patriotic Era* (Cambridge: Harvard University Press, 1984); Kay Saunders, "North American Women and the Second World War: Transformation or Consolidation," *Hecate* 15, no. 1 (1989); M. Higgonet, et al., eds, *Behind the Lines: Gender and the Two World Wars* (New Haven: Yale University Press, 1987).

3. A. J. Ray, *The Canadian Fur Trade in the Industrial Age* (Toronto: University of Toronto Press, 1990).

4. K. S. Coates, *Best Left as Indians* (Kingston: McGill-Queen's University Press, 1992).

5. *Edmonton Journal*, 12 July 1941.

6. *Edmonton Journal*, 12 July 1941.

7. L. E. Drummond to R. A. Gibson, 3 July 1942, NAC, RG 27, vol. 676, file 6-5-75-5-1.

8. T. R. L. MacInnes to L. E. Drummond, 23 June 1943, NAC, RG 27, vol. 676, file 6-5-75-5-1.

9. J. F. Marchand, "Tribal Epidemics in Yukon," *Journal of the American Medical Association* 123 (1943): pp. 1019-20.

10. The development of the Cyprus-Anvil mine near Faro, Y.T. in the late 1960s provides a similar example. The Native people at Ross River, located some forty miles away, avoided the mine and its perceived economic opportunities.

11. Questionnaire answered by A. Forgie, Edmonton, Alberta.

12. Questionnaire answered by Joe Garbus, Westhaven, Connecticut.

13. "Yukon: The Invisible History," part 1 of the "North of 60" television series, produced by TV Ontario, 1983.

14. *The Gravel Magnet*, a television program produced by Barbara Bardie and Ken Coates for Northern Native Broadcasting Yukon, January 1988.

15. Heath Twichell collection, 23 June 1942, YTA, Acc. #82/546, Misc. Manuscripts.

16. Questionnaire answered by Hampton Primeaux, Rayne, Louisiana.

17. Log Book, 18th Engineers, April 1942-January 1943, pp. 22-23, Glenbow-Alberta Institute, Seaton Papers, A. S441.

18. J. J. Honigmann, "On the Alaska Highway," *Dalhousie Review* (January 1944): 404.

19. Panel on Canadian-American Defence Construction Projects, 30 July 1942, NAC, RG 36/7, vol. 44, file D-19-4C, pt. 1.

20. Questionnaire answered by Charles Knott, London, Ontario.

21. Questionnaire answered by Frank Speer, White Rock, B.C.

22. Questionnaire answered by Hampton Primeaux, Rayne, Louisiana.

23. Richard Stuart, "The Impact of the Alaska Highway on Dawson City," in Ken Coates, ed., *The Alaska Highway*, p. 195.

24. J. E. Gibben to R. A. Gibson, 31 May 1946, NAC, RG 85, vol. 1872, file 550-2-1.

25. Barbara Kelcey, "Lost in the Rush: Women in the Klondike Gold Rush," Master's thesis, University of Victoria, 1989.

26. See Frank Peet, *Miners and Moonshiners: A Personal Account of Adventure and Survival in a Difficult Era* (Victoria: Sono Nis Press, 1983).

27. In 1940 American women made up sixteen percent of the labor force, in 1944 thirty-six percent, and in 1950 thirty-two percent. Between 1940 and 1944 the number of working wives rose from fifteen to twenty-three percent, the majority (three of five million) being thirty-five or older. Judith N. McArthur, "From Rosie the Riveter to the Feminine Mystique: An Historiographical Survey of American Women and World War II," *Bulletin of Bibliography* 44, no. 1 (1987): 10.

28. "Northwest Service Command News," *Whitehorse Star,* 11 February 1944, 3.

29. Questionnaire answered by Connie Bafford, Lusk, Wyoming.

30. Morely Cassidy, "U.S. Girls in Far Northland Experience 72 Below Zero," *Edmonton* (21 June 1943).

31. Questionnaire answered by Connie Bafford, Lusk, Wyoming.

32. "Personal interest items and observations," *The Highway Magazine* (Nov.-Dec. 1943).

33. G2 Report from 4 March 1944 to 11 March 1944, NA, RG 409, Box 32, file 91-DP1-2.1.

34. Questionnaire answered by Vera Brown, Cherhill, Alberta.

35. Questionnaire answered by D. T. Bath, Peterboro, Ontario, describes a camp with one married woman and a [single? unmarried? female?] cookhouse helper.

36. Questionnaire answered by Robert and Dell Black,

37. Ernest Manning to A. MacNamara, 14 January 1943, NAC, RG 27, vol. 676, file 6-5-75-3.

38. See G-2 Periodic Reports, NA, RG 407, Box 32, file 91DPI-2.1.

39. Questionnaire answered by Muriel Gwen Collip, Edmonton, Alberta.

40. Questionnaire answered by Colleen Bafford, Lusk, Wyoming.

41. E&SS Office at Edmonton, 3 May 1943, E&SS Office at Dawson Creek, B.C., 1 May 1943, NAC, RG 27, vol. 676, file 6-5-75-1.

42. E. A. W. Miles to Registrar, Division "M," 9 September 1944, NAC, RG 27, vol. 1488, file 2-171, pt. 1.

43. Statement Made by Major Thurston, Northwest Service Command, 9 January 1945, NAC, RG 27, vol. 1488, file 2-171, part 2.

44. Minute Book, June 43-Apr. 44, Minute of Meeting, 17 March 1944, NAC, RG 36/4, vol. 110, vol. 9.

45. Questionnaire answered by Muriel Gwen Collip, Edmonton, Alberta. As Ms. Collip noted, Canadian nurses were paid overtime, which "negated this as an irritant."

46. Belanger to Western Labour Board, 6 July 1944, NAC, RG 36/4, vol. 112, Agenda Book, Apr. 44-Sept. 44.

47. Audrey Coey to War Labour Board, 17 December 1945, NAC, RG 36/4, Vol. 112, Agenda Book, September 44—May 1946. "Surplused" meant laid off.

5

CIVILIAN WORKERS IN THE FAR NORTHWEST, 1942-1946

Historical writing about working people has recently begun to focus on the study of work experiences. This scholarship, which focuses primarily on the early factories of eastern North America, has done much to capture the essence of laboring life. The best of these studies, by historians such as Herbert Gutman, Bryan Palmer, Craig Heron,[1] and others, have attempted to describe the totality of working class life, documenting the close interrelationships between work, housing, education, social activities, and culture. This work, however, remains firmly placed in the transitional period to industrial capitalism and has made few inroads into the study of workers in middle decades of the twentieth century.

An examination of people's work experiences on the northwest defense projects represents a major departure from this historiographical mainstream, at least in the geographical sense. It steps outside the southern urban, industrial, agricultural, mining and forest focus of much of the work in the field, and moves to a northern frontier, construction-oriented setting. But this is not an unfamiliar nor an unimportant area. The workers on the northwest defense projects shared much in common with hardrock miners, lumber workers, railway navvies and others who worked in similarly isolated, masculine and corporate

AN EARLY VERSION OF THE FAMOUS WATSON LAKE SIGNPOST,
NOW GROWN TO A GREAT FOREST OF SIGNS.
Anchorage Museum, B62.X.15.12.

dominated situations. Like them, the workers in the Northwest during
World War II owed much of their circumstances, including high
wages and corporate paternalism, to the struggle between earlier
frontier workers and their employers. Employment practices, work-

ing conditions and salaries continued to improve after 1946, further entrenching the pattern of northern or frontier labor.

The men and women who came north to work on the wartime defense projects had a harder task then simply working a full day for a day's pay. They also had to adapt to subarctic conditions and modify their work habits and techniques to fit the demands of work under harsh circumstances. This transition would determine the success of the various construction projects and would provide the greatest test for those who accepted work with the civilian contractors.

For many of those who ventured northward, it was something of a grand adventure, a once-in-a-lifetime opportunity to work in the Land of the Midnight Sun. Others quickly soured on the region, and left as soon as they could. Workers faced many challenges, especially those of adapting their skills and work habits to conform to the climatic realities of the subarctic, a region unfamiliar to all but a few.

Few of those who signed on to work on the northwest defense projects had ever been in the region before. As supervisors were hired, professionals located and work crews put together—in Minnesota, Iowa, Washington and Ontario—many of the new employees were gripped with a sense of excitement and adventure. Despite the wartime rhetoric about the urgency of the northwest military projects, the men were drawn by the prospect of adventure and high salaries. As one of them put it, they were

> the adventurous, hard-working type who could see a few dollars at the same time helping the war effort. Most were in the late 35 to 50 year old range as the war had most of our young people overseas at that time . . . in general they were a good, hard-working lot that had just come through the depression of the 1930s and knew how to work.[2]

They left, many with a one-year contract in hand, certain of good pay but unsure of the climate, topography or working conditions that awaited them.

The workers from the United States faced a long trip to the Northwest. Most went overland, traveling by train across country to Edmonton. Those assigned to the CANOL project continued northward, by airplane, train or truck, constantly stalled in the transportation bottlenecks that plagued the start-up of the project. Workers for the Alaska Highway continued by train to the railhead at Dawson Creek or flew to Whitehorse.[3] From there, they traveled to their company's worksites, usually by way of a rough and extremely slow truck ride over the army's pioneer road. Other crews arrived by ship, traveling from Vancouver or Seattle to Skagway, Alaska,[4] and then by train to Whitehorse; a small number traveled via the Alaska Railway to Fairbanks, where they joined construction teams working on the north end of the Alaska Highway and pipeline projects. Julius Garbus, a recent engineering graduate, signed on with the Public Roads Administration Office in Albany, New York. He took a train to Buffalo, and then on to Toronto, where he boarded a Canadian National Railways train for the trip to Edmonton, where he transferred to yet another train for the leg to Dawson Creek. His office was to be in Fort St. John, so he hitched a ride by truck, car and ambulance to his work site.[5]

The journey northwest was slow and often uncomfortable, and there were few facilities available along the route. Workers arriving in Dawson Creek, Whitehorse and Fairbanks, for example, discovered that communities lacked the most basic amenities. There were few hotel rooms—in Whitehorse, incoming workers rented a bed, not a room, and for an eight-hour shift, not for a day—restaurants were continually filled to capacity and stores were short of basic supplies. The Northwest's transportation system, particularly during time of war shortages, was not well adapted for the movement of thousands of workers, to say nothing of tons of construction equipment and supplies.

Not all the workers faced a lengthy journey. The few Canadians in the Northwest, and Americans already in Alaska, had the jobs come to them, rather than the reverse. Dozens of regional workers quickly saw the monetary advantages of working with the construction crews. People from throughout the northern work force jumped at the opportunity to leave their work place to sign on with the high-paying American and Canadian contractors. For these workers, the decision to seek war work did not require a major separation from family and home, although most did move from settlements to isolated construction camps. For some, particularly in Edmonton, Dawson Creek, Whitehorse and Fairbanks, considerable work was available in their own community, much of it in the offices and supply shops established to service the northwest projects.

D. T. Bath, an engineering student at the University of Alberta, signed on with Dufferin Paving and was assigned to work north of Fort Nelson. He traveled on the Northern Alberta Railway as far as Dawson Creek. Then, with a couple of co-workers, he piled into the back of a transport truck for the journey of more than 300 miles:

> The ride was extremely uncomfortable; we couldn't see out of the truck and it was bumpy and dusty and long. During the night, the truck driver must have fallen asleep, we went off the road and ended beside a huge rock the size of the truck. With everyone now awake, we were able to proceed.[6]

The initial response of individual workers to the Northwest depended on the season when they arrived. While the soldiers had arrived en masse during the cold, damp weather of the early spring of 1942, the initial wave of civilians reached the area in the late spring and summer. The transition to long hours of daylight, which permitted equally long days of work, was more difficult than most had anticipated, but was not as hard as arriving in the middle of a subarctic winter.

The civilian workers, Americans and Canadians, were attracted by the promise of adventure and high wages. Canadian employers and employees were somewhat hamstrung by the limits imposed by the National War Labour Board and the Western Labour Board. For workers from both countries, however, northern wages, rates were set higher than southern averages. What is more, there was added benefit of exceptionally long hours—as many as twelve hours a day, seven days a week—which pushed monthly earnings far higher than those available elsewhere. Combined with free or subsidized room and board, the wages provided considerable compensation for the workers' hardships and loneliness. Gerry Pelletier, a self-employed truck driver from Vulcan, Alberta, later observed, "I was young at the time, and was not scared of work. And I had a lot of bush experience, so for the first time in my life I got well paid for what I knew, and I did real well under very tough conditions."[7]

The wages were, by the standards of that day, quite attractive. S. N. Long, working with Lytle and Green Construction Company, wrote to his wife:

I heard today that they want all the guys that can to stay till the first of Dec. then they pay us $3.00 a day for every day when home if we will come back next year and we can bring our wives along if they are willing to work and they will get $4.00 a day. Such as office or kitchen work. Don't tell any body but I am making $20.80 per day just think every 5 days a $100 bucks.[8]

One Canadian worker, who had earned sixty cents per hour the previous year for International Nickel Company (INCO), was paid $1.10 per hour, plus time and half after forty-four hours of work;[9] A. Forgie had earned $70 a month from Massey Harris and now made $165 a month plus room and board from the Public Roads Administration.[10] Frank Speer had been employed by McLeod's as a store manager, receiving $190 a month. As a cat skinner, he commented, "my deductions were about that."[11] Harvey Hayduk, who happily left behind a job that paid $45 a month for teaching forty-eight children in a single room, received $90 a month plus room and board from the Public Roads Administration.[12] Julius Garbus, an American engineer, had been paid $2,000 a year in his previous position; the Public Roads Administration gave him $3,000, a fifty percent increase, plus free room and board.[13] Robert Lockridge, writing to Imperial Oil to solicit support for a war bond drive, observed, "It is a well known fact that a very large percentage of the American employees presently working in Canada are receiving higher salaries than they have ever received before. With few exceptions, if any, the salaries of the lowest paid American citizens working in Canada far exceed their actual living expenses, and therefore, they are in no doubt in a position to invest a large percentage of their salaries in War Savings Bonds."[14] The high incomes included a few bizarre twists. Unable to find kitchen help, one contractor hired men as truck drivers, paid the going rate of $1.40 per hour, and then assigned them to wash dishes.[15]

The high incomes came, in large measure, from the extended hours of work on the construction projects. The urgency of the work, combined with the relative shortness of the summer season, ensured lengthy days and very full weeks. When Duncan Bath first arrived in the Northwest, he worked only during the day; by June 1942, however, the contractor had switched to a two-shift, twenty-four hour a day operation.[16] Frank Speer worked as a cat skinner for Harvey Construction. The men worked eleven hours a day and could work an additional three hours after supper if they wished. Some days, they pulled double shifts.[17] Miller Construction Company followed the standard seventy-hour work week,[18] broken into ten hours a day, seven days a week for its tree cutting crews.[19] Such a pace was not unusual, for the camp-based workers, typically far from home, seldom protested about the long hours. They were, after all, in the North to earn money and there was no better way to do that than by working the greatest number of hours possible.

Numerous questions surrounded payment for overtime, especially given the long hours worked during the first year of construction. Workers were understandably confused by the irregular connection between hours of work and the size of their pay packet and asked for clarification of the regulations.[20] A specific schedule was produced governing overtime work. Employees earning under $50 per week received straight time for overtime hours, except for double time for the seventh consecutive day of work. A graduated scale governed remaining workers, up to supervisory workers who were not entitled to additional compensation for any overtime.[21] The provisions were obviously unpopular with salaried workers. A quick amendment entitled civilian employees of the army to be paid for overtime, or time off in lieu of such pay, provided the extra work was authorized to "meet a specific emergency work situation."[22]

Workers on northwest defense projects were bound up in a baffling array of regulations and contractual details. To expedite hirings and to standardize working conditions, the army created a standard employment contract that was used by all employers and their American employees. The contract, limited to nine months duration, entitled all workers, except those in Edmonton, to receive free room and board. Wage workers were guaranteed a minimum of 240 hours paid work each month. Employers could set work schedules "for the purpose of completing the construction work as rapidly as possible," but the standard was declared to be ten-hour days, seven days a week, with a minimum of two days off per month. Workers could be dismissed for a range of offenses; a standard contract included the following provision:

> If the services of the Employee are not satisfactory to the Employer, or if he is not or does not show himself qualified for the position for which he is hired, or is negligent in his duties, or displays bad temper, or if he uses alcoholic drinks to a degree which, in the opinion of the Employer, is immoderate, or if he contracts or develops venereal disease, the Employee may be discharged . . .[23]

Workers also had to accept an open shop, agreeing to work alongside union or non-union workers as required by the employer.[24] There were later modifications. After May 1943, workers received time and a half for all hours in excess of eight hours per day or forty hours per week and for work on statutory holidays.[25]

Having Americans and Canadians on the same projects also created numerous administrative difficulties. American tax and labor laws differed significantly from Canadian regulations, forcing extended negotiations on these matters. Americans working on the northern defense projects were exempted from Canadian income tax. Canadians were forced to sign different contracts with U.S. companies than Americans did, due to different wage rates and regulations governing overtime pay.[26] Negotiations with the Alberta Compensation Board ensured that Canadians working for American companies were adequately covered by Workmen's Compensation. The greatest problem, however, lay with subsistence payments. American personnel received free room, board, and lodging. Because such payments were prohibited by the National War Labour Board, Canadians working in American camps, already receiving lower hourly pay than their U.S. counterparts, had to pay $1.25 per day for food and lodging.[27]

Some Canadians were angered by the differential wage rates (although others escaped the regulations and received American wages). A. Forgie "was not too happy about making a lot less than the Americans." His solution was to run a retail operation, selling watches to highway workers on the side.[28] Other Canadian workers expressed different sentiments. According to Frank Speer, "We envied them the higher pay but that caused no problems."[29]

The greatest difficulty on the wage front appeared at the beginning of construction activity. American contractors regularly ignored the standards set for Canadian employees by the War Labour Board, and hired whatever local Canadian workers they could find.[30] The result was that northern companies, locked into established Canadian wage rates, faced a mass exodus of workers to the Americans. General laborers in the Yukon, for example, earned seventy-five cents per hour under the War Labour Board regulations; American employers paid 96.5 cents plus ten percent exchange on Canadian funds.[31] Faced with such competition, Canadian contractors simply followed the American lead and did not submit their wage schedules to the labor board for approval.[32] The government moved quickly to quell the practice and to compel the Canadian contractors to honor the Western Labour Board rates.[33] For the workers, the knowledge that Americans doing similar work were receiving considerably higher wages created understandable resentment and increased the turnover among Canadian workers.[34]

The inequities of these wage rates were accepted by Canadian and American governments as essential to the construction of the project and national war efforts. The following wage schedules used by Bechtel-Price-Callahan, contractors on the CANOL project, in May 1943, are representative [see Table 5.1, page 150].[35]

Even these rates were not consistent throughout the North. Higher rates were permitted for workers assigned to northern posts to compensate for the isolation, lack of amenities, and the more difficult working conditions. Eventually, the effort to enforce uniformity was abandoned, leading to a range of salaries being offered for similar work. [See Table 5.2, page 150.]

Problems with inequality went beyond pay schedules, which were, after all, tied to national regulations and not subject to employers' whims. Towards the end of the war, the government lifted the rules prohibiting Canadians and Americans from working together. Under the new structure, however, evidence suggests that national favoritism continued. A survey of airfield employees in 1944, for example, revealed that Americans held the supervisory and well-

Table 5.1

Position	United States (U.S. $/hour)		Canada (Canadian $/hour)**	
	South*	North	South	North
Carpenter	1.50	1.65	1.00	1.20
Laborer	1.00	1.10	.50	.75
Bulldozer Op.	1.50	1.65	1.00	1.20
Welder	1.50	1.65	1.25	1.35
	(U.S. $/month)		(Candian $/month)	
	Min.	Max.	Min.	Max.
Accountants	250	350	150	300
Chief Stewards	500	600	250	400
Draftsmen	275	450	150	200
Sen. Engineers	500	700	350	500

*South or north of Resolution, NWT. Americans also received better benefits than Canadian employees.
**Through the war years, the U.S. dollar was worth approximately 10–20% more than the Candian.

Table 5.2
CONSTRUCTION WAGE RATES (PER HOUR)
VARIOUS EMPLOYERS, APRIL 1944[37]

Position	Edmonton	R.H. Smith Watson Lake	USED Yukon	BYNC Yukon
Carpenter	1.03	1.05	1.25	1.26
Driver	.60	.75	.75–.80	n/a
Shovel Oper.	1.17–1.30	1.30	1.40	1.45
Tractor Oper.	.80	.8	.95	1.00
Welder	1.00	1.30	1.15	1.20

paid positions, relegating Canadians to the lower ranks. At Fort Smith, the six Americans earned on average $3,145 per year; the fifteen Canadians earned $1,856. The Canadian section foreman received $250 per month, or $3,000 a year; an American tractor operator was paid $4,200 per year. At Fort Simpson, Superintendent M. Campbell, a Canadian, received $250 per month, while the American, N. C. Templeton, a tractor mechanic, was paid $4,200 per annum. The employment structure was the same at the airfields in Fort McMurray, Embarras, Fort Simpson, Hay River, Wrigley, and Mills Lake.[38]

Canadians also fell short of the Americans in other ways. Canadian camps had commissaries, where workers could buy clothing, tobacco, candy, gum, cards, magazines, and other similar goods.[39] The U.S. Army offered to provide Canadians access to its tax-free canteens in camps along the Alaska Highway. Such a privilege would have countered one of the more persistent complaints from Canadians—a shortage of luxury goods like cigarettes—but Ottawa denied the request, arguing that "Canadian citizens, wherever employed, will share equally the burdens of taxation and do their share in attaining maximum war effort."[40] The issue was not quickly resolved, however, for Canadian workers continued to complain that they were being discriminated against.[41] In fact, and despite the official attempts at prevention, some Canadian workers had access to American duty-free goods.[42] The government withheld its formal approval until the last months of the war, finally accepting the demands of its workers and the concurrence of the U.S. government in December 1944.[43]

For Americans, hundreds of miles from home and away for months at a time, the heavily subsidized canteen was a primary (and cheap) source of gifts and treats to be mailed to their families. Anxious to limit this practice—shipping consumer goods from the lower forty-eight states and back again was a terrible waste of transport—Lt. Col. Clifford ordered an end to such purchases. After December 1943, civilian and military personnel were forbidden to purchase gifts in the canteen. Other restrictions made sending presents from the Northwest difficult. Soldiers could send $50 worth of goods duty free; civilian workers, on the other hand, had to pay duty on any item valued at more than $1.00.[44] While the new regulations slowed—but

TRUCK AND BULLDOZER BADLY BOGGED DOWN AT THE
SOUTHERN END OF THE HIGHWAY NEAR DAWSON CREEK.
NAC, PA171417.

did not stop—the shipment of canteen supplies to the south, the
regulations proved a further burden on workers already suffering
from isolation and separation from their families. Many workers had
their employers deposit their monthly pay directly into a bank at
home, leaving out a small sum for casual expenses.[45] Some workers
mailed their pay check directly home[46] or arranged for the company
or government agency to do the same;[47] those living near the major
towns, of course, had access to banks.

Canadian workers were distressed by their evident second-class
status in their own country. Many were angered, too, by what they

CREW ERECTING A TELEPHONE POLE
AT MILE 10 OF THE CANOL ROAD, AUGUST 1943.
Photograph by R. S. Finnie.
NAC, Finnie collection, PA175983.

described as American arrogance in the work camps. A Canadian employee who had worked on the CANOL project wrote,

> Tell the Union not to send men up here and expect them to be satisfied. It is not a good place to send Union men. The Canadian has no chance here, all the best of the jobs are taken by the Yanks and the difference in wages is too great. The Yanks get away with almost murder...I know of cases where they took Yanks and put them over the top of Canadians that were fully qualified for the advance and paid them more money.[48]

Of course the money, whether paid at Canadian or U.S. rates, did not come easily. Workers had to face numerous hardships and extremely long hours in return for their pay. Working in the subarctic was a new experience for almost all the Americans and most of the Canadians. Many construction workers were used to working in isolated frontier settings under bad conditions, but the northwest defense projects required considerable adaptation, both in work habits and in construction techniques.

The greatest challenge to these workers came not from regulations but from the environment. In the summer months, the work days were stretched by the urgency of construction and the unaccustomed length of subarctic days. The pace of twelve-hour days, seven days a week proved exhausting, further complicated by the difficulty in adjusting to nights without darkness, the incessant noise of the construction camps, and the poor living accommodations. One junior American officer observed, "It is a fact that this post, like most outposts, is an officer's paradise and an enlisted man's concentration camp. It's really tough on the men living the restricted life they must …but everything to break the monotony of camp life is done that is possible."[49]

The worst hardship, noted by all northwest construction workers, was the legendary northern insect life—the mosquitoes and other bugs, particularly black flies, wasps, and no-see-ums.[50] Some workers made light of the bugs, which figured heavily in northwest folk lore, and joked about the abnormal size and viciousness of the mosquitoes. In reality, the insects were a serious problem, attacking the workers in the field and infiltrating cook house and sleeping quarters. Mosquito netting, including head coverings, were commonplace, particularly with the men who worked or lived near still water.[51] According to Willis Grafe, "The only reasonable remedy when at work was to wear two thicknesses of clothing and head nets. That way each time you moved your body it would torture their beaks and the face was protected."[52]

Spring and fall brought their own problems. In the spring, the melting snow and thawing permafrost combined to blanket the Northwest with mud. The mud and spring runoff caused numerous problems: bridges washed out, whole sections of road disappeared as the permafrost melted, trucks and construction equipment bogged down in the thick and slippery muck. Several workers were swept away by the raging creeks swollen by spring run-off. Workers were routinely covered in clinging sludge, which they tramped into their bunkhouses, cook houses, and workshops. In both seasons, frozen culverts created temporary dams, which quickly overflowed, flooding the road surface with several inches of water and ice. The first snow of fall, which usually came some time in September, caused numerous disruptions and provided solid warning of what lay ahead.

Winter was, of course, the most serious obstacle to be confronted. Work slowed appreciably as the days shortened and as cold weather gripped the Northwest. In the depths of winter, when the temperature often fell to -40°F, and occasionally -50°, work almost completely ceased, and the workers waited out the cold snap in their camps. Some workers, particularly survey crews, passed the winter of 1942 to 1943 in tents.[53] Robert Black, who worked for Campbell Construction Company northwest of Fort Nelson, recalled his accommodations the first year: "Our first lodgings were soldiers' tents with flaps, dirt floors, green wood in the camp stoves, 30-40 below weather."[54] Vern Kennedy described the beds in the survey camps: "Our beds were made with a pine frame, filled with spruce boughs—then a canvas ground sheet and army blankets."[55] Willis Grafe, working with a survey crew near Burwash Landing, spent most of the winter in similar conditions.

> Bunk tents were ten by twelve feet, with four men each except for the office tent, which held two men plus equipment for the office. In the center of each tent was a heating stove, a cone shaped creature of sheet metal with the stovepipe mounted atop the peak, pointing straight up. A door on the side provided access to the fire box. No bottom was attached, so it sat on the dirt floor of the tent, requiring some creativity on the part of the crew to provide some draft control. Clever use of cans from the kitchen enabled the fire to be adequately controlled, with draft designs improving as the season progressed.[56]

The frigid temperatures affected many aspects of northern work. Trucks and heavy equipment had to be kept running constantly; if they were turned off, they proved extremely difficult to restart. Workers dressed awkwardly in heavy parkas and other winter clothing, provided by their employer.[57] The extra clothing slowed their work considerably. Frostbite was winter's equivalent of the mosquitoes. For more than half the year, workers had to protect

A CIVILIAN CREW LUNCHING AT MILE 155
OF THE CANOL ROAD IN COLD WEATHER, 21 JANUARY 1944.
Photograph by R. S. Finnie.
NAC, Finnie collection, PA175982.

themselves against exposure. Hundreds, incautious or poorly equipped, froze fingers, toes, or parts of their face. A few failed to heed repeated warnings not to venture away from camp or vehicle during times of bitter cold and perished.[58] The dangers of winter were particularly noticeable along the CANOL pipeline route. The stretch through the Richardson Mountains, which offered little shelter from the harsh winds and extreme low temperatures of the winter months, was treacherous for as much as half the year.

Winter was particularly hard on construction equipment and its operators. Under the extreme subarctic cold, which turned tempered steel brittle, machinery routinely broke down. Mechanics and equipment operators continually battled against the cold, leaving their machines running for hours, even days, on end, afraid that they would not restart. The viscosity of oil proved no match for the northern winter, turning to a thick sludge that slowed, even stopped, the equipment. Workers often had to resort to warming engine blocks with blowtorches, an efficient but dangerous process.

These equipment problems were serious enough when they occurred in the construction camps. Difficulties often arose, however, when the operators were on the road. During the winter, drivers typically ran in convoys in an attempt to ensure that no one was stranded along the route. On occasion, a single vehicle was sent out—to deliver messages, repair a downed telephone line, or to deliver supplies or mail to the next camp up the road. Almost all operators carried a winter kit, including a sleeping bag, rations, and fire-making equipment and were ordered to remain with their vehicles. Relay stations stood every fifty miles along the highway, and all drivers were required to report to each post. If the vehicle did not arrive on schedule, a search team was quickly dispatched. Despite these precautions, a few men ignored the advice and, usually believing themselves to be only a short distance from the next camp, struck out on foot. Several of these foolhardy souls perished from exposure.

Despite the problems caused by spring run-off, lengthy summer days, mosquitoes and subzero winter temperatures, workers did not consider the northwest defense construction projects to be a particularly dangerous assignment. Army medical officers, supplemented in some civilian camps by first aid workers, tended to the inevitable cuts, bruises and more serious accidents that attended major construction projects. Although safety precautions were scarcely in evidence (there were few safety helmets or ear plugs in use), work generally proceeded within the limits of safety accepted at the time. Camps were often short of basic safety gear; one highway camp had only one proper welder's helmet, forcing the second welder to work with only welders' goggles on: "The result was almost comical—his eyes were two islands of white in a badly burned face. He was pretty uncomfortable for a few days."[59] Workers active in the Northwest consistently observed that skilled operators cared for their equipment and looked after their safety and that of their co-workers.

There were other, uniquely northern, dangers. Harvey Hayduk, driving on the highway outside of Fort St. John, came across a calf moose foundering in a water-filled ditch. He stopped to help the calf, only to be confronted by its mother: "She was certainly very angry and let me know it but did not trample me with her hooves."[60] A strategic retreat avoided injury.

The camp facilities, in the opinion of some workers, presented the greatest threat to worker safety. The buildings were often tinder-dry, with little means of controlling or putting out fires. J. Garbus, who worked on the lower part of the Alaska Highway, observed, "The greatest danger in my opinion was fire! This was due to the number of wood stoves and the lack of means including water to fight them."[61]

There were major exceptions to the general safety pattern. Given the high turn-over of personnel, it is not surprising that unqualified individuals occasionally found themselves in charge of equipment that they could not properly handle. Duncan Bath, who had considerable experience with farm equipment but no knowledge of caterpillar-type machines, hired on as a LeTourmeau operator and was forced to learn how to run the machine on the job.[62] Frank Speer observed that "at the start . . .men were put at work that was really out of their element. Road foremen were building latrines, jewelers trying to operate shovels and draglines, and, I might add, store managers trying to operate bulldozers. There were very few accidents although some very close misses."[63] Accidents followed, although little was done to punish the offenders or their supervisors. Perhaps more important, many operators were prepared to make allowance for their frontier setting. Under the circumstances of shortages of parts, equipment was kept in service that otherwise would have been sent to the shop. On occasion, for example, heavy trucks ran along the highway without brakes, at considerable risk to driver, passengers, and oncoming traffic. It was not as though there were not already enough problems. The army's rough pioneer road was ill-suited to regular traffic; several "Suicide Hills" along the route claimed their share of victims, as did the sharp shoulder of the road along Muncho Lake and many other danger spots along the Alaska Highway.

Many of the dangerous situations arising in the Northwest during World War II arose out of the perennial shortage of supplies and equipment. Trucks, bulldozers and other machinery were regularly cannibalized in order to keep at least a part of the fleet in operation. Drivers, for example, were extremely reluctant to leave their trucks unattended along a road, fearing that important parts (tires, distributor caps) in short supply would be stripped from their vehicle. Mechanics, in particular, became experts at making do without the proper components; jerry-rigged equipment was commonplace, as the top priority remained keeping the trucks and other equipment on the highway.

Money was not everything, not even to the northwest construction workers. Civilian workers quickly discovered that there was a price to pay for the high wages and long hours. Most of the civilian workers spent their time in the North in isolated construction camps, widely spaced along the CANOL pipeline and Alaska Highway. These hastily built camps, consisting of a series of insulated, tar paper bunkhouses, a large cook house, a small recreation hall and the required garages, warehouses and workshops, were far from attractive settings. Many were recycled, having been used on depression-era construction projects, and were transported north in sections.[64] Duncan Bath, based ninety-eight miles from Fort Nelson on the Alaska Highway, described his camp:

> We lived in bunk houses. The one I was in had, I would say, 12 to 14 bunks in it (one room). The bunks were iron-frame single cots with a "mattress," top and bottom sheets and a gray blanket with a rick pillow. Nothing happened to any of this over the four months I was there! My belongings (suit case) were under my cot. There was a small area at one end of the bunkhouse where one could take a bath in a round, steel, tub. We ate at long bare wooden tables in the central cook shack.[65]

Heating was typically provided by a wood stove, toilet facilities consisted of unheated outdoor latrines, and there was usually no running water.[66] There was little motivation, or need, to improve the camps, for most were slated for abandonment as soon as the contracts were completed. Toward the end of the war, as maintenance of the highway replaced construction as the top priority, the camps were upgraded somewhat, particularly through the addition of family quarters. These family units were not a great deal better. The Blacks, who worked near Muncho Lake, British Columbia, lived with their young son in a small cabin of "frame construction—3 feet high, 2 thicknesses of board floor, and a tent roof, extending over the board wall. Ours was 16 feet square." The families ate in the mess hall, showered in the camp facilities; it was, according to the Blacks, "regular camp living."[67]

Workers in the major centers enjoyed better surroundings. They also lived in prefabricated buildings but had running water, proper toilet facilities instead of outdoor latrines, electricity in most buildings, and proper heating systems.[68] Office facilities were similarly of a higher quality, befitting the seniority of the staff and the greater permanence of the headquarters.

Most of the buildings, constructed along standard army and construction lines, were not well suited for the northern setting. Sanitation was a constant problem. Most camps had outdoor latrines, acceptable during the summer months but a decided disadvantage during the winter. Most camp bunkhouses were heated with wood stoves, which presented problems in the winter: "With the tin stove in the middle of the room glowing, red hot, each roofing nail used to attach the sheeting to the studs had a button of ice that never melted from November to June." During the winter months, workers had trouble keeping warm, often sleeping with their hats on.[69] Fuel lines for those buildings with small and usually inefficient oil-burning furnaces were run on the outside of the buildings; in the extreme cold of subarctic winters, these fuel lines often froze, sending residents scrambling for warmer quarters. The cold was a memorable feature of the region:

> That first winter was a nightmare. Glyco, a fluid anti-freeze used in airplane cooling systems, was kept about four feet from stoves and yet congealed. At night the men would climb into their sleeping bags, leaving just their face out; in the morning a half-inch layer of frost would be around the opening of the sleeping bag. Metal frames of eyeglasses froze to the face. Pitchers of water (most bases had no running water then) sitting about five feet from stoves would be frozen solid. Ink in pens was always frozen. Typewriters (few of the bases had them) would freeze and had to be thawed out on a QM potbellied stove.[70]

COOK SHACK, SOMEWHERE ALONG THE HIGHWAY, 9 MAY 1943.
Photograph by R. Schubert. Schubert family collection.

Even with the heaters working, the buildings provided only passable comfort during the winter months and little protection from the dust, dirt and mosquitoes that plagued the countryside during the summer.

While workers could, and did, complain about their rustic accommodations, the civilians made fewer criticisms about the food than did military workers in the army camps. In most civilian camps, food of good quality and quantity was readily available. A. Forgie recalled the food fondly:

> This is one area where we lived like Kings. Our cook used to be the chef of the Brown Derby Rest. in Los Angeles. We had plenty of steak; the camp would get as many as 50 sides of beef in one shipment . . . Plenty of fresh fruit, dehydrated potatoes, powdered milk. No ice cream.[71]

Some, though not all, soldiers ate well. Heath Twichell, who accompanied the first troops to Fort St. John in the summer of 1942, reported

We . . . eat the best of chow. They have provided a special ration for us, which is more than adequate. We have 80 tons of fresh meat (steaks and chops) which have been stored in an ice house that we built. The quartermaster has set up a field bakery, and we will have fresh bread, rolls, and pastry. Some of the other items in the ration include powdered milk and eggs, dehydrated potatoes, all kinds of canned fruits, meats and vegetables, etc.[72]

There were, understandably, regular shortages of fresh produce and meat, and transportation problems (such as road washouts) often left some camps short of food.[73] Wild game was occasionally purchased from local Native hunters, and some construction workers shot moose, caribou or sheep and offered the meat to the camp cook. Project managers, however, correctly identified food as a crucial ingredient in keeping the workers content and expended considerable money (all returnable as part of the contractors' cost-plus contracts) on providing the kinds of meals that the workers demanded.

Another anecdote gives a rather different picture of the quality of northern cuisine:

First it was lady cooks we had. I remember this one. She made hotcakes in the morning. Big bowl under her arm and mixed up these hotcakes and throwing them on this griddle and "oh dear, oh dear" and kept making the cakes and saying "oh dear, oh dear." One of the other cooks said to her "What's the matter with you?" She said, "Well, I've got a hell of a head cold and my nose has been dripping in the hotcakes." But we never found out about it for months. But, you know, she was a good cook; a real good cook, and a fancy cook.[74]

Not all of the work associated with the northwest defense projects consisted of heavy construction hundreds of miles from the nearest settlements. From the beginning, hundreds of office workers, warehouse men, mechanics and other support workers were assigned to headquarters operations. The range of work was striking, reflecting the complexity of modern warfare and the logistical underpinnings of major construction projects. There were dozens of financial officers, secretaries, and other administrative staff in each of the major centers—Edmonton, Dawson Creek, Fort St. John, Whitehorse, and Fairbanks. The offices also had large professional staffs, particularly engineers and project managers, who worked feverishly to keep up with the work crews and to keep construction work on schedule.

Office workers experienced a very different work pattern than construction workers. The urgency so evident at the construction sites was not as much in evidence; bulldozer operators worked longer hours than did the U.S. officers in the film distribution center and truck drivers put in more time behind the wheel than secretaries did at their typewriters. The latter also worked under much more favorable conditions. Office accommodations were not much better than those in the camps—the ubiquitous army buildings and Quonset huts dotted the entire Northwest—but there were more amenities available in town, and many more distractions to fill the larger number of free hours.

Workers throughout the Northwest, whether in an isolated construction camp or in a contractors' office in Whitehorse, soon tired of the subarctic or, to be more accurate, missed their homes and families. For all but a few of those involved with the defense projects, letters provided the only contact with the people back home. High wages, and the promise of a better standard of living, provided some compensation, but that wore thin after many months of northern work. At Christmas 1942, when many northern employees had been away from home for six to eight months, intense loneliness set in: "In 1942 Christmas Day, the men in our camp had moved into dormitories from the tents we had occupied from November. However, we were an unhappy group as we thought of our families and friends in various parts of Canada."[75] Employees became increasingly anxious to return to their families, either on furlough or permanently. Most had signed up for one year's service, and many left, at company expense, as soon as their commitment expired.

The companies were understandably displeased with the turn-over of workers, which disrupted camp life and interrupted work schedules. In an attempt to hold onto the workers, companies offered more generous furlough arrangements, paying the costs of transporting employees to their homes for an extended visit on the condition that they returned to work in the North.[76] For most workers, however, one year (or less) was more than enough of a contribution to the North American war effort and long enough to spend away from home. Having served out their contracts and built up a savings account, most returned to the south.

Many of the contractors, anxious to staunch the flow of workers leaving the North, went even further to improve the attractiveness of their camps. They improved the quality of the food and the living quarters, provided entertainment for the workers and, within the limits of Canadian and American policy, offered what benefits they could. Carter-Halls Aldinger Company, working in northern British Columbia, applied to the Western Labour Board for permission to pay the railway fare for all employees so that they could go home over Christmas. The application was approved, subject to further review by the Selective Service Office, which made the final decisions on absences from places of employment.[77]

Operators often had great difficulty holding onto workers, particularly given the number of jobs available throughout the region.[78] For most workers it was a seller's market, and some took advantage of the situation. In the summer of 1942, an employee of McInnes Products Corporation requested a release so that he could secure employment with an American firm. When the request was refused, the company manager alleged, the man cut off the water supply to a $5,000 machine, "allowing it to seize and so tie up his plant."[79] C. J. Rogers of the White Pass and Yukon Railway complained to his Member of Parliament,

> Our Labour and Wage situation is all snarled up here on account of the arrival of American contractors who are competing for local labour and paying a wage scale away in excess of that prevailing for any similar kind of work such as on airfield here.... If this scale for local labour is maintained it is going to disorganize all work in the territory, government or private.[80]

George Simmons of Northern Airways petitioned the Yukon government to help find workers to assist with improvements on the Carcross airfield. Controller George Jeckell had to turn him down, reporting that surplus workers could not be found and that the government had to "beg" Canadian authorities for a couple of employees to work on graveling Whitehorse streets.[81] The Yukon Consolidated Gold Corporation took the unprecedented step of hiring Native people to work on the gold dredges. The experiment worked well in the short term, but the Natives left when hunting season arrived.[82]

Not all civilian workers were pleased with wages and working conditions. There were, however, few avenues of protest and little support for sustained job action. The standard workers' response of organized protest and strikes carried little clout in the Northwest. With wages determined by administrative fiat, and with the employees isolated in far-flung construction camps, there was little value in, or opportunity for, collective action. The unions carried workers' cases to the Western Labour Board, the special commissioner of northwest defence projects, and other appropriate government agencies; in this, they provided a useful counterbalance to the interests of management and government and ensured that workers' concerns remained in front of regulatory agencies.

Workers found ways to demonstrate their displeasure. There were scattered reports of sabotage, particularly along the CANOL pipeline project. In the Edmonton area, where defense project work pushed wages up and created serious labor shortages, there were a number of short strikes and walk-outs, most of which were quickly resolved in favor of the employer.[83]

Workers outside of the actual construction projects—working for employers not protected by cost-plus contracts—voiced their criticisms more vociferously. Local 884, Hotel and Restaurant Employees Union, based in Whitehorse, petitioned the Western Labour Board for a more realistic wage schedule. The existing rates, they argued, guaranteed a "lower standard of living, create discrimination, are detrimental to the intelligence and ability of the Canadian working men and women, create an inferiority complex,...remove all hopes of living a normal life,...leave no room for opportunities and

A MAN IDENTIFIED AS A "TEXAS OILMAN"
CHECKING A SECTION OF THE CANOL PIPELINE.
Photograph by H. Towed.
NAC, Finnie collection, PA174542.

promotions." They pointed to the continued wage gap between Americans and Canadians, who were often "employed in the same mess hall, doing the same work and assuming the same responsibilities." The bitterness was very real: "Through a padlocked income that is already heavy taxed, the Canadian worker finds himself in a position where he must, not by choice, but by forced necessity adopt a much inferior position in the society, as well as in the economical life of the community, a position much inferior to that adopted by his American co-worker who are performing the same duties for a much higher wage."[84] While there was obvious basis for grievance—American waitresses earned around $175 per month while the top Canadian rate was $108.50—the Western Labour Board was unwilling to adjust the wage schedules[85] and fell back on its policy of urging employers to keep Americans and Canadians apart.[86] The union would keep up the pressure in subsequent months, but to little avail.[87]

This was not the only grievance on this account from the Yukon. The newly formed Whitehorse and District Workers' Union (WDWU) made an appeal to the Western Labour Board in November 1944, asking for immediate attention to the wage differential between American and Canadian workers. The new association petitioned the board, meeting in Whitehorse, to address "the injustices, inequalities and discriminations that have been and are practiced against loyal Canadian workmen, who with their fellow-Canadians have given of their best to further Canada's war effort and victory, and far too often received scant consideration of their legitimate grievances by those in authority."[88] The Western Labour Board, while publicly sympathetic, did not change its policy. The WDWU protested the board's decision, and wondered if the Yukoners' complained had been fully understood.[89] The sense of grievance would remain throughout the war.

There were attempts to broaden the base of union activity on wartime construction projects. The Amalgamated Building Workers of Canada (ABWC), particularly active in the Edmonton area, presented itself to the Western Labour Board as the representative of nonunionized workers, offering a detailed wage schedule that it asked to have adopted for all employees in the area. Recruiting efforts did not go smoothly. Contractors refused to meet with the ABWC; organizers were often denied entry into company buildings. The unionists correctly identified that the concern lay with the unions, not the possibility that workers' pay would have to increase: "It is our understanding that the Contracts let, in the Edmonton Area, are on a cost plus basis with a fixed fee, whereby no contractor can make any more gain through the wages being brought up to the established Union Rates."[90]

Most of the complaints brought by the unions and workers to the Western Labour Board dealt with the poor wages of Canadian employees compared to their American counterparts. The Amalgamated Building Workers of Canada approached the board with a lengthy brief, outlining grievances ranging from hour wages to insurance coverage, asking the board to grant its workers equitable treatment.[91] Carl Berg of the Trades and Labour Council, already an outspoken critic of Canadian policy concerning northwestern defense work, requested freedom for Canadian workers to seek employment wherever possible and asked for improved wage rates and an immediate cost of living bonus of twenty-five percent.[92]

Workers moving to Edmonton, many of whom came from British Columbia, were a special case. The Alberta wage schedule was significantly lower than rates along the coast, and living costs were high—there was, for instance, a good deal of rent-gouging in the city. Employees accepting positions with the defense projects discovered to their dismay that they were earning less—not more—than in their previous employment. Unions representing the workers complained:

> We think that your Board should recognize the fact that most of the men who will man the construction jobs in Northern B.C. and outlying places, will come from the unions operating out of either Vancouver, Victoria or Prince Rupert. These men expect to work under the same wage scale and working conditions as they have formerly worked, and the men cannot be expected to go, nor can the union be expected to send men, to any jobs, where the wages and working conditions are lower because of the locality of the job.[93]

It is questionable, however, to what degree these complaints reflected real grievances on the workers' part, and to what degree they represented the unions' desire to strengthen their position. Virtually every worker interviewed for this book, Canadian or American, seems to have been delighted with his wages, which were often at least twice what they had been before the war.

Perhaps it was for this reason that labor unions did not play a particularly prominent role in the northwest defense projects. There was representation for workers in settled areas, particularly Edmonton and Whitehorse, and some very modest efforts to represent the interests of other Canadian workers. American unions were totally absent from the scene. Management clearly had little interest in involving unions in the construction projects, but the workers similarly were prepared to work without representation. There is an easy explanation. Civilian workers came north to make money, and the companies were coming up with the cash. While conditions were not great, wages were high and most employees outside the major centers considered it a fair exchange, at least in the short term.

Those who disliked the wages or working conditions in the Northwest could do what northern workers had done for decades: they could leave. As early as the fall of 1942, project managers were being warned that the frigid subarctic winters would cause problems with the work force. The doctor under contract to the Imperial Oil company at Norman Wells, for instance, warned his superiors that all workers should be rotated southward, preferably to their homes, for one or two weeks during the coldest part of the season. He argued that "the expense would be more than compensated by improvement in the morale of the men and the probability that a greater percentage of them would be willing to work through the next season." Logistical problems prevented the implementation of the doctor's advice. Project supervisors took pains to warn incoming workers of the vagaries of northern service. A 1943 circular letter, which was to be "transmitted by bulletin, memorandum, signs and posters at every occupied where employees are located," spelled out the "Dos and Don'ts" of winter preparation.[94] Not all workers heeded the warning; frostbite was endemic and there were some deaths due to exposure. The workers' intense dislike of winter became one of the greatest obstacles to the efficient management of the project work force.[95]

By 1943 morale among the civilian work force had slipped badly. A. W. Klieforth, American consul-general in Winnipeg, traveled along the southern part of the Alaska Highway in the fall of that year, and reported that since the Japanese threat seemed to be over, many workers saw no reason to exert themselves:

> ...they drop their tools on the minute of closing time, and within two minutes after quitting time the work places are as empty as the North Pole. ...The contractors informed me that there was not the slightest chance of having an audience listen to a War Bond talk, unless the speaker was either President Roosevelt or a well known movie star. I had to speak to them while they were eating, starting on the dot as the soup was served and stopping as the last bit of pie was washed down with coffee.... At a recent war relief contest, the first prize was a bottle of whiskey; the second, a dozen of beer; the third—a $100 war bond.[96]

Worker transiency was endemic, and continued throughout the war years. Standard Oil's Whitehorse refinery, one of the most stable and desirable work sites in the region, suffered continually from high turnover in its work force. The company lost almost eight percent of its employees in June 1944 alone, a slight increase over the previous month. Over half the employees cited personal reasons, rather than work related problems, as the reason for their departure.[97] This left the company continually scrambling to fill positions. The U.S. War Manpower Commission entered the Canadian field in a direct attempt to address this problem. An office was opened in Whitehorse in September 1943, aimed at reducing worker turn-over by offering disgruntled employees positions with other American contractors active in the area.[98] The on-site presence clearly helped. When Dowell Construction demobilized in the fall of 1943, "only" 2,700 of the 4,600 workers left the area; 1,900 workers were induced to remain with other contractors in the field, a great saving in recruitment time and transportation costs.[99] The same coordination was evident on the Canadian side, particularly as Canadian policy after 1944 called for greater participation of Canadian contractors and workers. The office of the special commissioner on northwest defence projects, the selective service and Western Labour Board worked closely together in an effort to stabilize and supply the northern labor force.[100]

The problem escalated as the end of the war neared. With much of the urgency of earlier years gone, overtime hours were slashed. For the boomers drawn north by promises of high wages and long hours, the changes stripped the military projects of their attractiveness. By January 1944 Bechtel-Price-Callahan was reporting 600 to 700 terminations per month in the Whitehorse District. Managers tried to address the situation by "working all employees seven days per week throughout the month without insistence upon the minimum of two days off per month."[101] Under normal conditions, workers would have protested such a work schedule; the employees' attitude to the North was such that these long, unbroken work days were expected, even welcomed.

The regular departure of hundreds of workers from northern camps opened opportunities for those remaining behind. Leonard Byran came north to work as a commissary officer, although he hoped for a more important position and a raise from his $225 month

A WARTIME PUBLICITY PHOTO, JUNE 1943. COLONEL J. LYONS (LEFT) AND
MAJOR GENERAL W. W. FOSTER "STOP TO CHAT WITH WELDERS
L. S. COOK AND C. R. DUNLOP, BUSY ON PIPELINE."
NAC, PA174543.

salary. An opening soon appeared, and he transferred to a new company as transportation assistant, complete with an increase of $100 per month.[102] John Blakely, brought north as a general foreman by Bechtel-Price-Callahan to work on the CANOL project, was hired away by Marine Operators and made superintendent responsible for road and marine equipment at Fort Smith. The change carried an increase in monthly salary from $350 to $450.[103] The companies and government agencies, of course, resented the inconvenience caused by workers' mobility. Elliott Construction Company was, in May 1944, paying workers at Norman Wells construction rates and offering longer hours than those available to maintenance workers in the Dawson Creek area. Faced with repeated transfers to the firm's employ, a company-government committee agreed that "no one can go to work for Elliott without approval from this office." Further, any person resigning to work with Elliott would be denied permission and would be out of work.[104] Such efforts, however, did little to stem the constant movement within the northern labor market.

Under the often unfavorable conditions extant in the North, and with a freedom that the American soldiers greatly envied, a number of civilians sought to return to the United States. Others were fired. It seemed, at times, as if as many workers were leaving the North as arriving. According to Public Roads Administration documents, Canadian laborers left the northwest at a rate of nineteen percent per month; American workers were considerably further behind, with approximately ten percent leaving each month, the difference no doubt partly due to the average hourly wage rate being $1.57 for Americans and 86 cents for Canadians.[105] One observer, capturing the army's hostility to the evident lack of commitment in the civilian work force, wrote, "Other quarters openly declaimed against 'boomer' tactics, particularly in Yukon areas supplied through Skagway. There, it was insisted, contractors had three crews, one working, one going and one coming to the job."[106] An intelligence officer reported, "After only a few weeks it is not uncommon to see many terminate and return to the States. This happens so frequently they came to be known as 'termites.' The turnover in labor has been extremely high and there has been a continual change of personnel."[107] The standard rule was that employees had to pay their own return fares if they left early; otherwise, the company was to pick up the cost of transportation.[108] Further, the government had to be informed before an employee was returned to the point of hiring.[109]

The termites were often not content simply to leave their jobs. They spread unfavorable stories, many of them true, about the camps, climate, rates of pay, and working conditions. A Denver man, returning from a stint of highway work, reported that he

> worked less than half the time but was paid time and one-half for overtime besides regular time all the time he was there. One time they laid idle for twenty-one days without reason. He made about $1,000 per month without much work but he says the men would rather work as the monotony of killing time and payrolls for the Contractor wears them down and they can't take it long. He quit in disgust and came back here.[110]

Other northern employees complained that their overtime hours were not being counted, denying them hundreds of dollars in earned income.[111] Workers gathered in Edmonton, ready to embark to the camps, were routinely subjected to stories from experienced highway hands on their way south.[112]

Measures were needed to control the out-migration from the Northwest. The United States government, in conjunction with the private contractors, laid down strict rules governing repatriation to the United States. Employees of Okes Construction Company and associated subcontractors had $10 docked from their pay each week for five weeks, leaving a pot of $50 to pay "the entire repatriation costs in the event a man leaves before the end of the season." Contractors had to collect the money; failure to do so left the contractor liable for the expenses. There was considerable demand for transportation to the south. Okes Construction ran trucks from Fort St. John to Dawson Creek on Sunday, Tuesday and Thursday of each week, coinciding with the trains leaving from Dawson Creek on Monday, Wednesday, and Friday. The trains carried departing workers to one of two locations, Sweetgrass, Montana, or Noyes, Minnesota. A cash payment of $10 was provided to cover the cost of food on the return trip to the United States. The worker was responsible for the costs of the rest of the trip. Workers injured on the job, or unable to continue for health reasons, were shipped back to the United States at government expense.[113]

These were not the only regulations. Following a meeting between contractors and the War Manpower Commission, a three-day cooling off period was established for any worker wishing to leave his position; it was hoped that the extra time would allow managers to settle minor grievances and keep more men in the field.[114] Bechtel-Price-Callahan had well-defined policies for dealing with termites or people fired for cause. American workers who quit while in isolated camps were charged $2 per day for room and board until they left; they often had to wait some time for a flight, since they were assigned the lowest priority. The cost of air transportation— which typically cost $165 for a Norman Wells to Edmonton flight— was deducted from the amount owed the employee. Not all employees understood the regulations. Workers who quit their northern postings nonetheless expected to have their travel costs covered by the company; the discovery that the considerable expense involved had been deducted from the final paycheck was a rude shock.[115]

The arrangements for Canadian employees, many of whom had not been hired on the same contract terms, were less favorable. Americans, for example, received paid travel and waiting time until arrival at destination; Canadians received no such consideration. U.S. workers discharged for reasons of health had their transportation costs met, but there were no similar provisions for Canadian employees.[116] Unlike the American government, which maintained a strong official presence in the region, Canadian authorities were scarce in the Northwest, offering little special help for workers who left their jobs.

Workers anxious to put the north behind them were not always willing to follow government or corporate guidelines. On 1 August 1942, two Americans arrived at the American consulate in Edmonton, demanding transportation back to the United States. They claimed to represent thirty other workers, stranded en route without train fare. The men, who had been in the north for only a few weeks, had apparently quit over the poor food in the camps. The contractor let them go and provided transportation to Sweetgrass, Montana, but the men lived in Minnesota. Accompanied by consular officials, they visited several Canadian and American representatives in an attempt to resolve the problem. When the contractor offered each man an extra $5 per person, the men boarded the train for Sweetgrass. One of the two men who initially approached the consulate, anxious to get home to his sick father, was provided free transportation on Northwest Airlines.

John Randolph, American consul in Edmonton, worried that the repatriation question would become a major problem. As part of the initial negotiations on the Alaska Highway project, American officials promised to "repatriate at its expense" any workers not shipped south by contractors. The arrival of thirty protesters raised the possibility of hundreds of similar applications. Randolph strongly favored the established method of collecting funds from the workers to pay for their transportation back to the United States. He believed that the contractors similarly supported this approach, although he cautioned that there might be later demands on the United States government for compensation in the case of "undeserving" cases.[117]

There were, of course, no promises of continuing work on the northwest defense projects. Workers knew from the beginning that their northern service would be limited, usually by the length of their contract, but also by the very nature of the work. When bridges or sections of highway were completed, pipe laid, or telephone lines strung, the company would close down operations and workers would be given termination notices. Because of the continuing demand for labor, however, efforts were made to keep the employees in the field. People still under contract who were given termination notices were required to report to the War Manpower Commission, with offices in Edmonton and Whitehorse, for reassignment to another contractor or to an American government agency for the remainder of the contract. Workers were encouraged to extend their contractual commitments. But by 1944, as war work wound down, increasing numbers of men were simply released from their contracts and, as required by agreement with their employer, provided with transportation to the south.[118]

The CANOL project stood, at least until 1945, as an exception to the impermanence of northern work. In most instances, men were expected to come north for a short time, usually nine months or a year, and then return to their families, much richer for the experience. Wives and children were not, as a rule, permitted to accompany the men. CANOL was different, for plans called for the use of the pipeline and Whitehorse refinery in the postwar period. As a result, company officials sought permanent employees for the refinery, and even permitted key workers to bring their families north. Those plans stalled in the summer of 1944, due to a shortage of housing rather than an abandonment of the plan.[119] The policy was, of course, reversed following the abandonment of the pipeline and refinery.

Civilian workers contacted about their time on the northwest defense projects express pride in their accomplishments—for most their only northern work experience—and remember their colleagues, camp life and subarctic adventure with genuine fondness. As Duncan Bath recalled,

I would still have to rate my summer on the Alaska Highway as a very significant event in my life. There was challenge, a lot of hard work, achievement, and adventure. I learned why one day off in seven is a good idea—the seven-day week did get monotonous even if work was exciting and there was nothing to do on a day off.[120]

Robin and Dell Black confessed that "Our main purpose when accepting was to accumulate a 'little nest egg' for beginning something more permanent, but we gained more perhaps than we shall ever realize."[121] Julius Garbus, an engineer with the Public Roads Administration, shared similar sentiments:

Where else could a 23 year old be offered the responsibilities of major construction projects of such varied scope. I accepted these responsibilities and gained experiences that shaped my career and my future. The rewards outdistance the few inconveniences encountered.[122]

Harvey Hayduk remembered his former colleagues with particular fondness: "I associated with extraordinarily fine people—honest, happy, sincere and very willing to go the extra mile. They were both American and Canadian. There were no complainers or shirkers. Each one was a positive thinker and a builder."[123] These memories, filtered by the passage of time, have lost some of the hard edge that is evident in the contemporary workers' descriptions of laboring activity in the Northwest during World War II. They do, nonetheless, reveal a great deal about the central patterns of work and life.

The northwest defense projects were suffused with a sense of immediacy and impermanence. The work was to be completed quickly and with only casual attention to cost and efficiency. Signs of haste and lack of concern for the future were evident everywhere, from the hastily located Alaska Highway to the jerry-built construction camps to the dozens of cannibalized trucks and pieces of heavy equipment that lay abandoned throughout the Northwest.

These two elements also dominated the lives of civilian workers. They came north to make money, and most did so at a pace they had seldom, if ever, known before. But the high wages did not inspire loyalty to the region or a desire to stay. Their point of reference was always to the south; they had decided to return home before they left

CUTTING ICE ON THE LIARD RIVER.
Photograph courtesy of J. Garbus.

in the first place. For the civilian workers, therefore, the priorities were to work as long as the regulations and the employer would permit, putting as much money into their pockets as possible.

Most quickly tired of the subarctic, especially during the long and frigid winters that limited their hours of work and added to a sense of boredom, isolation, and unease. Living in a large dormitory, which offered little privacy, eating in a noisy, hot cook house and surrounded by men of similar background, skill and ambition proved tiresome and, to some, endless. Some workers found this atmosphere exciting and were thrilled to be part of such an important and diverse venture. Others, constantly remembering the size of their pay packet, accepted the inconveniences and stayed out their term of work. Large numbers soon tired of northern work and, breaking their contracts, opted to leave altogether.

The North proved, in the final analysis, to be more tolerable and less of a threat than most workers had anticipated. The region presented certain environmental challenges—weeks of subzero temperatures, winter snow storms, spring runoff and long summer days—but these were confronted and handled with comparative ease. The human problems, more than the environmental ones, weighed most heavily on the minds of the civilian workers. Far from family and friends, stuck in an isolated work camp, and tied to an exhausting work schedule, most civilian workers longed for a return to the south.

Construction workers have historically worked under the most difficult of conditions. Railway crews, canal workers and road builders have traditionally been the vanguard of the modern work force into frontier areas. They were often among the most exploited of all workers, drawn from the immigrant classes and controlled by tough-minded contractors. The combination of worker desperation and the corporate firm hand had ensured the successful completion of the continent's canals and transcontinental railways and the expanding highway network. The frontier construction setting had long been among the most exploitative workplaces in the North American economy, as employers drove their workers to keep projects on time and on budget.

This pattern persisted through the nineteenth century and into the early twentieth century in both the United States and Canada during the Great Depression. In the United States, the Public Roads Administration supervised a series of makework highway projects, in which thousands of unemployed men were put to work building and improving rural roads. In Canada, the exploitation of workers during times of economic hardship was even more severe. Fearful that the unemployed might prove susceptible to radical ideologies, the Canadian government opened a series of frontier work camps and filled them with relief workers. In return for a pittance and room and board, the men had to accept rigid discipline and work on a series of labor-intensive construction projects, such as airfields and the Big Bend Highway in eastern British Columbia. In both cases, frontier construction remained low paid and relatively low skilled.

In more recent times, that pattern has been turned on its head. Contemporary frontier construction projects, like the building of the trans-Alaska pipeline across Alaska in the 1970s and many Canadian and American dams, have been among the most lucrative opportunities available for working people anywhere on the continent. Exceptionally high wages and remarkable generous benefit packages have completely transformed the image of construction labor from exploited immigrant workers to highly paid, unionized and even pampered personnel.

The World War II northwest defense projects fit in the middle of these extremes. The employment of civilian workers in the subarctic during World War II did not create this new work environment, but it is an excellent illustration of the transition to a highly paid frontier work force. Faced with a general labor shortage during the war, in possession of government cost-plus contracts that rendered wage scales substantially irrelevant, and knowing the limited enthusiasm of North American workers for frontier labor (understandable given the history of such work), employers offered generous salaries and additional benefits (free or subsidized room and board, transportation home and furloughs) in order to attract the necessary men northward. The effort worked. Thousands of men accepted the challenge—and the opportunity—presented by the northwest defense projects, came north, made their money, and returned home.

NOTES

1. Herbert Gutman, *Work, Culture, and Society in Industrializing America: Essays in American Working-class and Social History* (New York: Knopf, 1976); Bryan Palmer, *The Canadian Working Class Experience: The Rise and Reconstitution of Canadian Labour* (Toronto: Butterworths, 1983); and Craig Heron and Robert Storey, eds., *On the Job: Confronting the Labour Process in Canada* (Kingston: McGill-Queen's University Press, 1986).

2. Questionnaire answered by Cyril Griffith, Naicam, Saskatchewan.

3. Questionnaire answered by Bernice Sillemo, Edmonton, Alberta.

4. This trip is described in Willis Grafe, *The Summer of 1942, Yukon Style: Surveying the Alaska Highway* (private memoirs).

5. Questionnaire answered by Julius Garbus, West Hartford, Connecticut

6. Questionnaire answered by Duncan T. Bath, Peterborough, Ontario.

7. Questionnaire answered by Gerry Pelletier, Morinville, Alberta.

8. He need not have worried about his wife telling anyone, for the letter was confiscated by military censors. Paul Thompson to Colonel J. A. O'Connor, 5 September 1942, ACE, 72-A-3173, Box 16, file 50-26.

9. Questionnaire answered by Duncan Bath, Peterborough, Ontario.

10. Questionnaire answered by A. Forgie, Edmonton, Alberta.

11. Questionnaire answered by Frank Speer, White Rock, British Columbia.

12. Questionnaire answered by Harvey Hayduk, Edmonton, Alberta.

13. Questionnaire answered by J. Garbus, West Hartford, Connecticut.

14. Lockridge to Imperial Oil Limited, 22 September 1943, ACE, Main Collection, Box 418, file 20-15.

15. Questionnaire answered by A. Forgie, Edmonton, Alberta.

16. Questionnaire answered by Duncan Bath, Peterborough, Ontario.

17. Questionnaire answered by Frank Speer, White Rock, British Columbia.

18. James Connick to Lee Taylor, 5 February 1944, NA, RG 338, Box 23, "Policy and Procedures." The regulations noted that "The maximum number of hours per week that may be reimbursed shall be 70 hours and in no case shall it be exceeded."

19. ACE, Main Collection, Box 418, file 20-19, J. B. Miller to Division Engineer, 5 October 1943.

20. ACE, 72-A-3173, Box 16, file 50-26, A. H. Andersen to Chief of Engineers, U.S. Army, 18 May 1943. See also ACE, 52-A-434, Box 29, Robert Fell to National Labor Relations Board, 29 December 1944, Chief, Labor Relations, Corps of Engineers to Headquarters, Army Service Forces, 1 July 1944, Howard Kanouff to Department of Labor, 9 June 1944.

21. Ace, 72-A-3173, Box 18, Report on the Canol Project, Book 3, L. D. Worsham to District Engineers, Area Engineers, Contractors and Others Concerned, 29 May 1943.

22. USED, District Office Memorandum No. 21, Subject: Hours of Work and Overtime Compensation for Civilian Employees, 17 June 1943, NA, RG 338, Box 42.

23. Report on Canol Project, ACE, 72A3173, Box 18, Book 3.

24. Employment Contract (blank form), n.d. ACE, Miscellaneous, Box 411 (927731), file 7-2.

25. Division Circular Letter No. 97 (Labor Relations No. 13), Labor Policies for contractors' American Personnel, Laborers and Mechanics, 30 May 1943 ACE, Miscellaneous, Box 411 (927731), file 7-2.

26. One proposal early in the construction phase called for Americans and

Canadians to be paid the same rates. When the Americans returned to their country, they would "receive a sum equal to the accumulated difference between the United States and Canadian wage schedules." Memorandum handed to Alfred Kleiforth, American Consul General-Winnipeg, 29 May 1942, NAC, RG 27, vol. 676, file 6-5, file 6-5-75-5-1.

27. Ibid.

28. Questionnaire answered by A. Forgie, Edmonton, Alberta.

29. Questionnaire answered by Frank Speer, White Rock, British Columbia.

30. Questionnaire answered by J. Miller, London, Ontario.

31. George Black to Humphrey Mitchell, 4 June 1942, YTA, YRG 1, vol. 6, file 466iii.

32. Allan Mitchell to Managers of Edmonton and Prince Rupert Local Offices, 6 July 1942, YTA, YRG 1, vol. 6, file 466iii.

33. H. Mitchell to Clyde Wann, 4 June 1942, NAC, RG 27, vol. 676, file 6-5-75-3.

34. Report to Officer Commanding, R.C.M.P., "G" Division, 31 July 1942, NAC, RG 85, vol. 865, file 8327.

35. Wage Classification Schedules, May 1943, ACE, Main Collection, Misc. Wage-Rates and Personnel, file 22-53. For American wage rates in the north, see Report of Canol Project, L. D. Worsham to District Engineers, Area Engineers, Contractors and Others Concerned, 29 May 1943, plus attachments, ACE, 72-A-3173, Box 18, Box 3.

36. Sidney Shepherd, Foreign Exchange and Foreign Trade in Canada.

37. Agenda Book, April 1944 to September 1944, Wage Rates Established for Construction Operations, April 1944, NAC, RG 36, vol. 112. For a listing of wages at Consolidated Mining and Smelting Company operations at Yellowknife, see Schedule of Wages in the Northwest Territories—Return Form, c. 1945, RG 85, vol. 611, file 2725, Part 3.

38. Foster to Somerville, 8 June 1944, NAC, RG 36/7, vol. 18, file 5-2, pt. 1.

39. Questionnaire answered by Duncan Bath, Peterborough, Ontario.

40. V. C. Nauman to Gunner Swanson, 29 August 1944, NAC, RG 36/7, vol. 14, file 27-4. See the American response, Warren Gilbert to Swanson, 15 August 1944, W. C. Mauman to Major General W. W. Foster, 17 December 1943, NAC, RG 36/7, vol. 14, file 27-4.

41. Colonel F. S. Strong to Major General W. W. Foster, 18 May 1944, NAC,

RG 36/7, vol. 14, file 27-4. The U.S. Army recommended that the Army Exchanges at Whitehorse, Dawson Creek and Edmonton—places where private sources of supply were available—be exempt from the arrangement.

42. Questionnaire answered by J. Miller, London, Ontario; Questionnaire answered by Charles Knott, London Ontario.

43. Order in Council regarding sale of duty free goods to Canadian Nationals at isolated U.S. Army bases, PC 109/9267, 13 December 1944, NAC, RG 36/ 7, vol. 48, file "Privy Council."

44. C. M. Clifford to All Military and Civilian Personnel, 4 December 1943, NA, RG 338, NWSC, Box 10, Office Memos.

45. Questionnaire answered by Alex Forgie, Edmonton, Alberta.

46. Questionnaire answered by Duncan Bath, Peterborough, Ontario.

47. Questionnaire answered by J. Miller, London, Ontario.

48. G. Parkinson, Business Representative to G. B. Henwood, Chairman, Western Labour Board, 7 July 1944, NAC, RG 36/4, vol. 112, Apr. 44-Sept. 44.

49. Annex No. 3 to G-2 Periodic Report No. 108, 6 October 1944, NA, RG 407, Box 32, file 91-DP1-2.1.

50. Questionnaire answered by Vern Kennedy, North Vancouver, British Columbia.

51. Questionnaire answered by J. Miller, London, Ontario.

52. Willis Grafe, *The Summer of 1942, Yukon Style: Surveying on the Alaska Highway*, 30.

53. Questionnaire answered by J. Miller, London, Ontario.

54. Questionnaire answered by Robert and Dell Black,

55. Questionnaire answered by Vernon Kennedy, North Vancouver, British Columbia.

56. Willis Grafe, *The Summer of 1942, Yukon Style: Surveying on the Alaska Highway*, 29.

57. Questionnaire answered by Bernice Lillemo, Edmonton, April 1989.

58. The same thing happens during blizzards and cold snaps on the Canadian prairies and the northern Great Plains, but not as often.

59. Questionnaire answered by Duncan Bath, Peterborough, Ontario.

60. Questionnaire answered by Harvey Hayduk, Edmonton. Each year several drivers are killed in the Peace River region in collisions with moose, usually at night.

61. Questionnaire answered by J. Garbus, Westhaven, Connecticut.

62. Questionnaire answered by Duncan Bath, Peterborough, Ontario.

63. Questionnaire answered by Frank and Agatha Speer, White Rock, British Columbia.

64. Questionnaire answered by A. Forgie, Edmonton, Alberta.

65. Questionnaire answered by Duncan Bath, Peterborough, Ontario.

66. Questionnaire answered by J. Garbus, Westhaven, Connecticut.

67. Questionnaire answered by Robin and Dell Black.

68. Questionnaire answered by J. Garbus, Westhaven, Connecticut.

69. Questionnaire answered by J. Garbus, Westhaven, Connecticut.

70. *North Star Magazine*, November 1944, p. 19.

71. Questionnaire answered by A. Forgie, Edmonton, Alberta. 72 Heath Twichell Collection, letter of 3 April 1942, YTA, Misc. Manuscripts 82/546.

73. Questionnaire answered by Duncan Bath, Peterborough, Ontario.

74. Interview with Ray Talbot, April 1988.

75. Questionnaire answered by Robin and Dell Black.

76. Questionnaire answered by A. Forgie, Edmonton, Alberta.

77. Minutes of Meeting, 10 December 1943, NAC, RG 36/4, vol. 110, vol. 9, Minute Book, June 43-Apr. 44.

78. R. A. Gibson to MacNamara, 1 June 1942, NAC, RG 27, vol. 676, file 6-5-75-5-1.

79. Labour Conditions-Generally, Waterways and District, Alberta, 21 June 1942, NAC, RG 27, vol. 676, file 6-5-75-51.

80. C. J. Rogers to George Black, 20 May 1942, ACE, 72-A3173, Box 15, file 52-1. The problem persisted. See Jeckell to R. A. Gibson, 26 February 1943, YTA, YRG 1, vol. 59, file 34362, pt. 2.

81. G. A. Jeckell to George Simmons, 31 August 1942, YTA, YRG 1, Series 1, Vol. 8, file 476A. See also Controller to R. A. Gibson, 5 March 1943, YTA, YRG

1, Vol. 59, file 34362, file 2.

82. G. A. Jeckell to Gen. W. W. Hoge, 24 July 1942, NAC, RG 91, vol. 61, file 35402; Yukon Consolidated Gold Co. Report for 1942, ibid., vol. 66, file 3525.

83. Canada, Department of Labour, The Labour Gazette offers brief summaries of strikes and lock-outs across Canada, with an indication of the resolution of the conflict. Between 1942 and 1946, the labor conflicts recorded were restricted to the Edmonton area and involved waiters and waitresses and a few small construction companies.

84. Gerard Belanger to Western Wage Labour Board, 19 June 1944, NAC, RG 36/4, vol. 112, Agenda Book, Apr. 44-Sept. 44.

85. Belanger to Western Labour Board, 6 July 1944, NAC, RG 36/4, vol. 112, Agenda Book, Apr.44-Sept.44.

86. V. J. Macklin to H. W. Watts, 22 July 1944, NAC, RG 36/4, vol. 110, Minute Book, May 44 to Apr. 46; Macklin to Belanger, 9 August 1944, Ibid. Belanger pursued the case over the following year, applying to the Western Labour Board, the Regional Labour Board in Vancouver, and the National Labour Board, pointing the sizeable discrepancies in American and Canadian wages and the inappropriateness of existing wages in a boomtown like Whitehorse. See Belanger to National War Labour Board, 19 September 1944, Belanger to Western Labour Board, 20 September 1944, Belanger to Regional Labour Board (Vancouver), 22 September 1944, ibid., vol. 112, Agenda Book, Sept. 44-May 46. The union's request for increased wages was ultimately rejected. Macklin to Belanger, 13 December 1944, RG 36/4, vol. 112, Agenda Book, Sept. 44-May 46.

87. Belanger to Macklin, 22 December 1944, 16 December 1944, 30 December 1944, 3 January 1945, RG 36/4, vol. 112, Agenda Book, Sept. 44-May 46.

88. Garnet Bolton, Whitehorse and District Workers' Union, Local 815 Submission to Western Labour Board, 8 November 1944, NAC, RG 36/4, vol. 112, Agenda Book, Sept. 4 to May 46. As was commonplace, the Western Labour Board claimed that its mandate limited its options on such questions as national discrimination. See Minute Book, May 44—Apr. 46, Macklin to Whitehorse Workers Union, 8 November 1944, ibid., vol. 110.

89. Agenda Book, Sept. 44-May 46, RG 36/4, vol. 112.

90. Submission to the Western War Labour Board, Edmonton, Alberta, 1 October 1943 by S.C. Baxter, General Secretary and Organizer, A.B.W.C., NAC, RG 36/4, vol. 111, vol. 1.

91. Amalgamated Building Workers of Canada to Chairman, Western Labour Board, c. August 1943, NAC, RG 36/4, vol. 111, vol. 1.

92. Minutes of 3 August 1943, ibid., vol. 110, vol. 9, Minute Book, June 43-April 44.

93. Memorandum Presented to the Western Labour Board by the Vancouver, New Westminster and District Building Trades Council, 16 August 1943, NAC, RG 36/7, vol. 11, vol. 1.

94. Winter Precautions and District Circular Letter No. 73, 16 October 1943, NC, RG 112m Entry 54B, Box 15A, HD350.05.

95. P. W. Lambright to Theodore Wyman, Jr., 7 December 1943 [sic. 1942] ACE, 72-A-3173-3.

96. A. W. Klieforth to John Hickerson, 16 September 1943, NA, RG 165, ODP 336, Canada, Section I, case 1-21.

97. Canol Refinery Operations, Activities of Personnel Department, June 1944, NA, RG 338, Box 64.

98. Office of Division Engineer, Staff Meeting, 6 September 1943, NWSC, Reel 10, Conferences.

99. Office of the Division Engineer, Staff Meeting, 15 November 1943, NWSC, Reel 10, Conferences.

100. Special Commissioner's 10th Report, Part 16, Contracts and Employment, 31 March 1944, NAC, RG 22, vol. 107, file 84-32-6, pt. 1.

101. E. W. Davis, District Manager to District Engineer, Whitehorse District, 14 January 1944, NA, RG 338, Box 23, Policy and Procedure.

102. Lathan Smith to District Engineer, United States Engineer Office, 17 May 1943, ACE, Corps of Engineers Collection, Box 418, file 20-15.

103. Lathan Smith to District Engineer, United States Engineer Office, 16 May 1943, ACE, Corps of Engineers Collection, Box 418, file 20-15.

104. Staff Meeting, Dawson Creek, 10 May 1944, NA, RG 338, NWSC, Box 32, file 319.1 (Staff Meeting).

105. *The Alaska Highway: Interim Report of the Committee on Roads,* House Report No. 1705, 79th Congress, 2d Session (Washington: Government Printing Office, 1946), 179.

106. Annex to GS Report No. 20, 3 October 1942 to 10 October 1942, NA, RG 407, Box 6, 91-DCI-2.1, Part 2.

107. Report of Army Intelligence Officers' Conference, New Orleans, 17-19 November 1943, NA, RG 332, NWSC, Box 2.

108. Executive Officer for Labor Relations to R. C. Angstman, 15 January 1944, ACE, 52-A-434.

109. James Connick to J. Gordon Turnbull, 19 February 1944, NA, RG 338, Box 23, Policy and Procedure file.

110. E. C. Johnson to General Reybold, Chief of Engineers, 13 November 1943, ACE, 29-52A434.

111. A. H. Andresen to Chief of Engineers, 18 May 1943, ACE, 29-52A-434.

112. "Northwest Service Command News," *Whitehorse Star* (11 February 1944): 3.

113. George MacLean, Okes Construction Company, Bulletin 62, Termination of Employment, 3 August 1942, NA, RG 59 Decimal File 842.154, Seattle-Fairbanks Highway/450. Trains from Edmonton to Sweetgrass ran only Tuesday and Thursdays. The delivery of men to Fort St. John or Dawson Creek was coordinated with that schedule.

114. NWHS, Reel 10, Conferences, Division Engineer Office, Weekly Staff Meeting, 27 September 1943.

115. E. J. Spielman to Chief of Engineers, 31 May 1944, ACE, 29-52A434. This file deals with the case of George Eastey and Floyd Rinn, who left their jobs with Metcalfe-Hamilton, Kansas City Bridge Companies.

116. Conrad Hage to General Foster, 20 March 1944, NAC, RG 36/7, vol. 18, file 30-1. The report arose out of workers' complaints about their treatment by BPC.

117. John Randolph to Secretary of State, Washington, 6 August 1942, NA, RG 59, Decimal File 842.154, Seattle/Fairbanks Highway/439.

118. F. M. Tyvoll, War Manpower Commission to Charles Hood, U.S.E.D. Labor Relations Department, 27 March 1944, NA, RG 338, Box 23, Policy and Procedures file. The correspondence refers to three plumbers released by Bechtel-Price-Callahan due to a shortage of work.

119. Canol Refinery Operations, Administrative and Clerical report, June 1944, NA, RG 338, Box 64.

120. Questionnaire answered by Duncan Bath, Peterborough, Ontario.

121. Questionnaire answered by Robin and Dell Black, Dundalk, Ontario.

122. Questionnaire answered by J. Garbus, Westhaven, Connecticut.

123. Questionnaire answered by Harvey Hayduk, Edmonton, Alberta.

6 AFTER WORK

To what degree was the workers' time away from their bulldozer, cook hut, typewriter, or machine shop truly their own? A generation ago, the role of leisure time in the life of working people was for the most part ignored by labor historians, who concentrated on the organizational and political aspects of labor activism and ignored the culture of working class life. In recent years, however, there has been a new interest in this aspect of Canadian labor history. Bryan Palmer, starting with *Culture in Conflict*, has placed a new importance on the activities of working people away from the workplace. His research, drawing on the much richer American and British labor historiography, has challenged Canadian labor historians to give a fuller account of working class life, to follow working people from the shop floor into their homes, and to the meeting halls, churches, playing fields, libraries, taverns, and the other places that marked their daily lives. But such studies are still in their infancy.[1]

The phrase leisure or spare time activities suggests that such activities represent freedom, choice, or as one scholar noted, "relatively self-determined activity"[2]—a period when the worker can do as he pleases, free of the control of the boss. Other studies suggest, however, that

SINGSONG.
Photograph taken in a log schoolroom somewhere along the highway, 1943.
Photograph by R. Schubert. Schubert family collection.

they were sometimes used and shaped by management to control and influence the work force, or by the workers as a form of resistance and self-assertion.[3] Rex Lucas, a sociologist studying single-industry towns, has argued that "To the extent that there is active participation, recreational activities are effective agents of social control," though he qualifies this assertion by differentiating between organized activities and "voluntary associations," which serve various roles depending on the ideological, symbolic, social or performance functions of the association.[4] It seems clear that there is a relationship between the nature of the work being performed, the structure of workplace relations and the leisure activities selected by the workers.

The work that has been done on this aspect of working class life in Canada does illustrate the importance of after-work activities in the plans of employers and the lives of workers. Robert Storey's study of the Dofasco Company in Hamilton describes the "package of corporate welfare programs designed to defeat industrial unionism by fostering employee identification with the company." Important among this package were such things as a company magazine, picnics and Christmas parties, and an extensive company-funded recreation program. The goal was simple enough: "to subdue the militancy of workers, to drive down labour costs, and to increase productivity," three goals common to workplace managers.[5] Ian Radforth's examination of the Northern Ontario logging industry in the twentieth century includes an important chapter on camp life. Much as it was for workers in the Northwest during World War II, "the camp was an all encompassing experience." The logging camps, bleak by comparison to highway and pipeline establishments, had virtually nothing to offer in the way of formal recreation. The forest workers were very much on their own in the use and organization of their after-work hours; the absence of "wholesome" activities and decent facilities became, in the early twentieth century, a major target of reformers' criticisms of camp life.[6]

The nature of the evidence for the work experience in the Northwest makes it impossible to subject these theories to quantitative analysis. Applied to these defense projects, these arguments suggest that leisure activities may have been created (or in some cases prohibited) by employers as a means of controlling workers, and that the activities selected by the workers reflect the physical, social, and cultural structure of the workplace. Leisure pursuits may thus illustrate the efforts of managers to create a contented, productive work force and, on the other hand, illustrate workers' reaction to their work, and in this instance, to the war effort in general. It seems very likely that employers viewed recreational activities as an important means of reconciling workers to a harsh work environment, and that the way in which workers selected these activities (to the extent that they were allowed to choose) reflected their attitude to the environment and people of the North.

As soon as the troops and construction workers arrived in the Northwest, managers were looking for ways to fill their spare time with healthy and constructive recreational activities and entertainment. A staff officer, returning from a tour of the CANOL project, assessed the situation:

> Entertainment. So far, the soldiers, both white and black, on the CANOL project, have no means for entertainment. I saw no games of any kind and no movies or other stage entertainment. I do not believe that soldiers working as hard as those men are compelled to work, sometimes as many as fourteen to sixteen hours a day, can maintain a high state of morale without some sort of recreation. Negroes generally laugh, joke or sing while working. I witnessed none of these while I was there.[7]

It was clear to the authorities that if they did not provide some sort of diversion for the workers, the proverbial devil was likely to make work for idle hands, possibly in the form of organized complaints or other counterproductive activities. Recreational kits were quickly sent north. In August 1942, the Special Services Division shipped seventy-five sets of fishing gear and two 16-mm movie projectors with a supply of films north for the use of the troops.[8] Other equipment followed: gymnasium apparatus for a facility being built by a private contractor in Fort St. John, 200 books, twenty-five sets of athletic equipment, and $4,000 for recreational activities in Whitehorse. Thousands of song books and several dozen sets of "orchestra instrument kits" were sent north in December 1942 in time for Christmas celebrations.[9] Photographs taken of the Special Service storeroom in Prince Rupert show a room well stocked with fishing rods and gear, skis, poles and boots, snowshoes, and boxing gloves and equipment.[10]

The task of building the major recreational facilities for the soldiers fell to the U.S. Office of Supply, Special Services Division, whose main obligation was to the military work force, but whose activities usually took in civilian workers in a given area as well. Its plans called for the construction of recreational buildings in Dawson Creek, Whitehorse, Fairbanks, and fifteen smaller rest camps. In other centers, existing buildings were taken over and used for recreation. Each rest camp was to receive a theater and a recreational building, housing a hall/lounge, a post exchange, and a library. Each would also have a 16-mm projector, games, playing cards, 250 books, current periodicals, table tennis equipment, and a radio-phonograph

27. Saturday Night

SATURDAY NIGHT—PRIVATE GEORGE R. FUGITT,
"A" COMPANY, 341ST ENGINEERS, N.D. (1943?).
Photograph by R. Schubert. Schubert family collection.

set. Staffing was also required: Whitehorse was to have the largest
unit—three officers and six enlisted men—while Dawson Creek and
Fairbanks were allocated one officer and three enlisted men each.
The fifteen other camps were to have one officer part-time, two

entertainment directors, and one enlisted man. Where possible, Red Cross personnel were to replace the enlisted men.[11] Not all the facilities were a success: the social club provided for the U.S. troops in Prince Rupert, for example, was "very shabby and inadequate," located in a church basement, without enough space, lighting, or ventilation to be of much use. Local officers took matters into their own hands, got funding from the USO, drummed up volunteers to help with renovations to a barracks building, and created "one of the best developed USO facilities I have seen."[12]

In the larger centers, the local residents helped with recreational activities for the military and civilian workers, partly out of good will and partly in self-defense against a horde of bored, restless men with time on their hands. In the late summer of 1942 the citizens of Whitehorse donated a small building to the Red Cross. Next to the local library, the building was furnished by donations, fixed up by the soldiers, and was made available to anyone interested in playing games, ping-pong, reading, or writing. The local paper invited women to help out with the canteen, in order to lend a "feminine touch" to the clubhouse.[13] As a result there was plenty for the workers to do in their spare time in the town. When Joe Jacquot, a fifteen-year-old Yukoner returning home from school in British Columbia reached Whitehorse in the summer of 1943, he was dumbfounded with the activity both military and civilian.

> There seemed to be lineups for everything. If you wanted to eat in a cafe, you lined up; if you went to the theatre you lined up. As liquor was the only thing rationed line ups were 3 and 4 blocks long. If you went to the dance there were line ups. Gambling houses in tents ran wide open around the clock. Boot leggers had a field day. Moon shiners carried out a thriving business. Every shack in Whitehorse was occupied.[14]

But these amenities existed only in the large centers and in the semi-permanent rest camps. The men and women in the highway and pipeline camps, the majority of the workers during the war, had only occasional access to them. Those who lived in ill-equipped, isolated, often temporary camps had to provide their own amusements. Left to their own devices, the camps fell into a frontier rhythm of drinking and card playing. Even here, though, the guiding hand of authority was present, as the authorities permitted certain activities and

THE LINEUP OUTSIDE THE GOVERNMENT LIQUOR STORE
WAS A PERMANENT FEATURE OF WHITEHORSE DURING THE WAR.
YTA, Preston collection, 85/78 #68.

discouraged others, with a view to preserving order and encouraging productivity.

Gambling was a perennial problem in these camps, where card games, often for high stakes, were endemic. One American soldier, who boasted of having surrendered his sergeant's stripes and being busted to private so he "could be able to take care of my biz," claimed to have sent over $1,100 in winnings to his wife in a period of a few months. He wrote her that "I've kinda been in the money but its indefinite how long it will last. As soon as I'm back in the states things will be slow."[15]

Gambling for profit was prohibited under U.S. military and Canadian criminal law, but the authorities accepted it as inevitable, and within certain limits condoned it. Col. C. M. Clifford of the General Staff Corps circulated information on Canadian gambling regulations, pointing out that it was illegal to keep a common gaming house, to operate a game "for gain, even though the donations made by the players be voluntary," to charge a fee to enter a game, or to have one person maintain a "bank." He made it clear that the U.S. authorities would prosecute those who crossed the line between recreational card games, usually involving small sums of money, and ones organized for profit.[16] There were few objections to friendly games. One RCMP officer noted, "This is practically the only form of amusement for the men on this project, and if stopped would be very depressing on the morale of the men."[17] In Whitehorse, organized bridge evenings were held regularly, and for those not addicted to this game, there was always someone "eager to join you in a game of pinochle, gin-rummy, or cribbage."[18] There was no objection if the participants played for small stakes. Gambling for nickels was considered a harmless form of recreation; playing for large stakes, however, was a possible source of disorder. If a worker lost all his earnings in a poker game, might he not apply for a free ride home or otherwise make a nuisance of himself? And professional gamblers were notoriously bad characters, unwelcome in the Northwest.

Once the civilian workers moved in, however, large-scale gambling continued and even expanded. Many of the workers patronized regular, institutionalized card games. Some even proposed the establishment of casinos in the highway camps, a proposition that horrified the Canadian authorities. George Jeckell, controller for the Yukon, sniffed that such places "would be a mere cloak for gambling dives, and a harbouring place for undesirable characters, male and female."[19]

Although the contractors were reluctant to interfere with all gambling, government officials set limits on it, suppressing organized games as much as they could. In February 1944 there were rumors of rake-offs, supposedly intended for a camp recreation fund, in the Metcalfe-Hamilton, Kansas City Bridge Camp at Watson Lake. The U.S. Engineering Department was hesitant to take action, since this would have meant closing down all gambling, not just the offending game. But Canadian authorities argued that "These camps are definitely American, run by American companies and practically all U.S. personnel. It is better that any gambling be attended to by the U.S.E.D." The matter was settled when the gamblers, learning of the impending crackdown, visited the local RCMP detachment to inquire about their status. Learning that they were under criminal investigation, they immediately quit their jobs and returned to the United

BEER BUST, 1943.
Photograph by R. Schubert. Schubert family collection.

States. The RCMP commented that "anyone desiring to take a rake-off in any future games, will hesitate to do so for fear of the consequences."[20] This was the official line. But men who worked on the highway remember that there were always big-stakes games to be found, especially in the larger centers. A Montreal man who ran a private club in Dawson Creek, was reputed to have made $100,000, mostly from gambling, during the construction period.[21]

Another universal social outlet for the workers was drinking. Although the workers' seemingly insatiable appetite for alcohol was hard to satisfy, generous northern exemptions from the wartime liquor rationing went a long way towards filling the demand. "Beer busts" were routine; so, too, were visits to major centers like Whitehorse, where beer and liquor could be purchased at the government store. But there was never enough to go around, and the small Whitehorse store was under constant siege, with long lineups a familiar sight through the war. The problem was even worse in the isolated camps. One American official noted that "Whisky is expensive, starting at $51 a bottle at Dawson Creek and reaching $100 per bottle at the northern end [of the highway]. This is due, however, to the scarcity of whisky rather than to the presence of a heavy drinking crowd."[22]

Ration cards were mandatory throughout the war, but the ration varied from munificent to reasonably generous. The Whitehorse Army Exchange in 1944 permitted each enlisted man to buy two bottles of beer per day, uncapped so that it could not be hoarded or resold. A case of beer could be purchased once every fifteen days, but only with the permission of the commanding officer. Officers had the same ration, but did not need permission to buy it.[23]

Those who wanted more than this, and many did, as well as those who lived in camps far from the nearest PX, turned to highway bootleggers, a corps of part and full-time entrepreneurs whose numbers are difficult to determine. They were ingenious in their efforts to bring liquor to their customers, hiding it in hollowed-out loaves of bread, smuggling it in buses and maintenance vehicles. The trade was profitable, and despite official attempts to suppress it, did not slacken till the end of the war, when supplies increased, and a smaller work force lessened demand.

Some local residents tried to fill the demand. Frank Riddoch, a barber in Fort Smith, "reputed to be a total abstainer," bought $203 worth of liquor between July 9th and August 10th in 1942. The local RCMP constable watched him buy two bottles of whiskey one day, then went to his home,

> for the purpose of determining whether he still had the liquor in his possession. At the time Riddoch could not even produce the empty bottles. On instructions from N.C.O. I/C Fort Smith Detachment, the writer requested Riddoch to appear before Stip[endiary] Magistrate Dr. J. A. Urquhart...Riddoch could not give a satisfactory explanation...Liquor Permit No. 1740 made out in favour of Frank Riddoch, was surrendered to the Magistrate and the subject was placed on the Interdiction List for a period of three years. It is quite obvious that Riddoch has been trafficing liquor to the American soldiers, and the above course was taken to curtail it.[24]

Leaving workers to their own devices seemed generally to end in drinking, gambling, and other activities the managers considered counterproductive. They wanted instead to provide more healthy distractions by means of organized entertainment, particularly the shows put on by the United States Service Organization, a charitable organization based in New York. The USO operated worldwide during the war, carrying American humor, music, and popular culture generally to American troops wherever they were stationed. Some first-rank Hollywood stars—Bob Hope is the one best remembered—volunteered for USO tours.[25] Unfortunately for the workers on the northwest defense projects, the region lacked the high profile and glamour of other theaters of war—the troops and civilian workers had not after all been under enemy fire—and most of the big stars passed it by. Ingrid Bergman did stop off at Prince Rupert during a whirlwind tour of the West Coast and Alaska, but most of the task of entertaining the workers was left to an overworked band of lesser known performers.

The first USO performance in Whitehorse came about by accident, when in October 1942 bad weather forced the plane carrying USO Campshows Overseas Unit No. 17, en route to Alaska, to land in the town. The owner of the local movie theater turned his facility over to the troupe, which staged two performances for overflow crowds of military and civilian workers and local residents. The antics of singers, tumblers, a magician, and the star performer—"blonde, beautiful Carol Winters"—were welcomed by people starved for live professional entertainment.[26] Later on, other USO units made regular visits to the town.

Working for the USO in the Northwest was a far cry from Hollywood or Broadway. One group spent two weeks in January 1943 traveling with a truck convoy on the road between Whitehorse and Fairbanks, punching through the snowdrifts that often covered the highway. In fourteen days they put on seventeen shows. Some were in camps that had electricity; here they put on a full perfor-· mance—comedy, a magic show, and music. In other places, like Destruction Bay and Beaver Creek, there was no electricity, so the entertainment consisted of an extended magic show.[27] A 1944 production, appropriately entitled "Frosty Follies of '44," consisting of eleven servicemen and four USO performers, traveled over 5,000 miles on a grueling tour throughout the Northwest Service Command. The group put on sixty-three shows in eighty-three days, covering all the highway communities, military stations in Alaska, communities along the coast, as well as Prince George and Edmonton.[28] Most USO performers felt that the rapturous response they received from bored and lonely workers and servicemen made up for the rigors of the tour.

Some of the best entertainment came from local amateurs. In December 1942, soldiers from black units stationed in Whitehorse staged an "all-colored review," including singers, comedians, dancers, jitterbuggers (the jitterbug was then a novelty to white audiences), and "a swing trio that had the house tapping and swaying in time to its rhythm." An imitation of the popular "Amos 'n Andy" radio program was particularly well received. The performers' enthusiasm was heightened by the fact that their commanding officer had offered the ultimate highway prize—a furlough.[29]

The U.S. Army also sent military bands into the Northwest to entertain the workers. The bands gave regular performances along the Alaska Highway, which were always well received. An outdoor concert in Whitehorse, given in April 1942, attracted a large civilian crowd, undeterred by bitterly cold weather; American military personnel were later treated to a longer concert indoors.[30] In isolated areas like Camp Canol, however, such treats were rarer, and the men had to provide their own band music. In December 1943, Major J. B. McKenzie of Special Services visited the camp in advance of band equipment purchased by the contractor for use by the men and organized a small ensemble, which was labeled the "furthest north American military band."[31]

Ironically, as the military crisis in the Northwest eased, the number and variety of shows that reached the region increased. This was partly due to improved transportation but was also the result of an official belief that entertainment was essential to help dispel the workers' growing boredom in the postemergency period. Officials were always anxious that the shows be of the highest possible quality, for the workers, by all accounts, looked forward to them, and were bitterly disappointed if they were not up to standard. Heath Twichell, reporting on a performance in the Fort St. John sector, recommended a balanced program of four acts, and urged the actors to "use up to date material." He also noted that "Music, slight of hand work, acrobatics and good comedy skits are preferred by soldiers." In Dawson Creek, Frank de Scipio reported preferences for the "slapstick type" comedy, and "swing and semi-classic" music. He noted that one visiting group was somewhat of a flop; the men liked the comedian, but found the accordion player listless, the singer pretentious, and the Master of Ceremonies "flat due to the fact that he constantly told they [sic] audience how good they were going to be and did not come up to expectations." All camp commanders would have agreed with Scipio's conclusion that "Live entertainment is well received and more of it would be enthusiastically accepted."[32]

Naturally, the soldiers and construction crews were enthusiastic about female entertainers, particularly ones who resembled Betty Grable, whose photo—racy in the forties, but almost austere by modern standards—adorned tens of thousands of footlockers throughout the war. Sending women into the midst of isolated, overwhelming male camps raised some questions in the minds of tour organizers and other officials. Some feared that their presence would only frustrate workers and cause unrest. The authorities adopted an ambivalent policy, bringing female entertainers north while fretting about the reception they would get. When USO Show Overseas Unit #100 toured the Alaska Highway in 1943, they were issued detailed instructions that reveal the official uncertainties. The women were advised that this was the first time "we have had girls on the highway …whether or not we continue to have shows of this nature depends entirely on the success of your tour." They were warned to dress warmly, to expect rustic accommodations, unreliable performance schedules, poor performing conditions, and mediocre food. But throughout all the instructions ran a subtext of concern about the sexual aspect of the trip:

> On the questions of the girls wearing long or short wardrobe, it has been decided to leave it up to their own judgment. Long wardrobe would really be best, as the set up here is much different from the States. Some of these boys are in remote places and haven't been out of the rough for a long time.[33]

On the other hand, the female performers were reminded that they were in the Northwest for the purpose of alleviating discontent and raising morale with a view to increased productivity and efficiency. Moreover, the women were enjoined to put on a brave front: "members of the troupe should never complain about it if they wish to have favourable effect on morale. Your duty while on tour is to lift morale and if you complain about conditions the result will be just the opposite."[34]

There was some justification for this official ambivalence, for the female performers occasionally encountered sexual harassment from men who saw their arrival as an opportunity for a display of machismo. When late in 1943 USO Camp Shows Overseas Unit #112 visited Big Delta, Alaska, the performance was followed by an incident that was described by Carl Mondor, the unit's manager:

> Following the show we were invited for drinks at the officers quarters. I sensed a situation that is quite common with some officers in that part of the world and that was the idea to get rid of the two single fellows on the show, get the girls drunk and force them. I told the girls of this and after a few minutes at the party the three of us beat a hasty retreat to their quarters. They were afraid to be alone and asked me to stay with them until the party was over. B___ saw that we had left and invited the officers all over to the quarters. He had been telling the C.O. (a Major with the brain and ability of a latrine orderly) all sorts of lies about us and he came breaking into the girls' quarters with a couple of his officers. He saw me in the room with the girls (all three of us, by the way, were fully dressed) and demanded that they be allowed in there too. The girls asked him very courteously to please leave. He shouted an obscenity about our morals, grabbed me by the arm, threw me across the room and threatened to throw me in the guard house.[35]

Nothing more seems to have come from this incident of drunken boorishness, but it illustrated the sort of disorder that the authorities feared would accompany women into the region.

Of course, the entertainers were workers, too, a fact overlooked by soldiers and civilian workers who tended to compare the apparent glamour of performers' lives with their own boring routines. The lot of the entertainer, male or female, was not an easy one. Small troupes, generally of half a dozen or so, found themselves thrown together for weeks on end, traveling constantly, living in makeshift quarters, and performing before audiences which, though generally appreciative, sometimes gave the impression of a group of hungry lions eyeing a shipment of fresh meat. On occasion, artistic temperament led to squabbling among the performers. In November 1943, personal animosities flared up in Unit #112, which was traveling along the Alaska Highway. Hostilities caused by battles over the censorship of objectionable material (generally about how much sex could be put into the jokes and repartee) and the strains of travel erupted into nasty exchanges. After a series of quarrels, Ballard and Rae, an "eccentric tumbling act and pro tem co-master and mistress of ceremonies," were demoted, much to their rage. They complained long and bitterly and created scenes, leading Capt. B. C. Miller of the Adjunct General's office to note that

> Their subsequent actions went far beyond mere pique, and are considered inimical to the best interests of the Special Service Division, the USO and the military mission of this command. It is believed that the splendid record of USO Camp Shows is best served by the elimination of performers who, by ungentlemanly or unladylike comportment, reflect discredit upon the fine organization which they serve, or upon their fellow entertainers.[36]

The audiences often had different ideas on what constituted "entertainment" than their superiors did. While officers talked of slapstick comedy and acrobatics, the men clearly preferred cheese-cake and risqué jokes. In June 1943 a comedian named Russ Brown opened the show for USO Unit #56. His off-color humor quickly drove away the few women in attendance as well as an Oblate priest who was in the audience. The priest later complained to Brown about the language used, and asked him to stop saying "God damn it." Rebuffed, the priest wrote to the USO asking them to discipline the man. Brown's humor—he sang of having "caught a cold getting out of a warm bed and going home," and (in a parody of Bing Crosby's Christmas hit) "dreaming of a white mistress"—had been enthusiastically received by the men in the audience, belying the priest's contention that "The men themselves think that it was out of place and an insult to their character." Senior officials promised to "obviate a recurrence of objectionable entertainment," though it is not clear whether they actually tried to make the tone of the USO shows more like that of a Catholic parish social; one suspects that they actually took no action at all.

But such entertainments were only an occasional diversion. For many men, part of the attraction of working in the Northwest was the call of one of North America's last frontiers, a famous mecca for big-game hunters and sportsmen. Dropped in the midst of a vast wilderness, many workers were anxious to hunt and fish. As always, there were bureaucratic roadblocks. As foreign nationals, Americans were required to buy a nonresident hunting license—in the Yukon, the cost was $25 to $75—before they could legally head into the bush to shoot the local fauna. Moreover, since there were thousands of potential hunters, officials feared the possibility of a serious depletion of wildlife stocks.

Brigadier W. M. Hoge first raised the matter of hunting permits for Americans in April 1942. The RCMP had indicated, unofficially, that it would not require U.S. servicemen to have the necessary licenses. Hoge rejected this arrangement, arguing that the men would hunt and fish illegally, "which will sooner or later result in a conflict with local officials and then it will be too late to ask for special consideration."[37] He suggested that the licenses should be limited in number and used as rewards for diligent work.

When J. Pierrepont Moffatt, the American ambassador in Ottawa, took Hoge's suggestion to the Canadian authorities,[38] the reaction was less than enthusiastic. Canadian officials worried that issuing licenses would result in overhunting and complained that while Alaskan authorities were limiting hunting by service personnel there,[39] Canadians were being asked to open their wilderness to American hunters.[40] It was hard to ignore Hoge's argument about the inevitability of illegal hunting, though that was an unusual basis for amending the regulations.

The situation was further confused when comments came in from the governments of the Yukon and British Columbia. In Dawson City, Controller Jeckell recommended granting a limited number of hunting licenses to unit commanders, subject to Yukon game regulations,[41] an idea that would have involved American officials in the enforcement of Yukon hunting laws.[42] The government of British Columbia was not prepared to loosen its regulations, except for fishing, arguing that a "concession with respect to the hunting of big

MOOSE SHOT AT CAMP.
Anchorage Museum, b84.4.51.

game or game birds would be very detrimental and would seriously affect the game resources of the district in question which would upset many years of planned game conservation work in that portion of the Province."[43] Alberta, on the other hand, made no objection, and authorized American servicemen to hunt birds and big game freely in the province, subject to existing regulations.[44]

Things seemed hopelessly confused, with provincial and territorial policies contradictory, and advocates of conservation clashing with supporters of a policy of open hunting; as one observer commented, "In short, it was a beautiful mess."[45] The matter was resolved for the Yukon in July 1942, when the Territorial Council amended its game ordinance to permit U.S. military and civilian personnel to buy the cheaper resident hunting licenses.[46] The provision was soon extended to Canadian service personnel stationed in the territory,[47] and later to nonresident Canadian civilians as well.[48]

One factor limiting hunting in the Northwest was the reluctance of many men to venture far into the wilderness in search of game. As C. K. LeCapelain, Canadian liaison officer to the American authorities, noted,

> very few men will wander far from the beaten track without a guide owing to the fear of being lost. So that, although there may be intensive killing within a restricted area while there are these large numbers of men being employed in the Yukon, the game herds as a whole will probably not permanently suffer.[49]

The situation in the Northwest Territories was quite different. Here, large game preserves, including the Mackenzie Mountain preserve, were off-limits for hunting to all but status Indians. Regulations restricted the hunting rights of many non-Natives in the Northwest Territories; only those resident before May 1938 had full privileges.[50] Men carrying firearms into the country, even if properly registered for use in Canada, were required to surrender them to the RCMP until they left.[51] In September 1942 Lt. Col. Thomas Adcock, zone commander for the Forth Smith area, requested hunting rights for his troops, claiming that "recreational facilities and fresh meat are going to be scarce for the officers and men this winter. The men are in a strange climate, a long way from home."[52] In this case the Americans did not get their way. The Canadian position was that

> in the Northwest Territories the need for conserving the relatively scanty supply of game for the support of the native population is so great that relaxation of our policy in this regard might do serious harm.[53]

Such were the regulations; the reality was quite different. Soldiers and construction workers, particularly in the isolated camps, were going to hunt, regardless of what governments said. There were few RCMP officers in the territories—six to eight constables and a corporal at Whitehorse, and two more at Teslin in 1942—and they seldom had time to patrol the bush.[54] The Yukon had not a single game officer to enforce its regulations, making them ineffective on the ground. American authorities, ever sensitive to accusations that they were abusing Canadian hospitality, made some effort to supervise military and civilian personnel, but with little effect. The reality was expressed in a letter from a private in the 74th Engineers, intercepted by the censor:

> We get a lot of fresh meat up here. The fellows shot two moose & a mountain goat here last week. We ate all of it. The meat tastes pretty good. The Canadian Govt. has put out orders that we are not supposed to do any hunting or fishing up here. But who are they?[55]

Who indeed?

Long-time Yukon residents were distressed by the obvious disregard for the land and its animals displayed by many Americans. Whatever the death toll of game might have been, there was no doubt that many Americans were gun-happy and would shoot anything that moved, and a few things that did not. Whitehorse residents complained that all the wildlife along the river in the vicinity of town had been slaughtered or frightened away by the Americans; even the ubiquitous ravens had disappeared. Although most of the big game animals shot were eaten in the work camps, enough unused carcasses were found along the roads and near the airfields to lend credence to these complaints.[56]

Where game was scarce, civilian and military workers took potshots at other targets. In 1924, Whitehorse citizens had built a

"Robert Service Camp" at Whitehorse Rapids, including a pavilion and kitchen facilities. In 1943 the building was vandalized, the walls and roof riddled with bullet holes. A newspaper article on the incident concluded,

> Canadian citizens are not permitted to carry revolvers and discharge same at will. We certainly can suggest some better places for bullets than piercing the walls of a free public institution. It is high time that stricter measures are enforced concerning the carrying and use of firearms.

Inspector Matheson of the RCMP, who saw the item before publication, suggested that this passage, which seems mild enough under the circumstances, had too anti-American a tone, and the editor struck it out. The inspector did suggest, however, that tighter controls on the possession of firearms were required.[57]

The reaction of the American authorities to this incident, as so often happened during the war, was to take action to dispel any bad publicity or offended feelings that might arise from it. In May 1943, orders were issued requiring the registration of all firearms in private hands. These were to be securely stored in padlocked lockers and could be taken out only for the purpose of hunting. Civilians and soldiers were reminded of the necessity of obeying Yukon hunting regulations, particularly the prohibition on discharging firearms within a mile of the highway—a regulation routinely ignored by locals and nonresidents alike.[58]

Wherever possible, those who flouted the game laws were arrested and prosecuted and their firearms confiscated. The cases, which involved both military and civilian personnel, covered a wide range of infractions: shooting moose out of season, taking potshots at muskrats, possessing illegally taken pelts, and hunting without a license. In June 1943, for example, Captain H. L. Goodman of the USED shot and killed a small bear with his service revolver. It was hardly an act of great marksmanship: "The bear which had been shot was a pet of the residents of the McCrae area and was so tame that it would eat out of the hands of some of the persons in that district." Men in the area considered Goodman's action "very unsportsman-like," and one of them reported him to the authorities. Goodman was

PFC PAUL A. ALTEMAR, "A" COMPANY, 341ST ENGINEERS,
WASHING THE COMPANY'S PET BEARS, SUMMER 1943.
Photograph by R. Schubert. Schubert family collection.

unrepentant, berating the informant as "yellow, stool pigeon," and went so far as to "threaten bodily harm to the informant."[59]

Some of the hunters did as much damage to themselves as to the wildlife. With no knowledge of the region, a number of men wandered into the bush and became lost. Since officials had a responsibility for the safety for their men, and since searches in the bush were costly and time consuming, regulations were passed to protect hunters from their own inexperience. Procedures set down for the Dawson Creek district required all hunters to apply for a recreational leave ticket before they left camp. In addition, they had to produce a hunting license and a firearms registration permit. They also had to provide "evidence that some member of the party is entirely familiar with the area to be hunted. It is expected that this individual will be a native with previous experience in the woods."[60]

Similar efforts were made to regulate the use of boats on the lakes and rivers of the regions after a number of drownings and other accidents had occurred.[61]

In general, the Mounted Police and the Canadian authorities agreed that this system worked reasonably well. Most of the U.S. officers took their responsibilities as special game wardens seriously and did their best to supervise their men. Since hunting was a major form of recreation, most men were hesitant to risk losing their hunting rights. Control over hunting also gave the authorities a useful means of reward and punishment:

> Hunting permits were issued on the "reward" system, any infractions of the Game Ordinance observed by the officers resulted in the cancellation of the individual's license by the Officer. As a reward for long hours of work men were sometimes given a day or two's leave and allowed to go hunting, as a punishment any infraction of Army discipline or of the Game Ordinance, their leave was automatically cancelled, and their hunting activities, of course, restricted.[62]

In the first year of construction in the Yukon, 601 hunting permits were issued, with estimated animal kills of 100 moose, 60 bear, 100 caribou, 150 sheep, and 50 goats. Inspector D. J. Martin, commanding "G" Division of the RCMP, stated "I am satisfied that there has been no excessive killing of Game Animals by the United States Army in the Yukon Territory."[63]

This sanguine opinion was not shared by many local residents, who felt that there had been gross overhunting of local game stocks. Rumors and accusations about a great slaughter of game along the highway and pipeline routes circulated widely during the war and remain part of the mythology of the northwest defense projects. While it is impossible to quantify the impact of the hunting that took place, it seems clear that considerable overhunting did occur, particularly in the southwest Yukon. This was the major reason why the Yukon government withdrew a large area from Native and non-Native hunting altogether, and made it into the Kluane Game Sanctuary. It is worth noting, however, that an experienced observer attributed the scarcity of game near the highway to a different reason:

The officers of the leading units who pushed forward far ahead of the balance of the regiment expressed themselves as very surprised at the scarcity of game in practically a virgin country. This, of course is in my opinion chiefly due to the fact that the noise of their heavy equipment, such as "Bulldozers," "Carryalls" heavy trucks, etc., etc., had frightened all the game away long before these units actually arrived on the scene. . . [L]ocal Indians...stated that they had observed moose moving northwest through Lake Creek valley (through which the highway now passes) in droves for three weeks before the first Army caterpillars arrived on the scene.[64]

There are other indications that the depletion of game may have been worse than the authorities admitted. The *Northwest Newscast,* the official U.S. Army newspaper distributed along the highway, observed in April 1943,

The hunting season in this territory is officially closed until the first of September, 1945. Therefore, the promiscuous hunting of game that has been occurring in the past few weeks is unlawful. Any person who violates these regulations is subject to heavy fines. Mr. Higgins, the territorial agent in Whitehorse, requests all personnel in this area to help preserve game.[65]

Whether the hunting was regulated or "promiscuous," it is noteworthy that the Canadian authorities moved quickly to accommodate American requests for hunting privileges, further evidence of official desire to keep the workers happy. The Northwest, unfortunately, was to pay a price—how high is not clear—as animals along the construction corridors were overhunted or driven from the region.

For the men and women stationed in the larger centers— Edmonton, Dawson, Fort St. John, Whitehorse—off-duty life was quite different from that in the more isolated camps. Here, a wide variety of organized and informal social, sporting, and recreational activities were available, many of them reflecting American recreational patterns.

Chief among these was softball, which became a standard activity in the towns. Games ranged from informal pickup affairs in partially cleared fields to well-organized leagues and regional tournaments played in first-class facilities. A small league already existing in Whitehorse when the soldiers arrived in 1942 attracted dozens of eager American participants; in May of that year, an invitation was extended to the American army to form teams for league play.[66] The Americans proved to be tough competitors, winning most of their games against the hometown team, the Whitehorse Bears.[67] With troops regularly moving in and out of town, it was difficult to set up a stable league,[68] but by July 1942 the Whitehorse Softball League consisted of six teams: 691st Medicals, Military Police, Whitehorse Bears, 18th Engineers, Construction Workers.[69] Some small centers had teams as well. A team from Carcross made several trips into Whitehorse to play and challenged local teams to make the fifty-mile journey to Carcross for a series of return matches.[70] The games were extremely popular. A doubleheader involving the Carcross team and two Whitehorse squads attracted over 500 spectators; crowds of 200 to 250 were commonplace for league games.[71]

When the initial construction phase ended, it was possible to organize a more regular schedule of league and exhibition games. The Whitehorse league included teams from the Royal Canadian Air Force, Northwest Service Command, Standard Oil, the Whitehorse community, and civilians from the Northwest Service Command.[72] The 1944 league schedule called for as many as eight games per night, made possible by the eponymous "midnight sun," and utilizing town fields and softball diamonds built by the American military.[73] Also by that year, an International Army Softball League was in operation along the highway. Over 1,550 spectators turned out on July 4, 1944, to a battle between the Whitehorse All-Stars and the Dawson Creek All-Stars.[74] The Whitehorse team, bidding for the Northwest Service Command softball championship, journeyed to Skagway and other communities for games.[75] Such events were highlights of the social and athletic year.

Other activities were organized by private contractors and the Special Services for the less athletic. Night school classes and theater groups were organized, libraries set up, and movies shown. Newspapers, including the Northwest Service Command's *Northwest Newscast*,[76] several camp and community newsletters, and a regional radio broadcasting system provided entertainment and kept people abreast of current news and events.

None of these activities, however, addressed one of the workers' major complaints—the lack of immediate contact with the outside world. In 1942, there were newspapers in the major communities,[77] but the smaller places had to make do with papers brought in days late from outside. The same was true of radio. There was emergency coverage of sorts through the RCMP, the airfields and bush pilots, and in the Northwest Territories, through the Hudson's Bay Company, and there was of course an extensive military network. Some private citizens had shortwave sets. But there was no civilian radio broadcast service outside the major centers. The situation in regard to movies was equally third-hand. Once, during the salad days of the gold rush, when Dawson City was on the North American vaudeville and movie circuit, Yukon residents were treated to the best products of the American entertainment industry.[78] But by the 1920s the region had fallen off the circuit, and northwesterners had to wait months, if not years, for popular films to reach them.

All this was changed by the war. Military and civilian workers complained about their isolation, and demanded better newspaper, radio, and movie service. This was, of course, an era when movie going was far more frequent that it is now; weekly attendance in the U.S. roughly equalled the entire population of the country, and lack of movies was the equivalent of the disappearance of television today. The managers supported these demands. They naturally wanted to keep the work force happy, but they also realized that the absence of current news and entertainment media made it more difficult to keep information about the war constantly before the workers. The valuable propaganda tools of press, radio, and film were unavailable to managers anxious to translate wartime zeal into longer work hours, greater output, and fewer complaints about working conditions.

Little could be done to rectify this situation during the first few hectic months of construction. In September 1942, however, Captain Palmer Holmes of the U.S. Special Services Office visited the Northwest to draw up a plan for the "provision of radio and phonograph equipment with records, movies and winter equipment for the entire command."[79] During the following year, a wide variety of media services were provided throughout the region.

In 1943, a regional film distribution center was established in Edmonton to serve the highway, airfield, and pipeline camps. The

SARGENT FRANK S. HERMAN AND MISS H. DAKKEN AT WORK
IN THE FILM LIBRARY OF THE MILITARY SERVICES BRANCH,
EDMONTON DISTRIBUTION, MORALE, PLANS, AND TRAINING FILM
EXCHANGE, JULY 1944.
NA 111-SC323292.

first Edmonton program specifically targeted at Northwest Division workers opened on December 5, 1943, with a showing of a newsreel, a Popeye cartoon, and *Second Chorus*, starring Fred Astaire. Only Northwest Division employees, civilians and military, were permitted to purchase the twenty-five cent tickets. Following the opening show, movie nights were held on each Sunday, Tuesday, and Thursday.[80] Similar programs were circulated throughout the Northwest.

Private contractors also played an important role in bringing movies to the Northwest. Shortly after construction began, a theater was opened in Dawson Creek. Faced with the chronic overcrowding of the movie house in Whitehorse, Metcalfe-Hamilton, Kansas City Bridge Company loaded up three trucks with projection equipment and construction materials and carried the material to McCrae, just south of Whitehorse, where a new 500-seat theater opened in September 1943; the first show was Irving Berlin's *This is the Army*.[81] The U.S. Army did not immediately erect a movie house of its own. It did, however, make 16-mm projectors available to individual units based in the community and provided a regular flow of suitable films. In October 1944, a new motion picture theater was opened for headquarters staff in Whitehorse, with two shows on Monday, Wednesday, Thursday, Friday, and Sunday evenings; a second War Department Theater was operated at McCrae with a single show every night except Tuesday and Thursday. With the installation of the new service, the army withdrew most of the other 16-mm projectors, except those at the hospital and one other downtown location.[82] The theaters were open to all military personnel, their families and civilians "residing within the limits of the post, camp or station." With the installation of a 35-mm projector, admission charges of seventeen cents Canadian (eleven cents for children) were established.[83]

The extension of the motion picture network to the camps took a little longer. Not all of the camps had the facilities—electricity and a suitable meeting hall—for a show. By December 1943, however, roving operators were bringing their equipment and films into the isolated camps, providing much-needed recreation for workers and managers alike. The films were, not surprisingly, more enthusiastically received in the camps than in the larger centers, where other facilities and distractions were close at hand. In December 1943, Einar Fekjar delivered the first movie—Gary Cooper in *Pride of the Yankees*—to the line camps along the CANOL pipeline, inaugurating a service which would continue throughout the remainder of the war.[84]

Movies served more than a purely recreational function. During the war, both the United States and Canada produced dozens of films in which entertainment and propaganda were used to secure and increase the public commitment to the war effort. Health and hygiene films, particularly the memorable warnings against venereal disease, were regularly shown, and attendance at these as well special propaganda films was often compulsory. In October 1943, all employees of Northwest Division in Edmonton were required to watch a thirty-minute film called *Baptism by Fire*, which was accompanied by introductory and closing remarks by local officers.[85] The Canadians saw the value of such films, and in January 1945 the RCAF inaugurated a series of war films entitled *Why We Fight.*[86]

Workers throughout the region were also provided with a steady supply of books and current periodicals by the Special Services officer attached to the U.S. Engineers in Edmonton, who arranged to have them be shipped to highway and pipeline "outposts."[87] In the larger centers, the workers could use the facilities of local libraries, reading rooms established by the Red Cross, by government, by the construction companies, or by the Special Services Branch. There is unfortunately no record of the titles available in these libraries, but it is likely that the selection was carefully controlled and emphasized patriotic themes.[88]

Newspapers also played an important part in the tasks of information, entertainment, and propaganda. In the larger centers, the local papers, subject to wartime censorship regulations, met these objectives throughout the war. The *Whitehorse Star,* for example, published a regular column entitled "NWSC News," dealing with construction and military topics. A few entrepreneurs started new papers in the rapidly expanding highway communities. British Columbia's joyously outspoken "Ma" Murray, for example, founded a paper with her husband in Fort St. John to capitalize on the growing market. A number of agencies printed small papers for their employees: the Alaskan Division of the U.S. Air Transport Command published *North Star,* and the Dawson Creek headquarters of the NWSC produced *The Bulldozer.*[89] Some of the more permanent construction camps, such as the ones at Fort Smith and Camp Canol (Norman Wells), printed small news sheets emphasizing local items and patriotic themes as well.

The primary objective of these papers, large and small, was to entertain and inform, and at the same time remind their readers that, in the ubiquitous phrase, there was a war on, and that there was a connection between their hardships and the sacrifices of the servicemen overseas.

The December 11, 1943, issue of the *Canol Piper,* for example, included items on the activities of a volunteer safety group, the formation of a band, the disappearance of a slide rule, local gossip, poetry, announcements of movies, and upcoming social activities. Beyond the frivolity, which sounds very much like the social round of a frontier mining camp, were short reports from the battle lines and a lengthy story entitled "Something to Think About." The story dealt with an apocryphal pilot, now missing in action. The heart-wrenching tale had a moral:

> Too much for you, all of this? But it really happened last night just like that. You know…if people could only understand it, if they would just grind deep into their thinking the stark, terrible reality of it, every petty selfish interest would be swept away. They would sacrifice anything and everything just to make themselves worthy of that boy…He died last night, you see. Let's think of that the next time we gripe about our job.[90]

The connection between recreation, in this case a newspaper, and the requirements of management were seldom clearer.

The major wartime paper in the region was the *Northwest Newscast*, which was distributed to civilian and military camps throughout the Northwest. While most of the stories were lifted from the American military news services, there was considerable coverage of regional events and activities. The paper tried to foster a sense of community among highway workers by including generous amounts of local news. Regular columns with bowling, hockey and baseball scores, movie announcements and stories about regional personalities competed for space with accounts of fighting in Europe and the Pacific, political, sporting and social news from the home front, and a plethora of patriotic items. The news was reasonably current and was much appreciated by soldiers and civilian workers.

The news media also served to send information in the other direction. The northwest defense project was a newsworthy part of the North American defense effort, particularly during the first two years of the war. Journalists, filmmakers and radio announcers traveled along the highway, visited the pipeline camps, and flew into the airfields of the Northwest Staging Route. They filed hundreds of stories, most built around the "Man Against the Wilderness" theme, to newspapers and radio stations in the south. Films about the Alaska

Highway featured prominently in several American newsreels during 1942, though interest waned after that time. Richard Finnie, a noted northern filmmaker, shot thousands of feet of footage about the Alaska Highway and the CANOL pipeline, and produced two films, *The Alaska Highway* and *Canol*. They were not released during the war, largely due to the political controversy that surrounded northern defense projects after 1943, and were only declassified in the early 1980s.

The sacrifices made by northern workers figured heavily in stories from the north, serving to remind those in southern Canada and the lower forty-eight states of the work being done in the region. U.S. Army officials kept the patriotic information flowing throughout the war. In February 1944, Sgt. George Meyers, an army staff correspondent for *YANK* magazine, visited Whitehorse to prepare a story on the Northwest Service Command (NWSC).[91] Later that year, Hannah Grosvenor was named unit reporter for headquarters, Northwest Service Command. Each branch and section was urged to designate a subreporter to forward "items of interest" through channels for possible use by the Public Relations Division.[92] In this fashion, the southern media, particularly outlets in the hometowns of northern workers, would be supplied with a steady stream of reminders about the activities of the workers on the northern frontier.

But the medium with the most immediate impact on the troops and workers in the Northwest was radio. Initially, the American government had built a radio and telephone system in the region for military purposes, but as the initial sense of crisis faded, these facilities became available for entertainment purposes and were soon tied into the Canadian Broadcasting Corporation and the U.S. Mutual networks. As early as September 1942, the gala opening of the Tita Theatre in McCrae, near Whitehorse, was carried over both networks. Robert Service, the famous poet of the Yukon, was slated to give a speech, but could not attend; his message was taped in Vancouver and rebroadcast.[93]

Eventually a regional network was created, based in Edmonton, which provided extensive news coverage and entertainment for the Alaska Highway and CANOL camps. By the end of the war it was providing live coverage of major events including major league

T/5 VAN GELDIER AT THE MIKE, AND T/5 DEW
AT CONTROLS OF STATION CFWF, SPECIAL SERVICE, WHITEHORSE.
NA (U.S.), 111-SC 323150.

baseball and National League hockey games.[94] In February 1944, CFWH went on the air in Whitehorse, the first Army Expeditionary Forces radio station in the Northwest Services Command, operated "by and for the soldiers of this district." The station operated three hours per day during the week, four on Saturday, and eight on Sunday. Programming included "news while it is still news," music, military shows, and popular national shows broadcast without the commercials. As the staff gained experience, more local programming was added to the schedule, including live music, phone-in shows, and music request shows—a popular request was for "I'll be Glad When You're Dead You Rascal You," dedicated anonymously to the sergeants.

Radio, like the newspapers, was used by the military and civilian authorities as a means of boosting morale, encouraging a greater work effort, selling war savings bonds, and publicizing government policies in general. The Canadian government, the Canadian Broadcasting Corporation, and the Whitehorse station, for instance, ran a program called "The Servicemen's Forum," which the *Northwest Newscast* noted "should be of special interest to our ally Canada as well as to all servicemen now stationed here."[95] The NWSC Public Relations branch created a series aimed at encouraging Canadian-American friendship. Called "Welcome, American," it was produced at station CJCA in Edmonton and was broadcast throughout the western provinces and the Yukon in February 1944.[96] During the war, the idea of having an American write a series on why Canadians should welcome Americans into their midst seemed neither inappropriate or unusual.

Although the men and women who worked on the northwest defense projects were not an unusually pious group, the army, the civilian officials, and the churches were concerned for their spiritual well-being. The armed forces had always regarded religion as an important part of military life, though there were limits to official enthusiasm—as late as 1943, requests from various denominations for travel assistance or even permission to use the highway and military roads, were routinely denied.[97]

Beginning with the first arrival of American troops in the Yukon in the spring of 1942, the local clergy acknowledged their Christian responsibility to the newcomers. The Anglicans had long dominated the religious life of the Yukon, and they were well-placed to minister to the spiritual needs of the highway workers. Missions at Whitehorse (where the Bishop of the Yukon requested the use of an unused United Church building for additional services), Carcross, and Teslin were opened for civilian and military personnel. In Whitehorse, the Anglicans welcomed the Americans to their regular services and turned over the famous Old Log Church to the U.S. Army chaplains for evening prayers. In 1943, the Anglican Missionary Society provided additional money for a missionary at Kluane Lake. The American servicemen who attended these services must have experienced a certain amount of theological shock; few of the Americans, especially the black troops, were Episcopalians, and most were accustomed to a good deal more liveliness in their religion than they found in the churches of the Yukon. Nevertheless, even the austerities of Anglicanism were welcomed by those in need of spiritual comfort.

Providing church services in the communities was much easier than carrying the gospel to the remote camps. Radio provided a partial answer, and various denominations had regular programs on the radio stations. But this lacked the personal touch, and the principal denominations were compelled to send itinerant clergy to the camps on a regular basis. Father William O'Boyle, a Roman Catholic chaplain, traveled along the Alaska Highway visiting communicants in the region. William Brown, a Protestant chaplain stationed in McCrae, covered thousands of miles during his seventeen months in the Northwest. His traveling chapel, a miniature church built in the back of a truck by men working on the Haines Road, became a familiar sight as he drove between Dawson Creek and Fairbanks, and as far away as Valdez, Alaska. In June 1944 he was transferred to Edmonton, where he held services at the NWSC headquarters "in keeping with the spirit of the invasion."[98] Civilian clergyman from the major Protestant denominations divided the workload, making sure that a Baptist, Anglican, Presbyterian or United Church minister covered the highway every couple of months.

Religious minorities in the Northwest were even less well served. The official solution was ecumenism—let everyone worship together—and small groups who rejected this idea were left to their own devices. One group that worshipped on its own was the Jews; there were not many of them in the Northwest, but they did gather together when they could. In March 1945 a Passover dinner was held in Whitehorse,[99] and other services were held from time to time.[100]

In February 1945 Robert Ward, Anglican missionary assigned to the Alaska Highway and the Teslin region, traveled the route from Dawson Creek to Whitehorse. His journey was a difficult one, punctuated by car problems and the necessity of hitch-hiking between camps, but it gave him the opportunity of assessing the state of religious activity in the Northwest at the end of the war. He was not pleased by what he saw. There was confusion and poor communication among the Protestant denominations and even between members of his own church.[101] The Anglicans in Dawson

Creek had been outflanked by their rivals: the Roman Catholics, Lutherans, United Church, Pentecostals, and Salvation Army were each holding two services each Sunday, while the Anglican, Canon Hinchcliffe, could gather only enough followers for a single evening service. In the surrounding area, Ward reported, "The men in each case are doing valiant work but they need help." Thirty-six miles away, at Taylor Flats, a Bishop's Messenger (a lay woman) provided partial services, but had little success with the construction workers. At Mile 49, a mission worker offered regular services, and Rev. Mortimer from Fort St. John conducted a highway workers' service once a month. In addition, a U.S. armed forces chaplain conducted a regular Thursday evening service. At Blueberry, Mile 101, Monday services were held, attended by a military chaplain, every second week. The next highway camp with church services was Fort Nelson, Mile 300, where Protestant services were held weekly; a Roman Catholic priest visited the area twice a month. Weekly services were also available at the Watson Lake Maintenance Camp, Mile 635. The Anglicans maintained a mission, Ward's, at Teslin. Whitehorse, of course, was well-served by the various denominations. Protestant services were held at McCrae Headquarters Chapel, Air Base Chapel, and Standard Oil Chapel. There were also three Anglican services at Christ Church Cathedral and two at the Masonic Hall. Catholic mass was celebrated at the Station Hospital, Standard Oil, McCrae and the air base, with a series of services at Sacred Heart Church. The Mormons worshipped at the air base, as did the small Jewish community.[102]

There was much less religious activity at the north end of the Alaska Highway. The Anglicans maintained a small mission at Champagne, Mile 972, and the Roman Catholics had two priests based at Burwash Landing, Mile 1090. Permanent facilities were widely scattered, many families went without spiritual instruction and, to Ward's consternation, other denominations, particularly the Roman Catholics, seemed to be setting up permanent shop in the region.[103]

Although services in the larger community generally seemed to attract congregations, there does not seem to have been a strong religious impulse among the highway workers. This was partly the fault of the denominations themselves, who treated the northwest construction projects not only as an opportunity to do their Christian duty, but as a chance to get one up on the opposition. The struggle was for position—to be first into an area, or to stake out a congregation.

For many of the workers, church services were a welcome break in routine, an opportunity to relive family life in the south or to recall distantly remembered patterns of childhood. Others found the churches a source of social life. A NWSC choir was formed under church auspices in Edmonton, though posting and transfers created various difficulties,[104] and the choir eventually reformed in Whitehorse as the Chapel Choral Group, a social as well as a religious organization.[105] The arrival of a Marshall Electric Organ at the Whitehorse Headquarters Chapel similarly proved a boon to music buffs.[106]

Most of the recreational activities in the construction projects were fairly lowbrow in nature, yet the large number of engineers, accountants and other professionals, particularly in Whitehorse after the NWSC headquarters were moved there in 1944, gave rise to a demand for more cerebral pursuits than gambling, softball, and movies. There were a number of outlets for those with a taste for the beaux arts. The newspapers readily published the work of local poets, short-story writers, and comic artists.[107] Painters were encouraged to put their works on public display; Cpl. Will Barnett, with previous gallery credits to his name, exhibited a selection of his drawings at the NWSC headquarters building.[108] The radio was particularly useful in this regard; CFWH scheduled regular classical music shows, including a special 'Canadian Music in War' performance in January 1945.[109] The NWSC even sponsored a major Army Arts Contest (open to all employees of the NWSC), with competition in photography, graphic arts, and painting or sculpture.[110] By 1944, plays, recitals by well-known classical musicians, plays, and even evenings of artistic criticism were common, particularly in Whitehorse. In January 1945, for instance, Sgt. Alfred Urbach, Alaskan Division, ATC, visited the town to present several evenings of musical criticism and commentary. After he left, the newspaper reported, "the boys are now whistling Brahms, and discussing Beethoven."[111] It was the Yukon equivalent of Dame Myra Hess' famous noontime recitals for servicemen in London, and showed that "culture" was possible even in the Northwest—though not, apparently, along the remoter CANOL route, which was too rough for Brahms.

The authorities also attempted to make opportunities for self-improvement available to the workers. Some were purely informative, such as William Swan's missionary lectures on Borneo, or the Rev. Smith's film on England.[112] Others were more practical. Workers in Whitehorse could choose from a selection of night-school classes, ranging from blueprint reading, shorthand and typing, bookkeeping, accountancy, to French or Spanish—even, in those pre-Cold War days, the study of Russian.[113] The U.S. Air Force offered seven engineering night courses at the Whitehorse base, reminding potential students that "These courses will not be available to you at this low price ($2 per course) after you are out of uniform."[114] Not to be outdone, the army offered courses for headquarters personnel on foundations of American government.[115]

The Northwest has endless opportunities for those interested in exploring the subarctic wilderness, and the military and civilian authorities in charge of the defense construction projects made use of these for social and recreational outings. Organized hikes, guided nature walks, and bus tours were especially popular, particularly with headquarters staff in Whitehorse. There was, for instance, a NWSC Walking Club, a group that prided itself on its informality.[116] Picnics were well advertised and well attended; in the winter, there were skating parties, sleigh rides and skiing trips—a main attraction for servicemen was that there were generally women present. Special Services organized free bus trips each Sunday to points of interest along the Alaska Highway, including Kluane and Teslin lakes.[117] The wilderness was clearly viewed as compensation for isolation. In welcoming Edmonton workers transferred to Whitehorse, the *Northwest Newscast* observed:

> You will find here much of interest and much of value that you may recall in some distant future with pleasure and not a little regret. For here, as in few other parts of the world, there is much of the nature lover to gain in relaxation, sport and social benefit. You can, in your leisure moments, visit famed Lac LeBarge, take that weekend jaunt to Carcross at the head of Lake

Bennett, or fish in the Lewes River and its tributaries. And when it's all over and done with, and you have returned to your pre-war status, there will be for many of you regrets that you did not have a longer time to savor the many keen delights of this fabulous country. So, a final word of advice to you newcomers; make the most of this land in the fleeting time you are here; take advantage of the scenic beauty and this real down-to-earth outdoors.[118]

There were other distractions in the towns, particularly in Whitehorse, where a seemingly endless series of social and recreational activities, especially dances, were organized for civilian and military personnel. The U.S. Army and U.S. Air Force, the NWSC, Standard Oil, civilian contractors, and local residents took turns hosting these dances, large and small, formal and casual. The few dance bands in town, with names like the Alcanners and the Alaska Highway Maintenance Orchestra, performed almost nightly. Each Tuesday, the Red Cross held a dance, "with soft lights, a smooth floor and excellent music by the Alcanners drawing an increasing number of couples. There's always jitterbugging for you jive enthusiasts and sweet music for those who like it that way."[119]

Local women, both civilian and military, were much in demand at these functions and were encouraged as a morale boosting measure to attend; free transportation was provided. Jane Whitney, a USO director, wrote of the Whitehorse dance scene, in sexist language which today seems curiously, almost touchingly dated:

[A]ny wall-flower who is determined to get a man should unpack her snowshoes and trek northwards to Alaska. She said that at one recent dance there she counted only five girls against 250 men. "Of course, the girls get completely spoiled, but you can't blame them with men trailing them all the time."[120]

The shortage of women was so severe that the Special Services ran buses to take them from Whitehorse to dances in communities as far away as Skagway and Destruction Bay, and they were particularly urged to make the trip to all-male camps.[121] Dinner parties, especially farewell suppers—frequent events given the high turnover of highway workers—were also popular excuses to invite women out to the boondocks.[122] In the summer of 1944, fifty-five "of the prettiest girls the USAAF could find in Edmonton and Dawson Creek" were flown to Fort Nelson for a weekend of dancing and picnicking "with a bunch of fellows who wanted to show the girls a swell time. . . And the officers who check the morale of men in lonesome corners on the Alaskan highway decided this long-distance dating experiment was a success."[123]

These social gatherings brought Canadians and Americans together on an equal footing, and went a long way towards overcoming whatever national or occupational distrust existed in the community. A considerable spirit of cooperation existed in the region. In 1944, Bechtel-Price-Callahan and the U.S. Engineering Department organized the Polaris Club, dedicated to "developing the greatest spirit of cordiality between Americans and Canadians alike," expanding social opportunities and coordinating joint use of recreational facilities.[124] Their first event, a June 21st Midnight Sun celebration, suggested a solid future for cooperation between the different interests in the community and was praised by local leaders and project organizers alike.[125]

Nonetheless, despite all the efforts at encouraging official and personal goodwill, the tensions created by sexual, class, national and racial differences inevitably created a degree of social conflict in the region. Overcrowding was a perennial problem, particularly in the larger centers.[126] When things got out of hand, as they occasionally did, officials took quick action to calm the situation, often by separating the disputing parties. A rash of fistfights between soldiers and civilians in Dawson Creek, for instance, led to a directive in November 1943 reserving the Grandview Dance Hall for the military on Monday and Friday and for civilians on Wednesday and Saturday.[127] Hotels or restaurants that became trouble spots were declared off-limits to military personnel.[128] Whitehorse was off-limits to enlisted men between midnight and 6 A.M.[129] The army recreation hall in Edmonton was open to enlisted men and civilians only on Tuesdays, unless a movie was being shown or a bingo game held. The rest of the week it was reserved for officers and civilians. Throughout the Northwest Service Command, all civilian and military personnel were warned to stay out of "All houses, tents, buildings, or shelters, owned, occupied, or used by Indians or mixed bloods

MEALTIME, MOTHER'S DAY 1943.
Photograph by R. Schubert. Schubert family collection.

regardless of blood percentage."[130] Rooms occupied by female personnel were off-limits; barracks where they lived were to have a reception room for the entertainment of visitors. These rules were of course often broken, but they show the official determination to control the workers' social conduct, with a view to preventing disorder. They also give evidence, if any is needed, that the workers were not free to use their leisure time as they saw fit, but were expected to fit into the pattern of options set down by company or military leaders.

Recreation forms an integral part of the working experience, particularly in a situation of tough working conditions, labor shortage, and high worker turnover. Company managers had to provide more than high wages, decent food and housing to keep their workers reasonably content. They had to fill in the leisure hours, few though they were—though this was less true of the military authorities, who could call on military law to keep their workers in line.

In the first year or so of construction, a frontier atmosphere had prevailed. There was a job to do and, for civilians, boomtime wages to earn. Gambling, drinking and hunting marked the energy and confusion of that period. But by 1944, organized rather than individual events prevailed. The region had been transformed from a military theater to an economic zone on the northern frontier, and the changing nature of leisure pursuits mirrored that transformation.

Recreation was also used as a means of controlling the work force. Newspapers, USO performances, radio programs, periodicals, libraries, newsreels and movies were important propaganda tools, as well as means of entertainment, and were used to keep soldiers and civilian workers attuned to the war effort. After 1943, recreation was increasingly used to placate a work force that was growing increasingly weary of the northern experience. Hikes, bus tours, dances, skating parties and other activities were aimed at offsetting the cultural and human isolation of the Northwest. Dances also served the important function of providing contact between the sexes under controlled circumstances. By providing the men with an opportunity to meet the girls, who faced considerable pressure to attend dances regularly, the authorities hoped to lessen the level of sexual tension of an overwhelmingly male environment.

There was another side to the recreational activities associated with the northwest defense projects. The leisure programs were preponderantly American in character, representing a massive American cultural invasion of the Northwest. The Americans imported their recreational activities, from sports to reading materials, from frontline movies and newsreels to daily American radio broadcasts. The various imports had the desired effect. Americans clearly felt at home in the Canadian northwest; there was, in fact, little to remind the invading workers that they had left their home country. They also had a dramatic effect on the local population—ending their isolation and bringing modern technology and a new transportation and communication network to their doorsteps.

Viewed from one perspective, this wealth of recreational activities speaks well of the managers' concern for their workers. From a different perspective, however, it shows the influence the workers had over their working environment. As the bosses well knew, if suitable leisure activities were not provided, the military and civilian workers would create their own, less suitable diversions—drinking, gambling, and carousing[131]—all of which were feared as subversive of the war effort. Recreation, like other aspects of the northern work experience, demonstrates that authority between management and labor flowed in both directions.

NOTES

1. Bryan Palmer, *Working Class Experience: The Rise and Reconstitution of Canadian Labour, 1800-1900* (Toronto: Butterworth, 1983), 4.

2. Ken Roberts, *Contemporary Society and the Growth of Leisure* (London: Longman, 1978). See also Stanley Parker, *The Future of Work and Leisure* (London: Paladin, 1972).

3. Alan Tomlinson, ed., *Leisure and Social Control* (Brighton Polytechnic, 1981).

4 Rex Lucas, *Minetown, Milltown, Railtown: Life in Canadian Communities of Single Industry* (Toronto: University of Toronto Press, 1971), 220. See also, pp. 192-220.

5. Robert Storey, "Unionization Versus Corporate Welfare: The 'Dofasco Way'," *Labour/Le Travailleur* 12 (Fall 1983): 742.

6. Ian Radforth, *Bush Workers and Bosses: Logging in Northern Ontario, 1900-1980* (Toronto: University of Toronto Press, 1987), Chapter 5. Radforth's discussion, which is sketchy and often anecdotal on this topic, illustrates the difficulty of finding suitable sources on after-work activities. For American parallels, see Herbert Gutman, *Work, Culture and Society in Industrializing America: Essays in American Working-Class and Social History* (New York: Knopf, 1976); Stanley Aronowitz, *False Promises: The Shaping of American Working Class Consciousness* (New York: McGrawHill, 1973); and Harry Braverman, *Labor and Monopoly Capital: The Degradation of Work in the 20th Century* (New York: Monthly Review Press, 1974).

7. S. A. Howard to Adjutant General, 21 July 1942, NA, RG 338, NWSC, Box 7, file 353.8, Special Service-General 1944.

8. L. F. Nickel report re: Special Service—Alcan and Canon projects, 5 August 1942, NA, RG 338, NWSC, Box 7, file 353.8, Special Service-General 1944.

9. Headquarters, Fort St. John Sector to Commanding General, Northwest Service Command, Whitehorse, 31 December 1942, NA, RG 338, Box 7, Special Services-General, 1944.

10. Prince Rupert Subpost, NA, RG 336, Box 309.

11. Original Organization, NWSC, Memorandum for the Assistant Chief of Staff for Operations, S.S.S., 27 August 1942, NA, RG 338, Box 4, file 320.2.

12. Original Organization, NWSC, Memorandum for the Assistant Chief of Staff for Operations, S.S.S., 27 August 1942, NA, RG 338, Box 4, file 320.2. For an Australian parallel, see Ann-Mari Jordens, "Not Apocalypse Now: Government-Sponsored Australian Entertainers in Vietnam, 1965-71," *Labor History*, no. 58 (May 1990).

13. *Whitehorse Star*, 2 October 1942, p. 1.

14. NAC RG 126, vol. 27, Exhibit 618, Joe Jacquot, 21 Apr 1976.

15. Paul Thompson to Commanding General, Northern Sector, Alcan Highway, 18 August 1942. Excerpt from the censored mail of Lonnie Price, Company D, 93 Engineers, ACE, 72A3173, Box 16, File 50-26.

16. Office Memorandum No. 326, Violation of Canadian Gambling Laws, 26 October 1944, NA, RG 338, Box 10, NWSC, Office Memoranda, 1944.

17. Ibid.

18. *Northwest Newscast*, 27 January 1945, p. 4.

19. Jeckell to Gibson, 29 July 1943, NAC, RG 85, vol. 959, file 13515.

20. File re: B__, M__ Watson Lake, Yukon Territory—Operating a Common Gaming House, 8 February 1944, NA, RG 85, vol. 971, file 14062.

21. Interview with Cale Roberts, New Westminster, British Columbia, June 1988.

22. A. W. Klieforth, American Consul General to John Hickerson, 16 September 1943, NA, RG 165, ODP 336, Canada, Section I, Case 1-21.

23. Office Memorandum 316, PX Regulations, 15 September 1944, NA, RG 338, Box 10, NWSC, Office Memorandum, 1944.

24. RCMP G Division, Fort Smith, August 15th, 1942, NAC, RG 85, vol. 945, file 12806.

25. *Whitehorse Star*, 5 March 1943, p. 2, reported that several movie stars were coming north. The men, the paper noted, "are hoping the group will be headed by Hedy Lemarr and Betty Grable."

26. "USO Campshows Make First Visit to City—Give Great Performance," *Whitehorse Star*, 30 October 1942, p. 1.

27. Itinerary of Trip by Captain Russell Swan, January 1943, NA, RG 338, Box 3, file 314.7, Military Histories, 19421943.

28. Staff Meetings, 1943-1944, Monthly Report—June 1944, Military Services Branch, 4 July 1944, NA, RG 338, NWSC, Box 18.

29. *Whitehorse Star*, 11 December 1942. Three men tied for first prize, and the commander gave a furlough to all of them.

30. *Whitehorse Star*, 24 April 1942.

31. *Canol Piper*, 11 December 1943, NA, RG 338, Box 34, file 330.11 (NWD) 2.

32. Twitchell to Commanding General, 20 April 1943, De Scipio to Commanding General, 29 April 1943, NA, RG 338, NWSC, Box 7, file 353.8, Entertainers.

33. Entertaining Orientation of USO Show Overseas Unit #100, c. 1943, NA, RG 338, NWSC, Box 7, file 353.8.

34. Ibid.

35. Lawrence Phillips to director, Special Service Division, 21 December 1943, NA, RG 338, NWSC, Box 7, file 353.8, Entertaining.

36. Capt. B. C. Miller to War Department, Army Service Forces, Special Service Division, 11 November 1943, NA, RG 338, NWSC, Box 7, file 353.8, Entertainers.

37. W. M. Hoge to Brigadier General Sturdevant, 18 April 1942, ACE, 72-1-3173, Box 14, file 52-1.

38. Pierrepont Moffat to Norman Robertson, 4 May 1942, NAC, RG 22, vol. 251, file 40-7-4, pt. 3. See also Moffat to Secretary of State, 5 May 1942, ACE, 72-A-3173, Box 15, file 52-1.

39. Harrison Lewis to Mr. Cumming, 30 June 1942, YTA, YRG, Series 1, vol. 6, file 466ii.

40. Charles Camsell to Dr. Keenleyside, 11 May 1942, NAC, RG 22, vol. 251, file 40-7-4, pt. 3. In fact, Alaskan authorities did not provide resident hunting privileges to U.S. army personnel until the summer of 1943. Annex 3 to G2 Periodic Report No. 56, 12 June 1943-19 June 1943, NA, RG 407-7, file 91-DC1-2.1. The decision came after a year's agitation, topped off with a court challenge in Anchorage. American authorities reported "a jump in morale"

following the decision and observed that "numbers of soldiers are spending their extra time getting hunting gear together." Ibid., 10 July 1943-17 July 1943.

41. Views submitted by Mr. Jeckell, 19 May 1942, NAC, RG 22, vol. 251, file 40-7-4, pt. 3.

42. C. W. Jackson to H. L. Keenleyside, 25 June 1942, NAC, RG 22, vol. 251, file 40-7-4, pt. 3. Questions were also raised about whether or not the provisions would apply to all Americans, or only to the soldiers.

43. F. R. Butler to Hon. R. I. Maitland, 23 May 1942, NAC, RG 22, vol. 251, file 40-7-4, pt. 3. The Manitoba government, conversely, was prepared to make suitable arrangements for American troops stationed at Churchill. T. V. Sandys-Wunsch to Commissioner, RCMP, 4 September 1942, NAC, RG 85, vol. 944, file 12743, part I.

44. John Randolph to Colonel Theodore Wyman, 12 September 1942, NA, RG 338, Box 62, file 336, vol. 1.

45. J. D. Hickerson to Borjes, 12 February 1943, NA, FW 842.154, Seattle Fairbanks Highway/443.

46. Special Game Regulations, 24 July 1942, YTA, YRG1, Series 1, vol. 6, file 466ii.

47. Crossley to Jeckell, 21 September 1942, Jeckell to Crossley, 22 September 1942, YTA, YRG1, Series 3, vol. 10, file 12-20A. Canadian civilians later applied for similar treatment. In August 1943, Department of Transport officials requested similar resident permits for their employees.

48. An Ordinance to Amend "The Yukon Game Ordinance," 12 May 1944, YTA, YRG1, Series 3, vol. 10, file 12-20C. Resident hunting privileges were granted to employees of the RCMP Canadian Armed Forces, and all Dominion and Territorial employees serving in the Yukon, "irrespective of the length of time of actual residence in the Yukon Territory."

49. C. K. LeCapelain to R. A. Gibson, 29 December 1942, NAC, RG 85, vol. 944, file 12773, part I.

50. Memorandum: Hunting in Yukon Territory and Northwest Territories, 27 May 1943, NAC, RG 85, vol. 944, file 12743, pt. 1.

51. RCMP report regarding construction of oil pipeline from Normal Wells to Whitehorse, Yukon Territory, 14 August 1942, NAC, RG 85, vol. 865, file 8327. Similar registration was required of men in the Yukon who did not hold the appropriate big game licenses. See Jeckell to Cronkite, 17 August 1943 and Luper to Jeckell, 9 August 1943, YTA, YRG1, Series 3, vol. 10, file 12-20B.

52. Adcock to Urquhart, 11 September 1942, NAC, RG 85, vol. 944, file 12742, part I.

53. R. A. Gibson to Calvert, 27 October 1942, NAC, RG 85, vol. 944, file 12742, part I.

54. C. K. LeCapelain to R. A. Gibson, 29 December 1942, NAC, RG 85, vol. 944, file 12773, part I.

55. R. A. Gibson to commissioner, RCMP, 11 December 1942, YTA, YRG1, Series 3, vol. 10, file 12-20B.

56. See "The Gravel Magnet," Northern Native Broadcasting Production, January 1988, which includes interviews with Yukon residents.

57. Inspector Matheson to O.C. RCMP "G" Division, 14 April 1943, YTA, YRG1, Series 3, vol. 10, file 12-20B.

58. Colonel Hazeltine, Memorandum No. 106, Privately Owned Firearms, 18 May 1943, NA, RG 338, NWSC, Box 9, Numbered Memoranda, 1943. Such reminders were issued periodically, particularly when regulations changed. See Special Game Regulations in Yukon Territory, 31 July 1943, NA, RG 338, NWSC, Box 9, Numbered Memoranda, 1943, Memorandum No. 156. The bulk of this notice relates to the newly established Kluane Game Sanctuary.

59. Captain H. L. Goodman, USED—Section 6 Yukon Game Ordinance, 17 June 1943, YTA, YRG1, Series 3, vol. 10, file 12-20B. No action was taken, except seizing the bear skin. Local police later commented "It is perhaps fortunate that the bear was killed outright, if it had been only wounded, it is quite possible that persons living at McCrae would have been molested."

60. Memorandum to all District Employees, 18 October 1943, NA, RG 338, NWSC, Box 44, 300.6, Memos.

61. U.S. Engineers, District Circulars, NO(WH), District Circular Letter No. 170, Restrictions on Boating, 18 July 1944, NA, RG 338, Box 42. See also NA, RG 338, Box 17, Conferences, March-September 1945, p. 15.

62. Alleged killing of Game animals by U.S. Soldiers-Yukon Territory, 1 July 1943, NAC, RG 85, vol. 944, file 12743, part 1.

63. Addendum to letter, D. J. Martin to Commissioner, RCMP, n.d., ibid.

64. Alleged killing of Game animals and Fish by U.S. Soldiers—Yukon Territory, 1 July 1943, NAC, RG 85, vol. 944, file 12743, part 1.

65. *Northwest Newscast*, 18 April 1945, p. 3.

66. *Whitehorse Star*, 22 May 1942, p. 1.

67. The 691st Medicals won the first nine games against the Bears, their streak finally ending in mid-July. *Whitehorse Star*, p. 1.

68. *Whitehorse Star*, 6 June 1942, p. 1. It is noteworthy that softball stories were page one news in Whitehorse.

69. *Whitehorse Star*, 24 July 1942, p. 1

70. *Whitehorse Star*, 7 August 1942, p. 1

71. *Whitehorse Star*, 21 August 1942, p. 1 and 4.

72. *Northwest Newscast*, 3 May 1945, p. 3.

73. District of Whitehorse Military Softball League Conducted by Special Services, c. 1944, NA, RG 407, Box 22331, file ORCO-3470-0.1. The league included a Royal Canadian Airforce team.

74. *Whitehorse Star*, 7 July 1944, p. 1.

75. *Whitehorse Star*, 28 July 1944, p. 1.

76. For example, the *Northlander* from Camp Prairie, Fort Smith. Few of these community or camp newsletters are extant. ACE, 51A277, Box 29, file 461.

77. Edmonton and Fairbanks had daily papers, Dawson City and Whitehorse had weekly papers, Yellowknife had a locally produced sheet printed on a gestetner machine.

78. Dawson City was so remote that it did not pay to ship movies back from the town; after showing, they were thrown into an unused basement, where hundreds were found in the 1980s, preserved by the cold, many of them unique copies of long-lost silent films.

79. Memorandum for G-1 Northwest Service Command, 25 September 1942, NA, RG 338, NWSC, Box 7, Special Service—General, 1944.

80. Office Memos, 1943, Office Memorandum No. 202, Motion Pictures, C. M. Clifford, 1 December 1943, NA, RG 338, NWSC, Box 10.

81. *Whitehorse Star*, 17 September 1943, 24 September 1943. The theatre closed at war's end and McCrae was abandoned.

82. Office Memorandum No. 321, Opening of New Motion Picture Theatre, 4 October 1944, NA, RG 338, Box 10, NWSC, Office Memos, 1944.

83. Office Memorandum No. 331, War Department Theatres, 25 November 1944, NA, RG 338, Box 10, NWSC, Office Memorandum, 1944.

84. *Canol Piper*, 11 December 1943, NA, RG 338, Box 34, file 330.11(NWD)2.

85. Office Memorandum No. 191, Showing of Motion Picture, "Baptism by Fire," 8 October 1943, NA, RG 338, NWSC, Box 10, Office Memorandum, 1943.

86. *Northwest Newscast*, 12 January 1945, p. 4.

87. Office Memorandum No. 174, Magazines, periodicals and other reading material for outposts, 11 September 1943, NA, RG 338, NWSC, Box 10, Office Memorandum, 1943.

88. *Northwest Newscast*, 11 September 1944, p. 1.

89. *Whitehorse Star*, 16 February 1945, p. 1. *Northwest Newscast*, July 1944, vol. 1, no. 10, p. 2.

90. *Canol Piper*, 11 December 1943, NA, RG 338, Box 34, file 330.11(NWD)2.

91. *Whitehorse Star*, 18 February 1944.

92. Office Memorandum No. 234, Home Town New Items, 9 March 1944, NA, RG 338, NWSC, Box 10, Office Memorandum, 1944.

93. *Whitehorse Star*, 24 September 1943.

94. *Whitehorse Star*, 28 April 1944, p. 3. Telephone Repeater Officer, 28 November 1945, NA, RG 407, Box 23902, SGBN file 843 0.7, Daily Log, Jul-Dec. 1945.

95. *Northwest Newscast*, 27 January 1945, p. 3.

96. *Whitehorse Star*, 25 February 1944, p. 6.

97. J. A. O'Connor to Right Reverent Geddes, 26 June 1943, YTA, Anglican Church, 1-1c, Box 15, file 13. Problems eased in the summer of 1943, when bus service started along the highway. Until that time, ministers had to make their own travel arrangements.

98. *Northwest Newscast*, 10 January 1945, 15 July 1944, 10 June 1944; *Whitehorse Star*, 23 June 1944.

99. *Northwest Newscast*, 6 March 1945, p. 4.

100. *Northwest Newscast*, 24 March 1945, p. 3.

101. Robert Ward report, Diocese of Yukon, Chaplain Services on Alaskan Highway, Conditions on Highway, February 1945, YTA, Anglican Church, Series 1-1c, Box 11, folder 3.

102. *Northwest Newscast*, 28 April 1945, p. 2.

103. Highway Chart, Diocese of Yukon, Conditions on Highway, February 1945, YTA, Anglican Church, Series 1-1c, Box 11, folder 3.

104. *Northwest Newscast*, 28 August 1944, p. 4.

105. *Northwest Newscast*, 18 September 1944, p. 2.

106. *Northwest Newscast*, 25 January 1945, p. 4.

107. Lt. Charles Norman wrote a book of poems entitled "Northwest." *Northwest Newscast*, 3 March 1945, p. 3, and his work "A Soldier's Diary," was published by Scribners. *Northwest Newscast*, 13 May 1944, p. 4.

108. *Northwest Newscast*, 18 September 1945, p. 1.

109. *Northwest Newscast*, 11 January 1945, p. 2.

110. *Northwest Newscast*, 2 March 1945, p. 3.

111. *Northwest Newscast*, 1 and 12 January 1945.

112. *Northwest Newscast*, 27 January 1945, p. 3, 17 February 1945, p. 4.

113. *Northwest Newscast*, 9 and 10 January 1945, p. 3.

114. *Northwest Newscast*, 8 February 1945, p. 3.

115. *Northwest Newscast*, 5 March 1945, p. 3.

116. *Northwest Newscast*, 3 March 1945, p. 3. Hiking activities were not without mishaps; see *Northwest Newscast*, 23 February 1945, p. 3 for a description of the search for four lost women.

117. *Northwest Newscast*, 18 April 1945, p. 3.

118. *Northwest Newscast*, 19 August 1945, p. 2.

119. *Northwest Newscast*, 27 January 1945, p. 4.

120. *Northwest Newscast*, 26 January 1945, p. 4.

121. *Northwest Newscast*, 13 February 1945, p. 4; 27 January 1945, p. 2.

122. *Northwest Newscast*, 23 April 1945, p. 2.

123. *Edmonton Journal*, 24 July 1944.

124. *Northwest Newscast*, 23 April 1945, p. 2.

125. *Whitehorse Star*, 23 June 1944, p. 1. The 30 June issue of the newspaper was turned over to the Polaris Club.

126. Theodore Wyman to commanding general, Northwest Service Command, 25 November 1942, ACE, Box 419, Early Data on CANOL project, file 22-30.

127. Memorandum: Dances in Dawson Creek, c. November 1943, NA, RG 338, NWSC, Box 44, file 300.6 Memos.

128. General Orders No. 32: Off-Limits, 23 May 1944, NA, RG 338, NWSC, Box 9, file APOP-702. This order, one of many issued during the war, declared four premises off-limits and released three establishments from that status.

129. The men were permitted to stay in Whitehorse until 1 am on Sunday mornings.

130. Office Memorandum No. 237, 16 March 1944, NA, RG 338, Box 10, NWSC, Office Memorandum, 1944.

131. On the subject of sexual activity in the northwest defense projects, see K. S. Coates and W. R. Morrison, *The Alaska Highway in World War II,* chapter 5.

CONCLUSION

The situation of workers in the Northwest during the war sheds light on a much broader process—the recruitment and management of labor by large-scale corporations and government enterprises and the workers' response to these processes. Other studies have documented management styles and techniques aimed at ensuring the greatest efficiency in the workplace and keeping labor protest and radicalism to a minimum, stressing the importance of understanding the workers' ability to influence their working and living conditions. We have attempted to do the same for the Northwest during World War II, explaining the complex process by which the United States government and a variety of Canadian and American companies recruited, transported, paid and managed a massive work force, living in hastily prepared subarctic camps under wartime conditions, and examining the workers' response to these conditions.

The government and companies found the men and women that they needed for the tasks at hand. In the first instance, the U.S. government relied on soldier-workers to handle the difficult initial work. While their contribution has been much mythologized as representing an inspired "man against the wilderness" conquest conducted under duress of war, it is important to remember that the soldiers were workers first and foremost, using their hands, backs and skills to do the government's bidding. That they were cheap and readily controlled made them perfect candidates for the path-clearing and initial construction tasks.

Traditionally, labor historians have ignored soldiers within their conception of the working class. The soldiers were, for all purposes, "workers-minus," in that they encountered the same work as civilians, but had to accept much lower pay, worse conditions, and stricter discipline. Project managers were understandably pleased to have a pliant, easily controlled work force at their disposal. Civilian workers proved more troublesome.

Finding civilian workers, numbering in the tens of thousands, proved more difficult—the military workers were simply ordered north. A number of highly trained workers, particularly engineers, rose to meet a challenge; others worked for government departments and were simply assigned to northern duties. For the rest, the government and companies offered a combination of an appeal to patriotism—a chance for noncombatants to contribute directly to the war against Japan—and high wages. Since living circumstances were rustic at best, and families were not particularly welcome, employers had to resort to more basic enticements. They offered a chance for great adventure—and it is important not to forget the mythical attraction of the Northwest—good pay (in the case of Canadian workers officially sanctioned by the War Labour Board), and long hours. There was irony here, for working people had been fighting for years to overcome employer-enforced long work days. In the case of the North, where very few planned to stay, the workers wanted to make as much money as quickly as possible while boomtime conditions prevailed and actively sought to work as many hours as they could.

Managers did what they could to keep workers in the Northwest, for replacements were costly and scarce. Food was as good as could be provided under the circumstances and often far better than the workers were accustomed to. Efforts were made to fill their nonworking hours with a variety of recreational programs, although employ-

HIGHWAY CAMP IN WINTER.
YTA, MacBride Museum collection, 3551.

ers used these occasions to remind the workers of the war in an attempt to forestall protests about working conditions. The various inducements did not work particularly well, as there was a constant flow of workers out of the Northwest, forcing employers to maintain a constant recruitment drive in the south.

Employers, accepting the standard image of subarctic conditions and the allegedly limited working abilities of Natives and women, made few appeals to non-traditional sources of labor. Natives were hired only to work at select tasks—guiding and packing for survey crews, occasional unskilled work, and the like—that capitalized on their knowledge of the land. Hundreds of women were recruited for northern service but almost exclusively for traditional secretarial and domestic tasks. There were a few female truck and jeep drivers (although we have learned of no women bulldozer operators), but many female secretaries, office managers, cooks, and cleaners. A few women, usually only those with husbands working on the projects, were hired on in the remote construction camps, but most worked at the main headquarters stations during their time in the North.

Labor unions were virtually nonexistent in the Northwest during the war. There were organized labor protests by nonproject workers, particularly in the service sector, and unions did make frequent representations on behalf of Canadian workers to the Western Labour Board. The main employers, however, operated on a nonunion basis, and there is little evidence of the workers attempting to organize themselves. The workers were, however, far from powerless. If conditions at one company were not acceptable, a worker could seek employment with another northern contractor. Perhaps the best tool at the workers' disposal was the ability to leave the region altogether. Although company managers imposed strict penalties on the "termites," hundreds of workers, fed up with subarctic conditions, frustrated with lengthy separation from families and friends, or perhaps having made enough money, simply dropped their tools and quit their jobs. The ever-present prospect of losing their work force served as a powerful brake on the employers. They could not push the civilian workers too hard, nor attempt to cut wages or offer less than the best available working conditions lest they lose the bulk of their labor force. Even without unions, the workers exercised considerable control over their working conditions and ensured that northwest defense projects were not completed at their expense. And even in the military, the managers were always alert to the possibility of active or passive resistance.

The companies, in turn, had little reason to complain about employees' protests. In fact, they often supported workers' demands for higher wages, particularly in the case of Canadian employees, whose pay scales were set by the Western Labour Board. Canadian workers' anger was often directed toward the labour board and the perceived injustice of permitting American workers to be paid more than similarly skilled Canadian workers. The companies' support for high wages was not, of course, altruistic. Most of them worked on cost-plus contracts, which guaranteed a certain corporate profit, regardless of the cost of labor. As a result, there were few labor-management altercations during the course of the war.

PEACE RIVER BRIDGE, JULY 1944.
The footings under one end later gave way, and a new bridge had to be built.
NA, 111-SC 207151.

There is also evidence that the workers did not unthinkingly adopt the national and corporate rhetoric about patriotism and the war effort. Despite company and government efforts to keep the war alive through newspapers, radio, speeches, circulars and movies, the workers clearly saw that the companies were in the North for profit as well as patriotism; the details of their generous cost-plus contracts were widely known, and there was much evidence of corporate abuse of the system in order to pad company profits. Nor was the American government single-minded in its dedication to the war effort. There were numerous rumors about the diverse projects undertaken during the war, some of which seemed only distantly related to the war effort. Seeing through the facade of flag-wrapped patriotism, the workers expected to benefit as well, to gain a reasonable financial return for their months in the cold, isolation, boredom and hardships of the Northwest.

The projects were completed on schedule, and often ahead of it, although not as efficiently as the managers would have liked. Civilian worker mobility was a particular problem. Most workers stayed in the North for only a single season; a few hung around for two years or more. The structure of labor-management relations unquestionably added many thousands of dollars to the final cost of the projects; the wage and benefit structure was clearly in advance of anything likely to be offered under peacetime and so-called free market conditions. The constant turnover in the civilian labor force often left companies short of key personnel and, combined with chronic shortages of supplies and unexpected climatic and geographic problems, prevented the efficient and cost-effective completion of the highway, airfields, and pipeline projects.

Workers in the Northwest had enjoyed some of these benefits in the prewar period as well. Northern wages tended to be a bit higher than in the south, and employers requiring highly skilled workers often had to make concessions to attract and keep them in the region. Like their wartime counterparts, these workers had extracted these concessions largely through nonunion activities; although union-led actions were not unknown in the north, they were relatively rare. Companies recoiled at any threat to the short summer working season, and often made concessions in order to keep the labor force at work while weather conditions permitted. Similarly, workers exercised considerable control simply by their willingness and ability to leave, or not to return after a winter in the south. With no local work force at hand, employers were compelled to do their best to keep their workers on hand. During World War II, with the promise of virtually full employment in the south, companies had even more difficulty finding and keeping workers in the north.

The wartime experience in the Northwest also suggests that historians must continue to turn their attentions away from unions, important as they are, as the sole vehicles for improvement and change in working conditions. The situation in the Northwest demonstrates very clearly that the workers were able to turn the combination of wartime circumstances and northern location to their advantage. That most of them planned to stay only a short time in the region made it easier to make demands of employers and expect

ROADBUILDING AT KLUANE LAKE NEAR SOLDIER'S SUMMIT, SUMMER 1942.
YTA, R. A. Carter collecton, 1488.

results. If they did not get what they wanted, the workers often simply departed, leaving the employers shorthanded and slowing completion of the final project. With government-regulated conditions for Canadian workers and market forces determining pay schedules for Americans, unions had little role to play in the Northwest. They did their best to retain some kind of a presence, but the workers did well enough without them.

The construction boom ended with the Americans' withdrawal in 1946, and the Northwest began to retreat into its prewar patterns. But in the 1950s and 1960s, the region enjoyed another economic boom, stimulated by prospecting and mineral developments. A number of new mines opened, once again creating opportunities for skilled workers willing to live and work in the subarctic. Having learned from the situation in the past, and only too aware of the difficulties of keeping workers in the north, employers in the would-be "new" north opted for a management style that bore striking resemblance to the wartime arrangements.

The major difference after the war was that the new system relied heavily on a unionized work force. The major mines and transportation companies signed lucrative contracts with unions in an attempt to overcome worker resistance to life in the North.[1] The rationale was very simple. The companies had millions of dollars in capital investment committed to their northern operations in infrastructure, equipment, milling plants, and the company town. Wages and other benefits represented a comparatively small portion of overall operating costs, and if these concessions kept the plant functioning, they were, from management's perspective, a small price to pay for labor peace. The unions, by helping to recruit workers through hiring halls and international connections and by serving as an intermediary between labor and management, assisted in stabilizing the work force. The unions had, in fact, taken on a variety of the prewar management functions and aided in the rapid and profitable development of northern resources, while at the same time ensuring comparatively rich remuneration packages for their members.

The wartime experience represents a separate phase in the history of labor in the region, but the continuity is evident. It is clear that as a result of the unattractiveness of northern work and dozens of individual actions and protests by employees in the region, the workers during the war had gained generous wages and other benefits from the employers (or, more accurately, from the American and Canadian governments who paid for most of the cost).[2] Unorganized workers had overcome the tendency of corporations and governments to offer low wages and poor working conditions and secured boomtime pay for their work in the Northwest during the war.

The workers' response to opportunities on the northwest defense projects and the postwar mining boom says a great deal about southern attitudes toward life in the North. The tiny non-Native settlement in the Canadian northwest before 1942[3] provided mute testimony to the unwillingness of people to move permanently into the area. In fact, the northern non-Indian population was highly transient, with most people spending only a few years in the region. Many migrated on a seasonal basis, coming north each summer and leaving before the grip of winter set in.[4] Despite an extensive popular literature, much of it focusing on the Klondike gold rush, that promoted the Northwest as a land of adventure and opportunity, southerners had little more than a romantic interest in the region. Few Canadians or Americans wished to visit, let alone live in the Land of the Midnight Sun.

Working people were no exception to this pattern. Most came north as single people, fired by a sense of adventure or fleeing the depression-ridden south in search of a job. Only a very small number brought their families and settled permanently in the region. The major employers recognized the realities of life in the area and did most of their recruiting in the south, principally in Edmonton, Vancouver, Victoria, and Seattle. Few northern employers outside the fur trade made any effort to hire Native people. There was no pool of unemployed workers available in the Northwest; most of the jobless simply left the region for better opportunities in the south. This southern-based pattern of recruitment encouraged the continuation of the process, for the workers hired for northern jobs typically retained their attachments to the south.

Government and companies seeking to recruit workers for service during World War II ran headlong into this opposition to northern employment. Continent-wide resistance to living in the subarctic proved a very difficult barrier to breach, particularly in times of high employment in the south. Workers were secured only by providing enticements in the form of subsidized travel, high wages, long hours, and cheap room and board. The North, as it been from the days of the Klondike, was a place to make a killing, not a living; the wartime workers were no exception to that general pattern.

It is significant that only recently, when northern non-Native populations have grown, creating a more stable pool of skilled labor, have employers been able to get away from the boomtime wages typically associated with northern work. A severe recession across the Northwest in the early 1980s took the steam out of the resource-based economies, resulting in massive layoffs and a substantial out-migration from the territory. When several of the mines reopened, particularly the Curragh Resources property (formerly Cyprus-Anvil), the operators rejected the old salary and benefits scale and offered a package that was no more generous than most southern employers would provide. A surplus of skilled workers in the region, and in the industry, allowed the companies to secure the necessary workers to carry on full operations. These recent developments, which ironically are based on the fact that the North now has a more stable non-Native work force, suggest that the traditional pattern of northern labor is being eroded.

The reorganization of northern labor is not yet complete. There are still examples, such as the Beaufort Sea oil rigs and Polaris Mine in the Arctic Islands, of extremely remote operations that function as before. At the same time, however, most mining companies are abandoning the costly company-town approach to property development and are planning instead to transport workers from nearby large centers where their families will have great access to services and facilities. While these efforts will unquestionably limit development costs (and, incidentally, make it far easier to close the mine on a short- or long-term basis, since there will be no whole community dependent upon it for survival), it clearly represents a continued evolution of the hinterland labor market. Because employees will be drawn from a larger, more stable work force, and will be spared many of the personal and family inconveniences typically associated with frontier work camps, they will not be able to extract the same concessions from employers as hinterland workers have done in the past.[5]

The evidence from the Northwest suggests that workers have historically been able to extract significantly better than average wages and benefits from their employers compared to southern rates.[6] It appears that the basic unattractiveness to non-Natives of life in the subarctic has served as a valuable bargaining chip for workers, forcing managers to compete aggressively for their labor. As the regional work force increases in size, however, employers are able to turn its stability—based on the fact that families have been brought into the region and that permanent communities have developed—against the workers, providing lower wages and fewer benefits, and yet still establishing a greater hold over their employees.

Conditions in the Northwest during World War II, although clearly specific to the place and time, are not unique. They are, in fact, generally representative of the pattern of labor recruitment and

WHITEHORSE REFINERY, 1944.
NA, 111-SC 323079.

management in large-scale hinterland developments in the first half
of the twentieth century. The difficulties of recruitment and management were obviously increased by military urgency and the distance
from the labor markets and were made more complex by the mix of
Canadian and American, military and civilian labor. In general,
however, the management style and techniques were not significantly different from the mines, lumber camps and other hinterland
developments of this period.

It is important to recall, as well, that frontier workers had
considerable influence over the situation in which they found
themselves. Their work sites have often been described in unflatter-
ing terms, particularly when compared to urban conditions. The
workers who found their way into such employment were not,
however, powerless. They could demand better wages and working
conditions and, by exercising their ability to leave, could influence

the management of the operation. Managers adopted many techniques in an attempt to keep their employees, but they seldom worked very well, for in the absence of a complete social system—with opportunities for female companionship, families, social organizations and a means to escape the company's control—workers seldom stayed for long. In the nineteenth century, working people in such circumstances had fewer options and often endured hardships for longer times. One of the principal legacies of the twentieth century is that improvements in communications, knowledge of shifting labor market conditions, and greater ability to travel have provided more freedom and given workers improved ability to decide for themselves where and when they wanted to work. The opportunities in the Northwest between 1942 to 1946 are perhaps one of the best examples of the impact of labor force resistance and mobility on working conditions.

During World War II, tens of thousands of American and Canadian workers opted for employment in the Northwest. They saw an opportunity for adventure, work, and a high income; for some, the military projects also allowed them to contribute directly to the war effort. They came, made their money, experienced the North and then left. Only a tiny number stayed behind or returned at war's end. The workers knew what they wanted out of their war, and most of them got it. The managers had little reason to complain, for the work was finished quickly and, within the unusual limits laid down by geography and military concerns, successfully. Employers clearly hoped that the workers would stay longer and did their best to staunch the steady flow to the south, but their efforts were largely in vain.

To most North Americans, the subarctic was an inhospitable frontier, a place for adventure and sometimes to make money. The northwest defense projects were in a way simply a military version of the Klondike gold rush. And when the military spending dried up, as had the diggings in the Klondike fields, the workers, like most of the miners before them, returned to their homes in the south. Their northern work remained with them, an often-recalled and treasured experience, remembered fondly in later years. The Northwest was left with a mixed legacy from the war—a useless pipeline complex that was soon torn up and moved south, a partially completed highway, a series of airfields that would soon be rendered unnecessary by improvements to aircraft. But it would have few of the workers who had built the projects.

This book, finally, is about the employees, the thousands of men and hundreds of women who worked on the northwest construction projects. It is best not to focus on the legends that have now surrounded this era—of the soldiers and civilians battling against the cruel subarctic in a war-inspired race against time. This angle is best left for the poets and popularizers. A more significant story of the World War II projects rests with the workers—soldiers and civilians, Native, white and black, male and female, Canadian and American—assembled in the Northwest. Their part in these projects has been too often ignored or simplified. They were a unique group from across the continent who responded in a variety of ways to the conditions that they encountered in the subarctic. Theirs is not a story to mythologize, for that would only obscure the lessons to be gained from it. Rather, it is one that can be used to explore the relationship among government, capital and labor in the first half of the twentieth century. It is here, in the broader pattern of labor history, that the true significance of the workers' contribution to the northwest defense projects is to be found.

NOTES

1. Perhaps the best example of this is the impressive boomtime contracts signed with the Alaskan unions associated with the construction of the trans-Alaska pipeline in the 1970s, although the arrangements with mine workers at Pine Point, NWT, and Cyprus-Anvil and Clinton Creek in the Yukon the previous decade were significantly better than the pay arrangements for other northern workers.

2. The Canadian government exercised little control over the construction period, but because it repaid the U.S government for the investment in the Alaska Highway, the Canadians ultimately paid a portion of the cost of war-time labor practices.

3. The non-Native population of the Yukon in 1941 was 3,406; that of the NWT 2,572.

4. Ken Coates and Bill Morrison, *The Sinking of the Princess Sophia: Taking the North Down With Her* (Toronto: Oxford, 1990); Ken Coates and W. R. Morrison, "Transiency in the Far Northwest: The Case of the Princess Sophia," in K. Coates and W.R. Morrison, eds., *Interpreting Canada's North* (Toronto: Copp Clark Pitman, 1989).

5. Ken Coates and Judith Powell, *The Modern North: People, Politics and the Rejection of Colonialism* (Toronto: Lorimer, 1989).

6. There is, of course, a major question about the cost of living in the north and the relative standard of living in the north versus the south. Studies of this sort have not yet been conducted. It is important to keep in mind, however, that many workers migrated seasonally between regions, often leaving their families in the south.

BIBLIOGRAPHY

Archival Sources

Edmonton Municipal Archives (EMA).

Seaton, R. Papers. Glenbow-Alberta Institute.

Library of Congress, Harold Ickes Papers.

National Archives of Canada (NAC). Record Groups (RG) 10, 18, 22, 24, 36/7, 85.

National Archives of the United States (NA). Record Groups 30, 59, 92, 107,111, 112, 160, 165, 218, 253, 319, 335, 336, 338, 407. Washington, D.C., and Suitland, Md.

United States Army, Adjutant General's Office, Machine Records Branch.

United States Army Corps of Engineers. Office of History, Office of the Chief of Engineers, Fort Belvoir, Research Collections (ACE).

Yukon Territorial Archives (YTA). Yukon Government Records, White Pass and Yukon Route Collection, Anglican Church Diocese of Yukon Records. Yukon Record Group (YRG) 1.

Articles

Allen, Margaret. "The Domestic Ideal and the Mobilization of Womanpower in World War II." *Women's Studies International Forum* 6/4 (1983).

Barger, Cecil. "It's A Long Road." *Alaskan Sportsman* (November 1945).

Campbell, D'Ann. "Servicewomen of World War II." *Armed Forces and Society* 6, no. 2 (Winter 1990).

Cleveland, L. "When They Send the Last Yank Home: Wartime Images of Popular Culture." *Journal of Popular Culture* 18, 3 (Winter 1984).

Coates, K. S. "Best Left as Indians: The Federal Government and the Indians of the Yukon, 1894-1950." *Canadian Journal of Native Studies* 4, no. 2 (Fall 1984).

———. "Controlling the Periphery: A Comparison of the Territorial Administrations of Alaska and the Yukon Territory." *Pacific Northwest Quarterly* 78, 4 (October 1987).

———. "Upsetting the Rhythms: The Federal Government and Native Communities in the Yukon Territory, 1945 to 1973." In *Northern Communities: The Prospects for Empowerment*, ed. Gurston Dacks and Ken Coates. Edmonton: Boreal Institute for Northern Studies, 1988.

Coates, K. S. and W. R. Morrison. "More Than a Matter of Blood: The Churches, the Government and the Mixed Blood Populations of the Yukon and Mackenzie River Valley, 1890-1950." In *1885 and After,* ed. F. L. Barron and J. Waldrum. Regina: Canadian Plains Research Centre, 1986.

———. "War Comes to the Yukon." *The Beaver* (October/November 1989).

Cole, Terrence. "Klondike Contraptions." *The Northern Review* 3/4 (Summer/ Winter 1989).

de Wet, J. P. "Exploration for Oil in the Northwest Territories." *Canadian Mining Journal* (September 1944).

Diubaldo, Richard, "The Canol Project in Canadian-American Relations." *Canadian Historical Association, Historical Papers* (1977).

Fidock, Jane. "The Effect of the American 'Invasion' of Australia, 1942-1945." *Flinders Journal of History and Politics* 11 (1985).

Fisher, R. "T. D. Pattullo and the British Columbia to Alaska Highway." In *The Alaska Highway: Papers of the 40th Anniversary Symposium*, ed. K. S. Coates. Vancouver: University of British Columbia Press, 1985.

Freeman, Joshua. "Delivering the Goods: Industrial Unionism During World War II." *Labor History* (1978).

Friye, A. "Contemporary History as History: American Expansion into the Pacific Since 1941." *Pacific Historical Review* LIII (1984).

Gagnon, Jean-Pierre. "Canadian Soldiers in Bermuda During World War One." *Histoire Sociale/Social History* 23, no. 45 (May 1990).

Green, James. "Fighting on Two Fronts: Working Class Militancy in the 1940s." *Radical America* 8 (1975).

Guererard, Albert, Jr. "Novitiate." *Virginia Quarterly Review* 21, no. 1 (1945).

Hachey, T. "Jim Crow With a British Accent: Attitudes of London Government Officials Toward American Negro Soldiers in England During World War II." *Journal of Negro History* LIX, no. 1 (January 1974).

———. "Walter White and the American Negro Soldier in World War II: A Diplomatic Dilemma for Britain." *Phylon: The Atlanta University Review of Race and Culture* XXXIX, no. 3 (Fall 1978).

Hartmann, S. M. "Prescriptions for Penelope: Literature on Women's Obligations to Returning World War II Veterans." *Women's Studies* 5 (1978).

Honey, Maureen. "The Working Class Woman and Recruitment Propaganda During World War II: Class Differences in the Portrayal of War Work." *Signs* 8/4 (1983).

Honigman, J. J. "On the Alaska Highway." *Dalhousie Review* (January 1944).

Iriye, Akira. "Contemporary History as History: American Expansion into the Pacific Since 1941." *Pacific Historial Review* LIII (1984).

Johnston, H. "The Anglo-American Caribbean Commission and the Extension of American Influence in the British Caribbean, 1942-1945." *The Journal of Commonwealth and Comparative Politics* XXII, no. 2 (July 1984).

Jordens, Ann-Mari. "Not Apocalypse Now: Government-Sponsored Australian Entertainers in Vietnam, 1965-71." *Labor History* 58 (May 1990).

Kalisch, P. A. and M. Scobey. "Female Nurses in American Wars: Helplessness Suspended for the Duration." *Armed Forces and Society* 9, no. 2 (Winter 1983).

King, Archibald. "Further Development Concerning Jurisdiction Over Friendly Foreign Armed Forces." *American Journal of International Law* XL (1946).

Koppes, Clayton, and G. Black. "Blacks, Loyalty and Motion Picture Propaganda in World War II." *Journal of American History* 73, no. 2 (September 1976).

Levi, Steven. "Labor History and Alaska." *Labor History* 30, no 4 (1989).

McArthur, Judith N. "From Rosie the Riveter to the Feminine Mystique: An Historiographical Survey of American Women and World War II." *Bulletin of Bibliography* 44, no. 1 (1987).

McCusker, Knox F. "The Alaska Highway." *The Canadian Surveyor* 8 (July 1943).

MacDowell, Laurel Sefton. "The Formation of the Canadian Industrial Relations System During World War Two." *Labour/Le Travailleur* (1978).

Marchand, John. "Tribal Epidemics in the Yukon." *Journal of the American Medical Association* 123 (1943).

McGuire, Philip. "Desegregation of the Armed Forces: Black Leadership, Protest and World War II." *The Journal of Negro History* LXVIII, no. 2 (Spring 1983).

Modell, John and Diane Steffey. "Waging War and Marriage: Military Service and Family Formation, 1940-1950." *Journal of Family History* 13, no. 2 (1988).

Montgomerie, D. "The Limitations of Wartime Change: Women War Workers in New Zealand." *New Zealand Journal of History* 23, no. 1 (April 1989).

Morrison, W. R. "Alaska History." *The Northern Review* 5 (Summer 1990).

Morton, Desmond. "Aid to the Civil Power; The Canadian Militia in Support of Social Order, 1867-1914." *Canadian Historical Review* 51, no. 4 (1970).

Palmer, A. "The Politics of Race and War: Black American Soldiers in the Caribbean Theatre During the Second World War." *Military Affairs* XLVII, no. 2 (April 1983).

Powell, Judith. "Whitehorse and the Building of the Alaska Highway, 1942-1946." *Alaska History* (Spring 1989).

Rainey, F. "Alaskan Highway: An Engineering Epic." *National Geographic Magazine* LXXXIII, no. 2 (Feb.-Mar. 1943).

Reddicks, L. D. "Negro Policy in the United States Army, 1775-1945." *Journal of Negro History* 34 (1949).

Renshaw, P. "Organized Labor in the United States War Economy, 1939-1945." *Journal of Contemporary History* 21 (1986).

Reynold, David. "The Churchill Government and the Black American Troops in Britain During World War II." *Royal Historical Society, Transaction* 35 (1985).

Robson, Robert. "Flin Flon: A Study of Company-Community Relations in a Single Enterprise Community." *Urban History Review* (February 1984).

Saunders, Kay. "Conflict Between the American and Australian Governments over the Introduction of Black American Servicemen into Australia During World War Two." *Australian Journal of Politics and History* 33, no. 2 (1987).

Saunders, Kay and Helen Taylor. "The Reception of American Servicemen in Australia During Word War 2: The Resilience of 'White Australia.'" *Journal of Black Studies* (June 1988).

Sitkoff, H. "Racial Militancy and Interracial Violence in the Second World War." *Journal of American History,* 58 (December 1971).

Storey, Robert. "Unionization Versus Corporate Welfare: The 'Dofasco Way'." *Labour/Le Travaileur* 12 (Fall 1983).

Straub, Eleanor. "United States Government Policy Toward Civilian Women During World War II." *Prologue* 5 (1973).

Stuart, Richard. "The Yukon Schools Question, 1937." *Canadian Historical Review* LXIV, no. 1 (1983).

Sturma, M. "Loving the Alien: The Underside of Relations Between American Servicemen and Australian Women in Queensland, 1942-1945." *Journal of Australian Studies* 24 (1989).

———. "Public Health and Sexual Morality: Venereal Disease in World War II Australia." *Signs* 13, no. 4 (1988).

Schweitzer, Mary. "World War II and Female Labor Force Participation Rates." *Journal of Economic History* 40 (1980).

Taylor, Griffith. "Arctic Survey, IV: A Yukon Domesday: 1944." *Canadian Journal of Economics and Political Science* 14, no. 3 (August 1945).

Williams, G. O. "Share Croppers at Sea: The Whaler's 'Lay' and Events in the Arctic, 1905-1907." *Labor History* 29, no. 1 (1988).

Woodman, L. "CANOL: Pipeline of Brief Glory." *The Northern Engineer* 9, no. 2 (Summer 1977).

Wynn, Neill. "War and Social Change: The Black American in Two World Wars." In *War and Society,* vol. 2, ed. B. Bond and I. Roy. London: Crown Holm, 1977.

Books

Aieger, Robert. *American Workers, American Unions, 1920-1985.* Baltimore, Md.: Johns Hopkins University Press, 1986.

The Alaska Highway: Interim Report from the Committee on Roads, House of Representatives. Washington, D.C.: Government Printing Office, 1946.

Additional Report of the Special Committee Investigating the National Defense Program. 78th Congress, 1st Session, Report No. 10, Part 14. Washington, D.C.: Government Printing Office, 1944.

Aronowitz, Stanley. *False Promises: The Shaping of American Working Class Consciousness.* New York, N.Y.: McGraw-Hill, 1973.

Anderson, K. *Wartime Women: Sex Roles, Family Relations and the Status of Women.* Westport, Conn.: Greenwood, 1981.

Banner, Lois. *Women in Modern America: A Brief History.* New York, N.Y.: Harcourt Brace Jovanovich, 1984.

Baptiste, F. A. *War, Cooperation, and Conflict: The European Possessions in the Caribbean, 1939-1945.* New York, N.Y.: Greenwood Press, 1988.

Barry, P. S. *The Canol Project: An adventure of the U.S. War Department in Canada's Northwest.* Edmonton, Albert.: published by the author, 1985.

Beckles, Gordon. *Canada Comes to England.* London, U.K.: Hodder and Stoughton, 1941.

Bell, Roger. *Unequal Allies: Australian-American Relations in the Pacific War.* Melbourne, Victoria: Melbourne University Press, 1977.

Bennett, Gordon. *Yukon Transportation: a History.* Canadian Historic Sites Occasional Papers in Archaeology and History, No. 19. Ottawa, Ont.: Supply and Services Canada, 1978.

Berton, Pierre. *The Mysterious North.* Toronto, Ont.: McClelland and Stewart, 1956.

Bittner, Donald. *The Lion and the White Falcon: Britain and Iceland in the World War II Era.* Hamden, Conn.: Archon Books, 1983.

Bothwell, Robert. *Eldorado: Canada's National Uranium Company.* Toronto, Ont.: University of Toronto Press, 1984.

Bothwell, R., I. Drummond and J. English. *Canada, 1900 to 1945.* Toronto, Ont.: University of Toronto Press, 1988.

Bond, B. and I. Roy, eds. *War and Society,* vol. 2. London, U.K.: Crown Holm, 1977.

Braverman, Harry. *Labor and Monopoly Capital: The Degradation of Work in the 20th Century.* New York, N.Y.: Monthly Review Press, 1974.

British Columbia. *Report of the Commissioner of the Provincial Police . . . and Inspector of Gaols.* Victoria, Brit. Col.: King's Printer, 1941-1946.

British Columbia-Yukon-Alaska Highway Commission. *Preliminary Report on Proposed Highway Through British Columbia and the Yukon Territory to Alaska.* Ottawa, Ont.: Kings Printer, 1940.

Brody, David. *Workers in Industrial America: Essays on the Twentieth Century Struggle.* New York, N.Y.: Oxford University Press, 1980.

Brown, Jennifer. *Strangers in Blood: Families in Fur Trade Country*. Vancouver, Brit. Col.: University of British Columbia Press, 1980.

Brownmiller, Susan. *Against Our Will: Men, Women and Rape*. New York, N.Y.: Simon and Schuster, 1973.

Bryant, C. *Khaki-Collar Crime*. New York, N.Y.: Free Press, 1979.

Buchanan, A. Russell. *Black Americans in World War II*. Santa Barbara, Calif.: ABC-Clio Press, 1977.

Bykofsky, Joseph and Harold Larson. *The Transportation Corps: Operations Overseas*. Washington, D.C.: Department of the Army, 1957.

Campbell, D'Ann. *Women at War with America: Private Lives in a Patriotic Era*. Cambridge, Mass.: Harvard University Press, 1984.

Campbell, Rosemary. *Heroes and Lovers: A Question of National Identity*. Sydney, New South Wales: Allen & Unwin, 1989.

Canada. *Report of the R.C.M.P.*, 1940-1944. Ottawa, Ont.: King's Printer, 1941-1945.

Canada Year Book, 1932, 1938, 1950, 1952-53.

Census of Canada, 1901, 1911, 1921, 1931, 1941.

Coates, K. S. ed. *The Alaska Highway: Papers of the 40th Anniversary Symposium*. Vancouver, Brit. Col.: University of British Columbia Press, 1985.

Coates, K. S. *Best Left as Indians*. Kingston, Ont.: McGill-Queen's University Press, 1992.

Coates, K. S. and W. R. Morrison, eds. *Interpreting Canada's North*. Toronto, Ont.: Copp Clark Pitman, 1989.

Coates, K. S. and W. R. Morrison. *The Alaska Highway in World War II: The U.S. Army of Occupation in Canada's Northwest*. Norman, Okla.: University of Oklahoma Press and Toronto, Ont.: University of Toronto Press, 1992.

————. *Land of the Midnight Sun: A History of the Yukon*. Edmonton, Alberta: Hurtig, 1988.

————. *The Sinking of the Princess Sophia: Taking the North Down With Her*. Toronto, Ont.: Oxford University Press and Fairbanks, Alaska: University of Alaska Press, 1990.

————. *Treaty Report: Treaty 11*. Ottawa, Ont.: Treaties and Historical Research Centre, 1986.

Coates, Ken and Judith Powell. *The Modern North: People, Politics and the Rejection of Colonialism*. Toronto, Ont.: Lorimer, 1989.

Cohen, Stan. *The Trail of '42*. Missoula. Mont.: Pictorial Histories, 1988.

Costello, John. *Love, Sex and War: Changing Values, 1939-1945*. London, U.K.: Collins, 1985.

Creighton, Donald. *The Forked Road: Canada, 1939-1967*. Toronto, Ont.: McClelland and Stewart, 1976.

Dalfiume, Richard. *Desegregation of the United States Armed Forces: Fighting on Two Fronts, 1939-1953*. Columbia, Mo.: University of Missouri Press, 1989.

Dower, J. *War Without Mercy: Race and Power in the Pacific War*. New York, N.Y.: Pantheon, 1987.

Diubaldo, Richard. *Stefansson and the Canadian Arctic*. Montreal, Quebec: McGill-Queen's University Press, 1978.

Duffy, Quinn. *The Road to Nunavut: The Progress of the Eastern Arctic Inuit Since the Second World War*. Kingston, Ont.: McGill-Queen's University Press, 1988.

Dziuban, Stanley W. *Military Relations Between the United States and Canada 1939-1945*. Washington, D.C.: Department of the Army, 1959.

Eccles, William J. *Canada Under Louis XIV, 1663-1701*. Toronto, Ont.: McClelland and Stewart, 1964.

————. *The Canadian Frontier, 1534-1760*. New York, N.Y.: Holt, Rinehart, and Winston, 1969.

Finkel, Alvin. *Business and Social Reform in the Thirties*. Toronto, Ont.: James Lorimer, 1979.

Fletcher, Marvin. *The Black Soldier and Officer in the United States Army, 1891-1917*. Columbia: University of Missouri Press, 1974.

Flynn, George Q. *The Mess in Washington: Manpower, Mobilization and World War II*. Westport, Conn.: Greenwood Press, 1979.

Forbes-Robertson, Diana and Roger Straus, Jr., eds. *War Letters from Britain*. New York, N.Y.: G. P. Putnam, 1941.

Friesen, Gerald. *The Canadian Prairies*. Toronto, Ont.: University of Toronto Press, 1987.

Fumoleau, Rene. *As Long as This Land Shall Last*. Toronto, Ont.: McClelland and Stewart, 1973.

Getty, I. A. L. and A. S. Lussier, eds. *As Long As the Sun Shines and Water Flows*. Vancouver, Brit. Col.: University of British Columbia Press, 1983.

Gingrich, Earl. *Eastern passage to the Alaska Highway*. Winterburne, Alberta: self-published, 1986.

Griffith, Cyril. *Trucking the Tote Road to Alaska, 1942-1943: Memories of the Early Days of the Alaska Highway.* Self-published, 1989.

Glaberman, Martin. *Wartime Strikes: The Struggle Against the No-Strike Pledge in the UAW During World War II.* Detroit, Mich.: Bewich Editions, 1980.

Government of Yukon. *Revised Population Estimates of the Yukon.* Whitehorse,Yukon Terr.: Bureau of Statistics, June 1989.

Grant, Shelagh. *Sovereignty or Security? Government Policy in the Canadian North, 1939-1950.* Vancouver, Brit. Col.: University of British Columbia Press, 1988.

Green, Lewis. *The Gold Hustlers.* Anchorage, Alaska: Alaska Northwest Publishing, Co., 1977.

Gregory, C. *Women in Defense Work During World War II: An Analysis of the Labour Problem and Women's Rights.* New York, N.Y.: Exposition Press, 1974.

Gutman, Herbert. *Work, Culture, and Society in Industrializing America: Essays in American Working-class and Social History.* New York, N.Y.: Knopf, 1976.

Hall, David. *Clifford Sifton.* 2 vols. Vancouver, Brit. Col.: University of British Columbia Press, 1982 and 1984.

Hartmann, Susan. *The Home Front and Beyond: American Women in the 1940s.* Boston, Mass.: Twayne, 1982.

Heron, Craig ed. *On the Job: Confronting the Labour Process in Canada.* Kingston, Ont.: McGill-Queen's University Press, 1986.

Heron, Craig and R. Storey, eds. *Working in Steel: The Early Years in Canada 1883-1935.* Toronto, Ont.: McClelland and Stewart, 1988.

Hess, G. R. *The United States' Emergence as a Southeast Asia Power, 1940-1950.* New York, N.Y.: Columbia University Press, 1987.

Higgonet, M. et al., eds. *Behind the Lines: Gender and the Two World Wars.* New Haven, Conn.: Yale University Press, 1987.

Historical Statistics of the United States, Colonial Times to 1970, Part 1. Washington, D.C.: U.S. Bureau of the Census, 1975.

Isaksson, E., ed. *Women and the Military System.* New York, N. Y.: St. Martin's Press, 1988.

Jacobs, W. A. *The Alaska District: United States Army Corps of Engineers, 1946-1974.* Alaska: U.S. Army Corps of Engineers, 1976.

Kennett, Lee. *G.I.: The American Soldier in World War II.* New York, N.Y.: Charles Scribner's Sons, 1987.

Knight, Rolf. *Indians at Work: An Informal History of Native Indian Labour in British Columbia, 1858-1930.* Vancouver, Brit. Col.: New Star Books, 1978.

Large, R. G. *Prince Rupert: A Gateway to Alaska and the Pacific.* Vancouver, Brit Col.: Mitchell Press, 1960.

Lichtenstein, Nelson. *Labor's War at Home: The CIO in World War II.* New York, N.Y.: Cambridge University Press, 1982.

Longmate, Norman. *The G.I.'s: The Americans in Britain, 1942-1945.* London, U.K.: Hutchinson, 1975.

Louis, W. Roger. *Imperialism at Bay: The United States and the Decolonization of the British Empire, 1941-1945.* Oxford, U.K.: Clarendon Press, 1977. 1978.

Lotz, Jim. *People Outside: Studies of Squatters, Shack Towns, and Shanty Residents and Other Dwellings on the Fringe in Canada.* Ottawa, Ont.: St. Paul's University, 1971.

Lucas, Rex. *Minetown, Milltown, Railtown: Life in Canadian Communities of Single Industry.* Toronto, Ont.: University of Toronto Press, 1971.

Lynn, W. *From Working Girl to Working Mother: The Female Labor Force in the United States, 1820-1980.* Chapel Hill, N.C.: University of North Carolina Press, 1985.

Macdowell, Laurel Sefton. *Remember Kirkland Lake:The History and Effects of the Kirkland Lake Gold Miners' Strike, 1941-42.* Toronto, Ont.: University of Toronto Press, 1983.

MacGregor, J. D. *The Klondike Rush Through Edmonton, 1897-98.* Toronto, Ont.: McClelland and Stewart, 1970

Mackenzie, David. *Inside the North Atlantic Triangle.* Toronto, Ont.: University of Toronto Press, 1988.

Magnusson, S. A. *Northern Sphinx: Iceland and Icelanders from the Settlement to the Present.* Montreal, Quebec: McGill-Queen's University Press, 1977.

McCandless, Robert. *Yukon Wildlife: a Social History.* Edmonton, Alberta: University of Alberta Press, 1986.

McConachie, Grant. *Bush Pilot with a Briefcase: The Happy-go-lucky Story of Grant McConachie.* Toronto, Ont.: Doubleday, 1972.

McKernan, M. *All In! Australia During the Second World War.* Melbourne, Victoria: Thomas Nelson, 1983.

Michener, James. *The Journey.* Toronto, Ont.: McClelland and Stewart, 1989.

Milkman, Ruth. *Gender at Work: The Dynamics of Job Segregation by Sex During World War II.* Urbana, Ill.: University of Illinois Press, 1987.

Minter, Roy. *White Pass: Gateway to the Klondike.* Toronto, Ont.: McClelland and Stewart and Fairbanks, Alaska: University of Alaska Press, 1987.

Mitchell, David. *W. A. C. Bennett.* Vancouver, Brit. Col.: Douglas and McIntyre, 1983.

Moore, John H., ed. *The American Alliance: Australia, New Zealand and the United States, 1940-1970.* Melbourne, Victoria: Cassell Australia, 1970.

Moore, John H. *Over-Sexed, Over-Paid, and Over Here.* St. Lucia, Queensland: University of Queensland Press, 1981.

Morris, Richard, ed. *A History of the American Worker.* Princeton, N.J.: Princeton University Press, 1983.

Morrison, W. R. *Showing the Flag: The Mounted Police and Canadian Sovereignty in the North, 1894-1925.* Vancouver, Brit. Col.: University of British Columbia Press, 1985.

Morton, Desmond and Glenn Wright. *Winning the Second Battle: Canadian Veterans and the Return to Civilian Life, 1915-1930.* Toronto, Ont.: University of Toronto Press, 1987.

Morton, D. with Terry Copp. *Working People.* Ottawa, Ont.: Deneau, 1984.

Nalty, B. *Strength for the Fight: A History of Black Americans in the Military.* New York, N.Y.: Free Press, 1988.

Nash, G. *The American West Transformed: The Impact of the Second World War.* Bloomington, Ind.: Indiana University Press, 1985.

Naske, Claus-M. *Paving Alaska's Trails: The Work of the Alaska Road Commission.* New York, N.Y.: University Press of America, 1986.

Neufeld, Maurice. *American Working Class History: a Representative Bibliography.* Washington, D.C.: B.P. Inc., 1983.

North, Dick. *The Mad Trapper of Rat River.* Toronto, Ont.: Macmillan, 1972.

The North Pacific Planning Project, Report of Progress, May 1943. Washington, D.C.: National Resources Planning Board, 1943.

Palmer, Bryan. *The Canadian Working Class Experience: The Rise and Reconstitution of Canadian Labour.* Toronto, Ont.: Butterworths, 1983.

Parker, Stanley. *The Future of Work and Leisure.* London, U.K.: Paladin, 1972.

Peet, Fred. *Miners and Moonshiners: A Personal Account of Adventure and Survival in a Difficult Era.* Victoria, Brit. Col.: Sono Nis Press, 1983.

Pierson, Ruth. *They're Still Women After All: The Second World War and Canadian Womenhood.* Toronto, Ont.: McClelland and Stewart, 1986.

Polenberg, Richard. *War and Society in the United States, 1941-1945.* New York, N.Y.: J.B. Lippincott, 1972.

Potts, E. D. and A. Potts. *Yanks Down Under, 1941-45.* Melbourne, Victoria: Oxford University Press, 1985.

Powell, A. *The Shadow's Edge: Australia's Northern War.* Melbourne, Victoria: Melbourne University Press, 1988.

Radforth, Ian. *Bush Workers and Bosses: Logging in Northern Ontario, 1900-1980.* Toronto, Ont.: University of Toronto Press, 1987.

Ray, A. J. *The Canadian Fur Trade in the Industrial Age.* Toronto, Ont.: University of Toronto Press, 1990.

Remley, David. *Crooked Road: The Story of the Alaska Highway.* New York, N.Y.: McGraw Hill, 1976.

Report of the Alaskan International Highway Commission. Washington, D.C.: Government Printing Office, 1940.

Roberts, Ken. *Contemporary Society and the Growth of Leisure.* London, U.K.: Longman, 1978.

Rogers, George and Richard Cooley. *Alaska's Population and Economy: Regional Growth, Development, and Future Outlook.* Vol. 1. Fairbanks, Alaska: University of Alaska Institute of Business, Economic and Government Research, 1963.

Schmidt, John. *This was No @#$%% Picnic: 2.4 Years of Wild and Woolly Mayhem in Dawson Creek.* Hanna, Alberta: Gorman and Gorman, 1991.

Schuurman, Herbert. *Canada's Eastern Neighbour: A View on Change in Greenland.* Ottawa, Ont.: Supply and Services Canada, 1976.

Smith, Graham. *When Jim Crow Met John Bull: Black American Soldiers in World War II Britain.* London, U.K.: Tauris, 1967.

Stacey, C. P. and Barbara Wilson. *The Half Million: The Canadians in Britain, 1939-1946.* Toronto, Ont.: University of Toronto Press, 1987.

Stambuk, George. *American Military Forces Abroad: Their Impact on the Western State System.* Columbia, Ohio: Ohio State University Press, 1963.

Stiehm, Judith, ed. *Women and Men's Wars.* Oxford: Pergamon Press, 1983.

————. *Women's View of the Political World of Men.* New York, N.Y.: Transnational Publishers, 1984.

Strong, F. S., Jr. *What's it all About?: Thoughts from the Nineties*. Privately published, 1985.

Tanlons, C. L. *The State and the Unions: Labor Relations, Law and the Organized Labor Movement in America, 1880-1960*. Cambridge, Mass.: Cambridge University Press, 1985.

Thompson, John H. *The Harvests of War: The Prairie West, 1914-1918*. Toronto, Ont.: McClelland and Stewart, 1978.

Tomlinson, Alan, ed. *Leisure and Social Control*. Brighton, U.K.: Brighton Polytechnic, 1981.

Treadwell, Mattie. *The Women's Army Corps*. Washington, D.C.: Department of the Army, 1954.

Trofimenkoff, Susan Mann. *The Dream of Nation: a Social and Intellectual History of Quebec*. Toronto, Ont.: Macmillan, 1982.

U.S. Army Corps of Engineers, *The History of the US Army Corps of Engineers*. Washington, D.C.: U.S. Corps of Engineers, 1986.

United States House of Representatives. *The Alaska Highway: An Interim Report*. Washington, D.C.: Government Printing Office, 1946.

Usher, Peter. *Fur Trade Posts of the Northwest Territories, 1870-1910*. Ottawa, Ont.: Department of Indian Affairs and Northern Development, 1971.

Van Kirk, Sylvia. *Many Tender Ties: Women in Fur Trade Society, 1670-1870*. Winnipeg, Manitoba: Watson and Dyer, 1980.

Watt, F. B. *Great Bear: A Journey Remebered*. Yellowknife, Northwest Terr.: Outcrop Press, 1980.

White, G. and L. Lindstrom, eds. *The Pacific Theatre: Island Representation of World War II*. Melbourne, Victoria: Melbourne University Press, 1990.

Winkler, Allan. *The Politics of Propaganda: The Office of War Information, 1942-1945*. New Haven, Conn.: Yale University Press, 1978.

Wynn, Neil. *The Afro-American and the Second World War*. New York, N.Y.: Holmes and Meier, 1976.

Yukon Historical Museums Association. *Whitehorse Heritage Buildings*. Whitehorse, Yukon Terr.: Yukon Historical Museums Association, 1983.

Zaslow, Morris. *The Northward Expansion of Canada*. Toronto, Ont.: McClelland and Stewart, 1988.

———. *Reading the Rocks: The Story of the Geological Survey of Canada, 1842-1972*. Toronto, Ont.: Macmillan, 1975.

Unpublished Works

Grafe, Willis. *The Summer of 1942, Yukon Style: Surveying the Alaska Highway.* Private memoirs.

Zaslow, Morris. "The Development of the Mackenzie Basin, 1922-1940." Ph.D. Dissertation, University of Toronto, 1957.

Newspapers and Periodicals

Calgary *Albertan*

Canol Piper

Dawson Daily News

Edmonton Bulletin

Edmonton Journal

Financial Times

Fort St. John *Alaska Highway News*

Northern Lights

Northern Miner

Northwest Newscast

North Star Magazine

Ottawa Citizen

Ottawa Journal

Prince Rupert *Daily News*

Regina *Leader Post*

Stewart News and Northern B.C. Miner

Toronto *Star Weekly*

Vancouver *News-Herald*

Victoria *Daily Colonist*

Washington Post

Whitehorse Star

INDEX

Riggs, Thomas, 38
Robson, Robert, 2
Rogers, Clifford, 117, 164
Royal Canadian Air Force, 210, 214
Royal Canadian Mounted Police,
    17-18, 84, 85, 87, 194, 195, 202,
    204, 205, 206, 211
Royal Engineers, 35
Sager, Eric, xi
San Francisco, CA, 82
Saskatchewan Farm Labour Ser-
    vice, 89
Seaton, Bob, 39
Seattle, WA, 20, 144
Selective Service Commission, 73
Service, Robert, 216
Shackleford, R. B., 83
Simmons, George, 165
Sinclair, Gordon, 116-117
Skagway, AK, 26, 36, 144, 172, 223
Smith, R. Melville Co., 70, 78, 131
Snag, Yukon, 122
Softball, 209-210
Soldier's Summit, 243
Spear, Ralph, 79
Speer, Frank, 122, 146, 148
Standard Oil Co., 70, 77, 90-91, 170,
    210
Storey, Robert, 189
Sturdevant, Brigadier-Gen. C. L.,
    81, 87
Swann, William, 222
Sweetgrass, MT, 173, 174
Tanana, AK, 12
Tatum, W., 43
Taylor and Drury Co., 13
Templeton, N. C., 151
Teslin, Yukon, 119, 122, 218, 219
Thompson, Lt. Col. P., 71
Thurston, Major Henry, 75, 97, 98
Trade unions, 20, 31, 67-69, 72, 73,
    77-78, 92, 93, 94, 165-167, 240,
    244

Turnbull-Sverdrup-Parcel Co., 81
Twichell, Heath, xi, 121, 162, 198
USO. See United States Service
    Organization
United States Air Transport Com-
    mand, 214
United States Army Corps of Engi-
    neers, 37-38, 80; history, 29-30
United States Employment Service,
    82
United States Engineering Depart-
    ment, 78, 131, 194, 206
United States Service Organization
    (USO), 197-202, 223, 226
United States War Manpower Com-
    mission, 73, 82, 83, 170, 175
Urbach, Sgt. Alfred, 221
Vancouver, BC, 20, 76, 92, 144, 216
Victoria, BC, 76
Walton, J. S., 81
War Measures Act, 74
Ward, Robert, 219
Waterways, NWT, 76, 87
Watson Lake, Yukon, 76, 142, 194,
    220
Western Labour Board, 75, 76, 96,
    98, 145, 149, 165, 166, 167, 170
White Pass and Yukon Railway, 11,
    19, 117, 164
Whitehorse All-Stars, 210
Whitehorse and District Workers'
    Union, 167
Whitehorse Star, 214
Whitehorse refinery, 70, 81, 82,
    133, 169, 247
Whitehorse, Yukon, 17, 26, 40, 42,
    43, 52, 54, 76, 77, 97, 116, 127,
    144, 162, 163, 170, 175, 190, 191,
    192, 195, 212, 218, 220, 222, 223
Whitney, Jane, 223
Whyte, Doug, vii
Wilson Freightways, 130
Winnipeg general strike, 31

Winters, Carol, 197
Women workers, 73, 91, 114-115, 125-136, 239-240. *See also* Black women
Workers, and climate, 42-43; control over conditions, 8, 100, 242, 246; diet, 160-162, 164; and the environment, 154-157, 176-178; leisure activities, 187-227; numbers of 96-97, 132; pay of, 69, 71, 76, 77, 91-93, 95, 98, 100-101, 103, 133, 145-151, 152-153, 159, 165-168, 170, 172, 180n, 184n, 245; protests, 165-168; recruitment of, 4-6, 69-72, 79-95, 98-100, 103, 245; regulation of, 69, 74, 86, 100, 103, 147-148, 238-239, 247-248. *See also* accidents, alcohol, black workers, hunting, gambling, morale, movies, newspapers, Native workers, radio, religion, softball, USO., women workers

Worsham, Brigadier-Gen. L.D., 89
Wrigley, NWT, 151
YANK, 216
Yellowknife, NWT, 17
Yukon Consolidated Gold Co., 164
Yukon Trade Union Co-ordinating Council, 94

William R. Morrison

Kenneth A. Coates

William. R. Morrison, dean of research and graduate studies, and Kenneth A. Coates, vice president (academic), work at the University of Northern British Columbia. They have co-authored a number of books on northern history, including *The Alaska Highway in World War II: The U.S. Army of Occupation in Canada's Northwest* (University of Toronto/Oklahoma, 1992), *The Sinking of the Princess Sophia* (University of Alaska Press, 1991), and *Land of the Midnight Sun: A History of the Yukon Territory* (Edmonton, 1988). They are currently completing three projects, "Strange Things Done 'Neath the Midnight Sun: Murder in the Yukon," "A Favoured Colony: The Federal Government and the Transformation of the Yukon, 1946-1979," and "Wilderness Saint: Bishop William Carpenter Bompas of the Yukon."